Insight

This book explores the clinical processes of psychoanalysis by charting modern developments in logic and applying them to the study of insight. Offering an epistemic approach to clinical psychoanalysis this book places value on the clinical interpretations of both the analysand and analyst and engages in a critique on purely linguistic approaches to psychoanalysis, which forsake crucial dimensions of clinical practice.

Drawing on the work of key twentieth century thinkers including Jerome Richfield, Ignacio Matte-Blanco, Gregory Bateson and the pioneering contribution on insight made by James Strachey, topics of discussion include:

- the structure and role of clinical interpretation
- interpretation and creationism
- body, meaning and language
- logical levels and transference.

As such, this book will be of great interest to all those in the psychoanalytic field, in particular those wanting to learn more about the study of insight and its relationship to clinical processes of psychoanalysis.

Jorge L. Ahumada is a training analyst of the Argentine Psychoanalytic Association and a Distinguished Fellow in the British Pychoanalytical Society. He is Mary S. Sigourney Awardee for 1996 and is a past Editor for Latin America of *The Internationl Journal of Psychoanalysis.*

THE NEW LIBRARY OF PSYCHOANALYSIS

General Editor: Alessandra Lemma

The New Library of Psychoanalysis was launched in 1987 in association with the Institute of Psycho-Analysis, London. It took over from the International Psychoanalytical Library which published many of the early translations of the works of Freud and the writings of most of the leading British and Continental psychoanalysts.

The purpose of the New Library of Psychoanalysis is to facilitate a greater and more widespread appreciation of psychoanalysis and to provide a forum for increasing mutual understanding between psychoanalysts and those working in other disciplines such as the social sciences, medicine, philosophy, history, linguistics, literature and the arts. It aims to represent different trends both in British psychoanalysis and in psychoanalysis generally. The New Library of Psychoanalysis is well placed to make available to the English-speaking world psychoanalytic writings from other European countries and to increase the interchange of ideas between British and American psychoanalysts. Through the *Teaching Series*, the New Library of Psychoanalysis now also publishes books that provide comprehensive, yet accessible, overviews of selected subject areas aimed at those studying psychoanalysis and related fields such as the social sciences, philosophy, literature and the arts.

The Institute, together with the British Psychoanalytical Society, runs a low-fee psychoanalytic clinic, organizes lectures and scientific events concerned with psychoanalysis and publishes *The International Journal of Psychoanalysis*. It also runs the only UK training course in psychoanalysis which leads to membership of the International Psychoanalytical Association – the body which preserves internationally agreed standards of training, of professional entry, and of professional ethics and practice for psychoanalysis as initiated and developed by Sigmund Freud. Distinguished members of the Institute have included Michael Balint, Wilfred Bion, Ronald Fairbairn, Anna Freud, Ernest Jones, Melanie Klein, John Rickman and Donald Winnicott.

Previous General Editors have included David Tuckett, who played a very active role in the establishment of the New Library. He was followed as General Editor by Elizabeth Bott Spillius, who was in turn followed by Susan Budd and then Dana Birksted-Breen.

The current General Editor of the New Library of Psychoanalysis is Alessandra Lemma, but this book was initiated and edited by Dana Birksted-Breen, former General Editor.

ALSO IN THIS SERIES

Impasse and Interpretation Herbert Rosenfeld
Psychoanalysis and Discourse Patrick Mahony
The Suppressed Madness of Sane Men Marion Milner
The Riddle of Freud Estelle Roith
Thinking, Feeling, and Being Ignacio Matte-Blanco
The Theatre of the Dream Salomon Resnik
Melanie Klein Today: Volume 1, Mainly Theory Edited by Elizabeth Bott Spillius
Melanie Klein Today: Volume 2, Mainly Practice Edited by Elizabeth Bott Spillius
Psychic Equilibrium and Psychic Change: Selected Papers of Betty Joseph Edited by Michael Feldman and Elizabeth Bott Spillius
About Children and Children-No-Longer: Collected Papers 1942–80 Paula Heimann. Edited by Margret Tonnesmann
The Freud–Klein Controversies 1941–45 Edited by Pearl King and Riccardo Steiner
Dream, Phantasy and Art Hanna Segal
Psychic Experience and Problems of Technique Harold Stewart
Clinical Lectures on Klein and Bion Edited by Robin Anderson
From Fetus to Child Alessandra Piontelli
A Psychoanalytic Theory of Infantile Experience: Conceptual and Clinical Reflections E. Gaddini. Edited by Adam Limentani
The Dream Discourse Today Edited and introduced by Sara Flanders
The Gender Conundrum: Contemporary Psychoanalytic Perspectives on Feminitity and Masculinity Edited and introduced by Dana Birksted-Breen
Psychic Retreats John Steiner
The Taming of Solitude: Separation Anxiety in Psychoanalysis Jean-Michel Quinodoz
Unconscious Logic: An Introduction to Matte-Blanco's Bi-logic and its Uses Eric Rayner
Understanding Mental Objects Meir Perlow
Life, Sex and Death: Selected Writings of William Gillespie Edited and introduced by Michael Sinason
What Do Psychoanalysts Want?: The Problem of Aims in Psychoanalytic Therapy Joseph Sandler and Anna Ursula Dreher
Michael Balint: Object Relations, Pure and Applied Harold Stewart
Hope: A Shield in the Economy of Borderline States Anna Potamianou
Psychoanalysis, Literature and War: Papers 1972–1995 Hanna Segal
Emotional Vertigo: Between Anxiety and Pleasure Danielle Quinodoz
Early Freud and Late Freud Ilse Grubrich-Simitis

A History of Child Psychoanalysis Claudine and Pierre Geissmann
Belief and Imagination: Explorations in Psychoanalysis Ronald Britton
A Mind of One's Own: A Kleinian View of Self and Object Robert A. Caper
Psychoanalytic Understanding of Violence and Suicide Edited by Rosine Jozef Perelberg
On Bearing Unbearable States of Mind Ruth Riesenberg-Malcolm. Edited by Priscilla Roth
Psychoanalysis on the Move: The Work of Joseph Sandler Edited by Peter Fonagy, Arnold M. Cooper and Robert S. Wallerstein
The Dead Mother: The Work of André Green Edited by Gregorio Kohon
The Fabric of Affect in the Psychoanalytic Discourse André Green
The Bi-Personal Field: Experiences of Child Analysis Antonino Ferro
The Dove that Returns, the Dove that Vanishes: Paradox and Creativity in Psychoanalysis Michael Parsons
Ordinary People, Extra-ordinary Protections: A Post-Kleinian Approach to the Treatment of Primitive Mental States Judith Mitrani
The Violence of Interpretation: From Pictogram to Statement Piera Aulagnier
The Importance of Fathers: A Psychoanalytic Re-Evaluation Judith Trowell and Alicia Etchegoyen
Dreams That Turn Over a Page: Paradoxical Dreams in Psychoanalysis Jean-Michel Quinodoz
The Couch and the Silver Screen: Psychoanalytic Reflections on European Cinema Edited and introduced by Andrea Sabbadini
In Pursuit of Psychic Change: The Betty Joseph Workshop Edited by Edith Hargreaves and Arturo Varchevker
The Quiet Revolution in American Psychoanalysis: Selected Papers of Arnold M. Cooper Arnold M. Cooper. Edited and introduced by Elizabeth L. Auchincloss
Seeds of Illness and Seeds of Recovery: The Genesis of Suffering and the Role of Psychoanalysis Antonino Ferro
The Work of Psychic Figurability: Mental States Without Representation César Botella and Sára Botella
Key Ideas for a Contemporary Psychoanalysis: Misrecognition and Recognition of the Unconscious André Green
The Telescoping of Generations: Listening to the Narcissistic Links Between Generations Haydée Faimberg
Glacial Times: A Journey Through the World of Madness Salomon Resnik
This Art of Psychoanalysis: Dreaming Undreamt Dreams and Interrupted Cries Thomas H. Ogden
Psychoanalysis as Therapy and Storytelling Antonino Ferro
Psychoanalysis and Religion in the 21st Century: Competitors or Collaborators? Edited by David M. Black

Recovery of the Lost Good Object Eric Brenman. Edited and introduced by Gigliola Fornari Spoto
The Many Voices of Psychoanalysis Roger Kennedy
Feeling the Words: Neuropsychoanalytic Understanding of Memory and the Unconscious Mauro Mancia
Projected Shadows: Psychoanalytic Reflections on the Representation of Loss in European Cinema Edited by Andrea Sabbadini
Encounters with Melanie Klein: Selected Papers of Elizabeth Spillius Elizabeth Spillius. Edited by Priscilla Roth and Richard Rusbridger
Constructions and the Analytic Field: History, Scenes and Destiny Domenico Chianese
Yesterday, Today and Tomorrow Hanna Segal. Edited by Nicola Abel-Hirsch
Psychoanalysis Comparable and Incomparable: The Evolution of a Method to Describe and Compare Psychoanalytic Approaches David Tuckett, Roberto Basile, Dana Birksted-Breen, Tomas Böhm, Paul Denis, Antonino Ferro, Helmut Hinz, Arne Jemstedt, Paola Mariotti and Johan Schubert
Time, Space and Phantasy Rosine Jozef Perelberg
Rediscovering Psychoanalysis: Thinking and Dreaming, Learning and Forgetting Thomas H. Ogden
Mind Works: Technique and Creativity in Psychoanalysis Antonino Ferro
Doubt, Conviction and the Analytic Process: Selected Papers of Michael Feldman Michael Feldman. Edited by Betty Joseph
Melanie Klein in Berlin: Her First Psychoanalysis of Children Claudia Frank. Edited by Elizabeth Spillius
The Psychotic Wavelength: A Psychoanalytic Perspective for Psychiatry Richard Lucas
Betweenity: A Discussion of the Concept of Borderline Judy Gammelgaard
The Intimate Room: Theory and Technique of the Analytic Field Giuseppe Civitarese
Bion Today Edited by Chris Mawson
Secret Passages: The Theory and Technique of Interpsychic Relations Stefano Bolognini
Intersubjective Processes and the Unconscious: An Integration of Freudian, Kleinian and Bionian Perspectives Lawrence J. Brown
Seeing and Being Seen: Emerging from a Psychic Retreat John Steiner
Avoiding Emotions, Living Emotions Antonino Ferro
Insight: Essays on Psychoanalytic Knowing Jorge L. Ahumada
Projective Identification: The Fate of a Concept Edited by Elizabeth Spillius and Edna O'Shaughnessy

TITLES IN THE NEW LIBRARY OF PSYCHOANALYSIS TEACHING SERIES

Reading Freud: A Chronological Exploration of Freud's Writings Jean-Michel Quinodoz
Listening to Hanna Segal: Her Contribution to Psychoanalysis Jean-Michel Quinodoz
Reading French Psychoanalysis Edited by Dana Birksted-Breen, Sara Flanders and Alain Gibeault
Reading Winnicott Edited by Lesley Caldwell and Angela Joyce

THE NEW LIBRARY OF PSYCHOANALYSIS

General Editor: Alessandra Lemma

Insight

Essays on Psychoanalytic Knowing

Jorge L. Ahumada

Foreword by Dale Boesky

Routledge
Taylor & Francis Group
LONDON AND NEW YORK

First published 2011
by Routledge
27 Church Road, Hove, East Sussex BN3 2FA

Simultaneously published in the USA and Canada
by Routledge
711 Third Avenue, New York NY 10017

Routledge is an imprint of the Taylor & Francis Group, an Informa business

British Library Cataloguing in Publication Data
A catalogue record for this book is available from the British Library

Library of Congress Cataloging-in-Publication Data
Ahumada, Jorge L., 1940–
Insight : essays on psychoanalytic knowing / Jorge L. Ahumada.
p. cm.
ISBN 978–0–415–61880–9 (hbk.)—ISBN 978–0–415–61881–6 (pbk.)
1. Psychoanalysis. 2. Insight. 3. Insight in psychotherapy. I. Title.
BF175.A543 2011
150.19′5—dc22
2011001228

ISBN: 978–0–415–61880–9 (hbk)
ISBN: 978–0–415–61881–6 (pbk)
ISBN: 978–0–203–15784–8 (ebk)

Typeset in Bembo by RefineCatch Limited, Bungay, Suffolk
Printed and bound in Great Britain by TJ International Ltd, Padstow, Cornwall
Cover design by Sandra Heath

Contents

Foreword

Dale Boesky

This is an important, illuminating book by one of the few psychoanalysts who are intellectually equipped to deal authoritatively with the crucially important links between our failure to improve our methods for evaluating clinical evidence and the culture wars in psychoanalysis in recent decades. We must be more wary about either agreeing or disagreeing among ourselves if we lack information about how an author has linked his theoretic assertions and truth claims to the clinical material alleged to have generated these claims. Profound misunderstandings about the actual nature of science have fuelled and perpetuated the argument in some quarters that the very idea that there can be such a thing as 'evidence' is like a Prussian boot crushing the perfumed garden of psychoanalysis. In this argument it is held that the pursuit of evidence is a fool's errand perpetuated by a few surviving positivists who have failed to understand that their irreducible subjectivity disqualifies them from being 'observers'. Our conclusions according to this argument are not to be confused with 'truth' and are contingent on the vagaries of constructed contexts that are valid only in the constraints of a unique psychoanalytic dyad. There can be no such thing as trans-contextual reality, because there can be no such thing as trans-contextual meaning.

The opposing argument in these culture wars holds that the anti-scientists are uninformed about the true nature of science and argue that the view of all reality as context-dependent or as an intersubjectively generated construction are equating patients with texts and using hermeneutics as a warrant to disregard the rigorous criteria of evidential challenge. In this argument, those who challenge the notion of evidence across the boards are merely pragmatic opportunists who wish to be freed of the constraints of evidential challenge.

A minority of authors, gradually increasing in their number, have identified this polemic as a spuriously dichotomous opposition of straw men masking serious misunderstandings about the nature of science, but also about the neglected effect of our ignorance about epistemology as the study of knowledge and our justification methods for supporting knowledge claims. The controversy about whether there can be such a thing as trans-contextual 'evidence' that can be carried over from the realm of inference to the realm of 'knowledge' is at its heart dependent on basic principles of epistemology often neglected by both warring factions.

'Clinical Epistemology' does not appear as a course title in the catalogues of seminars in psychoanalytic institutes throughout the world. Instead we see many seminars devoted to 'Comparative Psychoanalysis', but sadly, these well intended and respectfully taught seminars do not investigate exactly what we are comparing at the level where it matters most: how were the disputed theoretic explanations of various rival theories derived from the clinical material? It is all too easy to debate at lofty levels of theoretic abstraction, but these debates too often degenerate into Babel because the points of disagreement are incongruent. An example is the deceptively plausible proposal to define psychoanalysis as a hermeneutic science. This is the hybrid conceptual equivalent of a centaur, half man and half horse. Hermeneutics and science are distinguished by arbitrary definitions, and not by conceptually comparable categorical boundaries. Hermeneutics refers to interpretive methods and all sciences depend on the interpretation of data of widely varying kinds. The principles of hermeneutic interpretation can be applied to both artistic as well as scientific questions, but that does not mean that hermeneutics per se is either an art or a science. Thus the term 'hermeneutic science' enshrines a category error analogous to speaking of purple patriotism.

By this point the reader may wonder what these arcane matters have to do with me as a psychoanalytic clinician. The answer lies in whether or not one believes, as I do, that our failure to improve our methods for evaluating clinical evidence is a crucially important problem and that whether or not we do something about this problem may very well determine the fate of psychoanalysis. And here is the relevant point. The entire problem of evaluating clinical evidence is rendered moot by those who argue that it is futile to say that any particular intervention is better or worse than any other. Those who adhere to this radical relativism rest their arguments in large measure on just those assumptions noted above: since there is no such thing as trans-contextual reality, we can forget about the entire issue of evidence. What is true in one psychoanalytic dyad may or may not be true in another. There is simply no trans-contextual reality. That view has gained considerable acceptance in our literature and in our meetings and also in the curricula of many institutes. The assumptions on which this notion depends are in my opinion rooted in a fundamental misunderstanding of the nature of science but also in a misunderstanding or ignorance about certain basic philosophical problems that have engaged the attention of professional philosophers for three millennia.

I noted the absence of attention in our curricula to this vital problem: the average psychoanalytic candidate and the average psychoanalyst has no formal acquaintance with basic epistemological concepts as they relate to this debate about whether or not psychoanalysis should be viewed as a science and, if so, what kind of science it is. Enter Ahumada, who with this book provides us with a basic contribution to an unborn discipline: psychoanalytic epistemology. It will be immensely valuable not only for candidates but for experienced clinicians too. Indeed, this volume could well serve as a textbook in seminars on remedial epistemology for psychoanalysts. There is, of course, a very large literature about psychoanalysis and the philosophy of science, but much of it has been written by experts outside our field who know little about psychoanalysis. Other authors who are psychoanalysts do not have sufficient acquaintance with the philosophic issues. Ahumada is one of the very few who is both a master clinician and also deeply conversant with the relevant philosophic literature. In this volume he extends the groundbreaking contributions of his earlier book, *The Logics of the Mind: A Clinical View*.

In the Dora case, Freud spoke of his omission of information about his method for developing his interpretations about his patient and fatefully dismissed this omission quite casually and superficially. He compared it to two other forms of 'incompleteness'. Those were the incompleteness required by discretion and concern for the privacy of the patient and the incompleteness of practicality, since it would be too taxing for the reader to plough through the reams of paper required to give all of the relevant details. He clearly believed that he knew what he needed to know about how he formed his interpretations to the patient on the basis of his theories, just as he clearly believed at the end of his life that he knew very well why patients got better as a consequence of his interpretations. Both Fenichel and Glover referred to this 'incompleteness' as the Achilles heel of psychoanalysis. This absence of a reliable method to describe how analysts make their interpretations out of the associations of the patient is a fundamental and long neglected problem for psychoanalysis. Arguments in favour of pragmatic criteria of truth and radical relativism thrive on this very confusion and the ultimate consequences of this neglect can become the death of hope for ever developing a method for the consensual evaluation of evidence. I predict that Ahumada's new book will be viewed in years to come as an essential addition to clarifying these problems.

Preface

This volume is a companion to my *The Logics of the Mind: A Clinical View*, published in London by Karnac (Ahumada, 2001b), which comprised mostly clinical papers. This book deals with the psychoanalytic method and its epistemological place and with the pluralities of empiry and the sciences. It focuses upon insight as dual work on the evidence by both analysand and analyst, building upon a line of thought at the core of Freud's contribution and unfolded in the work of Strachey, Racker, and Etchegoyen, which seems pertinent at this time when the role of insight is contested in the wider culture even more than in psychoanalytic circles. It strives to clarify the nature of insight following on conceptual developments introduced by Jerome Richfield, Ignacio Matte-Blanco, and Gregory Bateson.

A notion that Strachey got from Freud, says Winnicott (1969, p. 508), and that he, in his turn, got it from his analysis with Strachey, is that a process develops in the patient, and what transpires cannot be produced but can be made use of. In such spirit, my approach centres on helping the analysand to explore her/his 'unconscious theories' in order to attain an evolving 'evidence-realism'.

Except for deletions to avoid repetition, some corrections, and further explanation or quotation here and there, the papers are reprinted as published; in order to follow their inner logic, the order is that of their genesis rather than that of publication. Four chapters had not been available in English. Four had been published in *The International Journal of Psychoanalysis*, and another in *The Journal of the American Psychoanalytic Association*. Three had appeared in books: 'What is a clinical fact? Clinical psychoanalysis as inductive method', presented at the International Journal of Psychoanalysis 75th

Anniversary Celebration Conference and published in the *IJP*, was also part of the earlier book mentioned above (Ahumada, 1994b), while 'Counterinduction in psychoanalytic practice: Epistemic and technical aspects' was published in *The Perverse Transference and Other Matters: Essays in Honour of R. Horacio Etchegoyen*, published by Jason Aronson (Ahumada, 1997c). 'Counterinductive knowledge and the blunders of so-called "theory of science"', was published by Whurr/ Wiley in *From Practice to Theory*, edited by Jorge Canestri (Ahumada, 2006a).

My training analyst, the late Dr. Joel Zac, R. Horacio Etchegoyen, and my wife Luisa Busch de Ahumada must be thanked first. David Tuckett, Elias M. da Rocha Barros, Eric Rayner, Marianne Leuzinger-Bohleber, Arnold D. Richards, María Rosa Senet, Alfredo Gazzano, Roberto Doria Medina, Manuel J. Gálvez, Jorge Luis Maldonado, Vincenzo Bonaminio, Salvador Adroer, Inge Wise, Maria Inês Carneiro, Jorge Canestri, Warren Poland, and, most especially, Dale Boesky have provided generous friendship and much-appreciated intellectual support. Last but not least I thank the anonymous reviewers of *The New Library of Psychoanalysis* and its then Editor, Dana Birksted-Breen, for their valuable and patient help and suggestions in putting together the manuscript, and to Kate Hawes, Sarah Gibson, and Kate Moysen at Routledge and Klara King for getting it into readable English.

Permissions acknowledgements

Chapter 1 was originally published as: J. L. Ahumada, 'Logical types and ostensive insight'. *International Journal of Psychoanalysis*, 72: 683–691, 1991. © Institute of Psychoanalysis, London, UK. Reprinted with permission.

Chapter 2 was originally published as: J. L. Ahumada, 'Interpretation and creationism'. *International Journal of Psychoanalysis*, 75: 695–707, 1994. © Institute of Psychoanalysis, London, UK. Reprinted with permission.

Chapter 3 was originally published as: J. L. Ahumada, 'What is a clinical fact? Clinical psychoanalysis as inductive method'. *International Journal of Psychoanalysis*, 75: 949–962, 1994. © Institute of Psychoanalysis, London, UK. Reprinted with permission. It was also presented at the International Journal of Psychoanalysis 75th Anniversary Celebration Conference, São Paulo, Brazil, 31 March–2 April 1995.

Chapter 4 was originally published in Spanish as: J. L. Ahumada, 'Cuerpo, significación y lenguaje' [Body, meaning and language]. *Revista de Psicanálisis*, Special International Issue No 4: 9–30, 1995. © Revista de Psicoanálisis. Reprinted with permission.

Chapter 5 was originally published in Portuguese as: J. L. Ahumada, 'Fato, contexto, imagem, relato: uma aproximação biológica' [Fact, context, image, narrative: A bio-logical approach]. *Revista Brasileira de Psicanálise*, 32: 9–27, 1998. © Revista Brasileira de Psicanálise. Reprinted with permission.

Chapter 6 was originally published as: J. L. Ahumada, 'Toward the epistemology of clinical psychoanalysis'. The final, definitive version of this paper has been published in *Journal of the American*

Psychoanalytic Association, 45: 507–530, 1997, by SAGE Publications, Inc., All rights reserved. © American Psychoanalytic Association. http://online.sagepub.com. Reprinted with permission.

Chapter 7 was originally published as: J. L. Ahumada, 'Disclosures and refutations: Clinical psychoanalysis as a logic of enquiry'. *International Journal of Psychoanalysis*, 78: 1105–1118, 1997. © Institute of Psychoanalysis, London, UK. Reprinted with permission.

Chapter 8 was originally published as: J. L. Ahumada (1997), 'Counterinduction in psychoanalytic practice: Epistemic and technical aspects', in J. L. Ahumada, J. Olagaray, A. K. Richards, and A. D. Richards (Eds.), *The Perverse Transference and Other Matters: Essays in Honor of R. Horacio Etchegoyen* (pp. 181–202). Northvale, NJ and London, UK: Jason Aronson. © 1997 Jason Aronson, Inc., MA, USA. Reprinted with permission.

Chapter 9 was originally published in Portuguese as: J. L. Ahumada, 'Níveis lógicos e comunicacionais da transferência' [Logical and communicational levels of transference]. *Revista de Psicanálise (Porto Alegre)*, 4: 82–91, 1996. © Revista de Psicanálise (Porto Alegre). Reprinted with permission.

Chapter 10 is based on an IPA New Orleans Congress presentation, 'Objectivity in the clinical setting: the double work on the evidences', at the panel 'Idea and observation evaluate interpretations and theories?', chaired by Professor Charles Hanly. An extended version of this presentation was originally published in Italian at the invitation of Dr. Agostino Racalbuto, then Editor, as 'Il doppio lavoro sulle prove cliniche. Natura e limite della simbolizzazione' [The double work on the clinical evidences, and the nature and limits of symbolization]. *Rivista di Psicoanalisi*, 51: 1065–1086, 2005. © Rivista di Psicoanalisi. Reprinted with permission. The paper was republished in German as J. L. Ahumada, 'Die doppelte Arbeit an den klinischen Evidenzen. Symbolisierung und ihre Grenzen'. *Psyche: Zeitschrift für Psychoanalyse*, 61: 889–912, 2007, and in Catalan as 'El doble treball de les evidències cliniques, i la naturalesa i limits de la simbolizació'. *Revista Catalana de Psicoanàlisi*, 25: 7–24, 2008. The current chapter in this volume is published with some additions to previous versions.

Chapter 11 was originally published as: J. L. Ahumada (2006), 'The analytic mind at work: Counterinductive knowledge and the blunders of so-called "theory of science"', in J. Canestri (Ed.), *Psychoanalysis: From Practice to Theory* (pp. 127–146). Chichester, UK: Wiley. © Wiley. Reprinted by permission.

INTRODUCTION

On the place and limits of psychoanalytic knowing

This book has two intertwined purposes: first, to enquire on how insight is gained in clinical psychoanalysis and, second, to clarify the epistemic place of psychoanalysis and of its concepts, for which the main hurdle is a conflation of knowledge and certainty in philosophical notions on science.[1] About such an obstacle, Freud said: 'Science, as you know, is not a revelation; long after its beginnings it still lacks the attributes of definiteness, immutability and infallibility for which human thought so deeply longs' (1926, p. 191).

Did Freud rightly assume that science is *not* a revelation? At the dawn of Western science, in its Pythagorean origins, science was indeed a holy revelation, with definiteness, immutability, and infallibility as keystones at its geometrical–mathematical core. Things look different at the humbler start of mathematics two millennia earlier in Egypt and Mesopotamia, emerging as rules of thumb for solving practical problems: the division of agricultural plots after the yearly floodings, the dredging of channels for irrigation, the construction of buildings, stock-keeping, and accounting. The most famous rule of thumb, which divided a cord into segments of lengths of 3–4–5 so that joining its tips resulted in a right angle, was used by Egyptian and Babylonian builders since time immemorial: they were after practice, not theory. With Pythagoras, who spent two decades studying in the Middle East before returning to Samos and then Croton in Sicily to found his school, geometry became 'theoretical':

upon the rule of 3–4–5 he built his theorem, which launched geometry as an endeavour grounded on deductive reason. Deduction, which allowed the complex to be built up starting from simple elements, gained for the Pythagoreans a sacred imprint, based on the conviction that, in the veritable secret structure of the universe, numbers carried the eternal and immutable. Finding a numerical relation between the length of the chords in the four-stringed lyre and harmony in music, they concluded that – from musical harmony to the orbits of the celestial bodies – an eternal order based on number ruled the *Harmonia Mundi* despite apparent diversity, disorder, and chaos: 'Everything is Number', knowledge of which brought man closer to the gods. The holy simplicity of number primed the rupture that resulted from the finding of what came to be called *irrational* numbers: expressing the relation between the length of the sides of a square and its diagonals required an indefinite series of numbers, which broke their holy certainty about the simplicity of the cosmos. That the discoverer, Hipassus, was taken out to sea and left to drown – condemned, even beyond his death, to what to the ancient Greeks was the utmost disgrace: not to be buried in their native soil – highlights the religious fervour lodging in the thirst for simplicity and certainty. However, faith in simplicity is not readily abdicated: the simplest motion representing ultimate order – uniform circular motion – remained to rule the attempts to reduce the complex planetary motions to simple components in Ptolomean astronomy, just as, fifteen centuries later, it guided the Copernican revolution and was later on stoutly hailed as a cosmological certainty by Galileo (Lindberg, 2007, p. 102). The deductivistic tradition found its summit centuries after Pythagoras – in the Hellenistic period – in Euclid's *Elements*, articulating geometry in an axiomatic that remains to this day the epistemic ideal for science: it is built on a few basic elements – 23 definitions, 5 postulates, and 5 general axioms – upon which an initial proposition was construed, followed by a second, and so on.

What does this have to do with psychoanalysis? It shows that whoever dares to question the certainties of those around him is in for a rough journey! Such is the fate of psychoanalysis: definiteness, immutability, and infallibility – that is, certainties – it cannot provide; nor are certainty and simplicity offered by everyday learning from experience, on which sanity depends. Psychoanalytic knowing *cannot be fixed beyond a doubt or respond to pleas for certainty*: clinical thinking is concerned with our everyday life and merges with it. Psychoanalytic practice, however, leads to nets of concepts forming a conceptual discipline. Freud's appraisal of psychoanalysis as part of the natural sciences has lately taken a polemical turn due to misconceptions on the varied status of what fits beneath the umbrella term 'natural science'. That in Greek antiquity knowledge (*episteme*) was conceivable only as relating to the immutable and the eternal marks the *infallibilist* tradition in science, exemplified by the Pythagoreans, which prioritizes formal theory over practice and equates knowledge to certainty – two ambitions later renounced by *fallibilist* traditions.

The philosopher of history Roger Collingwood expressed it thus: 'For the Greeks it had been an axiom that nothing is knowable unless it is unchanging' (1945, p. 11). To the Renaissance, continues Collingwood, nature as it appears to our senses, the changing world of 'secondary qualities', was unknowable: behind it lay the true objects of natural science, the 'primary qualities', knowable because unchanging. Galileo's dictum 'the Book of the Universe is written in mathematical language' – its occult, mathematically expressible characteristics being the 'primary qualities', harking back to the Pythagoreans and to the atomists Leucippus and Democritus – came to philosophy with Descartes, and is the mark of positivism.

To the Pythagoreans, and at the Galilean birth of modern science, the repetitious, unchanging, mathematically graspable realm of celestial mechanics was paradigmatic for empiry, moulding ideas of knowledge and science. The celestial clockwork and the mechanical realms of statics and dynamics stood at the root of science; the methodical study of living beings came later, and psychology and the human sciences did not emerge as disciplines until the nineteenth century. Their advance posed the need to re-work the idea of 'knowledge' giving place to change, and foremost to the concepts of development and conflict required by the domains of biology and the psyche. Lacking a pretence to certainty, psychoanalysis' scientific aspirations find their place in fallibilistic outlooks on science. Nicholas Rescher wrote in his book *The Limits of Science*:

> The idea that reason, proceeding from a vast body of empirical observations, will in the end discern a single definitive structure reflects the grand aspiration of classical metaphysics: that reason in nature will deliver unto reason in the mind of enquirers a clear, determinate, all-embracing formula.
>
> (1999, p. 75)

It may seem obvious nowadays that the objects of mathematics and logic are not empirical objects, only objects of thought – namely ideal or formal objects. However, quite recently, in the nineteenth century, with the emerging new geometries of Lobachewsky and Riemann, Euclid's geometry (and logic) has been fully acknowledged as being purely formal or ideal rather than empirical; therefore, as Bertrand Russell put it, 'we must only assert . . . that the axioms imply the propositions, not that the axioms are true and therefore the propositions are true' (1938, p. vii), and we must also admit that 'none of the raw material of the world has smooth logical properties' (p. ix). Moreover, in what was probably the first attempt to develop a symbolic logic that would be a workable instrument for mathematicians, Rosser (1953) warns his reader that the artificiality of a formal system turns harmful when users ignore the fact that it is artificial, that the logic he presents is unsuitable for other fields, and that even within mathematics the user should not forget that his intuition is the final authority, while formal methods are just a supplement.

The spell of certainty brands, however, most 'philosophy of science' (epistemology) and the academic public's grasp on 'empiry' and 'natural science'. From Descartes on, the impetus of calculative Reason's thrust for certainties – *pura atque abstracta mathesis,* pure and abstract mathematical thinking – defined 'empiry' and 'natural science', the nature of the observations in the various fields of enquiry playing second fiddle to the axiomatic deductive systems. Upon Descartes' influence, Husserl affirmed, 'the whole modern conviction is rationalistic' (1954, p. 313), while to Cottingham 'the writings of the philosophical giants of the early modern period, Spinoza, Malebranche and Leibniz, on the Continent, and Locke, Berkeley and Hume, in the British Isles, all, in different ways, bear the unmistakable imprint of Descartes' thought concerning the structure of human knowledge, the nature of the mind and the relationship between mind and matter' (1986, p. xxxvii). Descartes' *Discourse on the Method* (1637) proposed a model for intellectual theory applying algebraic methods to Euclid's geometry, capable of being extended to any scientific field that lends itself to formal analysis (Toulmin, 1990, p. 72); from Newton on, by way of Euler to Kant or later, the attractions of certainty were as powerful as they were for Descartes (p. 75). Descartes' work, avers Cottingham, 'has been enormously influential in the development of the modern life sciences: the guiding model is that of an animal machine governed by stimulus–response mechanisms, whose complex behaviour is to be explained purely on the basis of the structure and organization of the internal organs' (1992, p. 15).

The demise of the idea of nature as unchanging hit the mid-nineteenth century largely with Darwin's *Origin of Species* in 1859, attesting that species emerged in an ages-long process: as a result, argues Collingwood (1946, p. 129), at long last nature entered a historical dimension. It then became obvious that concepts born out of physics did not suit other realms.

What is at stake as a result of the longstanding aegis of epistemological physicalism is summarized by the British philosopher of ethics Bernard Williams:

> We may say that what naturalism recognizes are just those things recognized by the natural sciences. But then is biology a natural science? If biology is, is ethology? If ethology, what about the ethology of human beings, which includes culture? At this point, it may be that the screw is tightened, and naturalism is required to represent everything – plants, the behaviour of animals, human cultures – in terms of the universally applicable natural science, physics. So naturalism gets tied to the project of physicalistic reductionism. Physicalistic reductionism is an entirely implausible undertaking in itself; and it surely cannot be that the interests of a naturalistic approach to ethics, for instance, must be essentially tied to it. We should get away from the preoccupation with reductionism. . . . Questions about naturalism . . . are questions not about reduction but about explanation. Of course I recognize that this leaves almost everything open.
>
> (2002, pp. 22–23)

Open indeed has it long been for those working in the field – in biology in Darwin's case, or in depth-psychology in Freud's. Thus two quite different epistemic versions of 'natural science' need to be firmly distinguished.

1 A *physicalistic reductionism* considering 'empirical' what fits deductivism under the notions of 'variable' and 'natural law'. Euclidean axiomatic as epistemic model shines in Ernest Nagel's avowal, in *The Structure of Science*, that scientific knowledge seeks a system of

explanations whereby 'with the help of a small number of explanatory principles an indefinitely large number of propositions about these facts can be shown to constitute a logically unified body of knowledge' (1961, p. 4). Though conceding that not all sciences present the highly integrated form of systematic explanation exhibited by mechanics, this being valid for social enquiry and various divisions of natural science, he insists that the notion that the explicandum must be a logically necessary consequence of the explanatory premises 'has been widely regarded as the paradigm for any 'genuine' explanation' (1961, p. 21). There, as in positivisms generally, physics is held to be the ideal science the epistemic structure of which must ultimately encompass all fields, the mind included: such reductionism, which marks the hypothetico-deductive approach, equates, following Descartes, animals with mindless machines, restricting mind to man's calculative reason and conscious will.

2 A *naturalism* taking as given change and context-dependency, including enquiry on the researcher's inescapable but not incorrigible concepts. In contrast to the deductivism marking the reductive physicalistic approach, this leaves almost everything open. About such wide naturalism Darwin claimed in *The Descent of Man* that it is far from easy to distinguish between instinct and reason, and this can only be judged by the circumstances (1879, pp. 96–97), and that the difference in mind between man and the higher animals, great as it is, is one of degree and not of kind (1879, p. 151): in such a conceptual frame Freud set psychoanalysis within the natural sciences. In fact, argues Stephen Toulmin (1990, p. 151), the task of fully calling into question the Cartesian equation of 'mentality' and 'conscious calculation', and of 'reasonableness' with 'formal rationality', fell to Freud and the psychoanalysts.

A 20-month-old boy coping with the birth of a baby sister exemplifies the naturalistic build-up of knowing. In pregnancy, at his parents' prompting, he often caressed mother's belly tenderly saying '*Bebé*' (baby); by this time he had stopped calling himself '*Bebé*', switching to *Nené* (kid): when asked about his sister, he joined the tips of his fingers, leaving no space at all, laughingly evincing how small she was. On meeting his newborn sister at the hospital, and then at home, he dotingly related to the *Bebé* for some days – until he seemed to realize she had come to stay: he was desolate for a while, and then pulled himself together and resumed his tender relationship. However, though a nonverbal boy who deftly handled issues by gestures and pointing, he caught an on-the-fly comment that the baby was 'mini', repeating it time and again; also, out in the park he started to select the smallest pebbles, saying 'mini' or, more explicitly, 'mini-*Bebé*': whereby we assist *in statu nascendi* to a contradiction in the events – a contradiction of impulse on the one hand, and conscious affect on the other. As far as can be ascertained, his sister's birth elicited counterpoised 'natural interpretations' arising from tenderness and jealous rivalry: here our knowledge was gained mostly from observations, in contrast to the deductivistic bent that rules physicalistic reductionism and rationalistic 'theories of science'.

This shows a primacy of affective pragmatics over semantics, and of deixis (pointing) over verbalization: months earlier this boy, who at the time did not yet verbally name grandpa or grandma, asked about grandpa by insistently pointing at his empty armchair. Noticing this, his caretaker asked *Abu?* [grandfather?] and he readily nodded; when she explained that *Abu* was at work and would come later, he was content. Patently, anxiety/emotion about grandpa's physical absence motivated the original act: knowing and insight, in turn, allayed the anxiety and opened up psychic spaces. At about that time, when grandma went away for a week, the baby, up in his caretaker's arms, forced her to carry him through the house, looking for himself where he had known her to be before accepting grandmother's absence.

Can naturalistic knowledge build-up grounded in observation and insight be deemed 'rational'? Far from formal deduction, it grounds everyday rationality and the 'eureka' processes of discovery in all science, including the cutting edge in 'exact' science and the purely 'ideal' formal sciences, as witnessed by the mathematician Andrew Wiles' account, at a time when he contemplated failure after seven years of painstaking work, of his sudden insight concerning that foremost mathematical challenge, Fermat's last theorem:

> I was sitting at my desk one Monday morning, September 19, examining the Kolyvagin–Flach method. It wasn't that I believed I could make it work, but I thought that at least I could explain why it didn't work. I thought I was clutching at straws, but I wanted to reassure myself. Suddenly, totally unexpectedly, I had

> this incredible revelation . . . out of the ashes of the Kolyvagin–Flach method seemed to rise the true answer to the problem. . . . It was so indescribably beautiful; it was so simple and so elegant. I couldn't understand how I had missed it and I just stared at it in disbelief for twenty minutes. Then during the day I walked around the department, and I'd keep coming back to my desk looking to see if it was still there. I couldn't contain myself, I was so excited. It was the most important moment of my working life. Nothing I will ever do will mean as much.
>
> (Singh, 1997, pp. 274–275)

It goes without saying that on speaking of his 'incredible revelation' Wiles refers to the unexpectedness of his crucial insight, not to a belief of accessing holy truths; while preceded by long years of deductive exercise, this crucial sudden insight is as such far removed from the deliberateness of formal deduction.

Psychoanalysis as a methodical enquiry into our hitherto unknown psychic processes started with the twentieth century, in Freud's *Traumdeutung* (*The Interpretation of Dreams*, 1900). Efforts at self-understanding are, however, consubstantial with culture: in the ages prior to the invention of the written alphabet, such efforts were embedded in myths and in folk wisdom; later in literature and in the quite diverse of thought called philosophy; much of which, from Descartes on, took the form of a philosophy of consciousness that, considering an assumedly self-transparent consciousness equivalent to mind, claimed sovereignty over the realm of the psyche.

Thus self-understandings issuing from the psychoanalytic method competed in a crowded field. Unable to compete with the appeal of philosophy or literature, it survived on dealing in the flesh with dire human necessity, its patients' felt need for relief or, indeed, psychic survival. Besides, on a par with its claim to access hitherto unavailable findings on the human psyche, a main epistemic contribution was its enquiry into the psychic issues of *un*knowing in the Freudian dynamics of repression and negation, but mainly of denial (*Verleugnung*). Issues of *un*knowing, alien to philosophy, are not alien to myth, folk wisdom, and common sense, as vouchsafed by a Spanish saying: 'none more deaf than he who seeks not to listen'; *un*knowing is found by psychoanalysis to be an *active* psychic process, distinct from the philosophical themes of the validity of knowledge.

Philosophical conceptions of scientific knowledge and logic start from *formulaic or linguistically stated propositions*, while psychoanalysis reaches beyond language, enquiring on levels of *psychic meaning to be traversed so that consciously graspable and verbally statable propositions are attained.* Those preverbal levels of psychic dynamics, the level of Freudian thing-presentations linked to impulse and affect, require, additionally, to allow for self–object differentiations unfolding from early infancy on, which philosophies ignore. That psychoanalysis addresses this conundrum sets the stage for its conflicting reception in academic and scientific circles. In addition, the psychoanalytic experiential query on the evidence has no witnesses. Clinical work is private, not public, in a *dual* work on psychic evidence by patient and analyst. Its privacy and singularity places it in antithesis to the universalistic goals of the philosophies.

What, issuing from the immediacy of its clinical experiences, psychoanalysis makes public as its 'literature' or, worse, its 'theory' comes out opaquely: we meet here the gap between what Bertrand Russell (1911) set apart as direct, unmediated 'knowledge by acquaintance' and verbally mediated 'knowledge by description'. The clinical method works at the experiential level of knowledge by acquaintance; psychoanalytic literature, though, conveys a somewhat rigidified knowledge by description, that is of use mostly to those who are able to access their own background of clinical experience. Inability to jump the gap between private knowledge by acquaintance and publishable description is the reverse to a main epistemic strength: the challenge that in-depth personal enquiry poses to the universalistic aims of philosophers. Philosophy, says the philosopher Simon Blackburn, is thinking about 'the big themes: knowledge, reason, truth, mind, freedom, destiny, identity, God, goodness, justice' (1999, p. 1); it aims at the universal and at securing universal foundations for knowledge – an ambition often pursued at the cost of forsaking or obliterating the obvious.

It was on biology's prompting that an antecedent to a pluralistic notion of science emerged in antiquity. 'As is the science, so is the truth: for each science takes cognizance of its peculiar truths', said Aristotle (1995, p. 49) 25 centuries ago, speaking from his much too forgotten prominence as a scientist investigating disparate fields of enquiry, from the study of minerals to, and mostly, biology, as well as language, psychology, and political science. 'Natural science' was there meant in the plural, and respect for the particular in each field forsook pretensions to unity and univocity. In a final work Paul Feyerabend explains how, while 'theoreticist' approaches such as Plato's that built mathematical models in order to find the principles of planetary motion, leaving observations for a later stage, Aristotle's approach began with 'phenomena', taking experience at face value and striving to articulate observations, common sense, and abstract thought. He analysed the phenomena in a particular field, extrapolating and removing contradictions, staying close to observation in empirical issues, or to linguistic usage in abstract ones, and finally he brought in definitions to summarize what he had obtained; the deductive structure proposed for explanations served the exposition, not the discovery, of knowledge. Signalling the primacy of biology-driven thinking in Aristotle's pluralism on the sciences, Feyerabend (1995, p. 807) quotes the eminent biologist Ernst Mayr: 'No one prior to Darwin has made a greater contribution to our understanding of the living world than Aristotle.'

Fallibilist postures are espoused by working scientists but disowned by philosophies of science: Descartes' attempt to seek absolute knowledge by way of axiomatics coupled with a mechanical ontology was a daunting attempt to cut the Gordian knot of reality, which the philosopher does not easily renounce. The clinical approach of psychoanalysis attempting to untie, rather than cut, psychic Gordian knots poses to the universalistic ambitions of the philosophies of consciousness the charge of indulging in what to John Stuart Mill (1852) was the foremost fallacy, the fallacy of observation – that is, the error of *not*-observing. A main tenet of this book is that clinical psychoanalysis works to a greater extent on the basis of a reliance on access to discrepancies and errors than upon access to elusive 'truths' – an approach that is profitable in the session insofar as unconscious psychic facts attain representability. A brief example comes from an analysand who, at a time when a long-standing idealizing transference was in the process of breaking down, realized on entering her session that my eyes were not blue, as she had thought up to then, but (vulgar) brown eyes: this bluntly evidenced to her the might of her idealizations, opening the way to relevant new insights. Neatness in the access to evidence for error often contrasts with the vagaries of a search for indisputable 'truths': one might differ on my eyes' 'true' tinge, but elementary observation confirms that they are *not* blue. It falls to the omnipotent primitive parts of the personality to impose 'deductively' a logic of 'certainties' that is as valid as is the 'blue' colour of my eyes. Such a vignette summarizes well the main tenets deployed in *Insight: Essays in Psychoanalytic Knowing*.

Is the Pythagorean–Cartesian enthrallment with certainties alive and well? Yes, indeed. The need to sustain the epistemic autonomy of our clinical method focusing on insight arises today vis-à-vis 'empirical research' in psychoanalysis and the currently fashionable neurosciences. So-called psychoanalytic 'empirical research' proceeds as 'variable-research' upon a generalizing approach that, though indispensable for therapy outcome studies, has yet to show its ability to deal with the multifariousness of the psychoanalytic process. What is questionable there is a bent for displacing the findings of clinical psychoanalytic enquiry, giving *a priori* pride of place to what are assumed to be epistemically supraordinate 'empirical' ones in terms of the simplicities of 'variables'. The deductivistic bent backing such a stance is apparent in the complaint that 'It is our impression that psychoanalytic clinical practice is not logically deducible from currently available theory' (Fonagy, 2006, p. 72). However, as it happens, in no empirical realm is scientific practice deducible from theory.

Similar issues arise concerning the neurosciences. Psychoanalysis can gain valid knowledge from them: a case being, in the 1960s, the physiological studies on REM sleep establishing that sleep, beyond its Freudian function as the guardian of sleep, has a wider function as a guardian of sanity – a finding that can be clinically well appreciated. Let us hope that this happens to mutual benefit. A quite different issue is the proposal that clinical psychoanalysis should bind itself epistemically to the neurosciences, as was requested a decade ago by the Nobel-winning neuroscientist Eric Kandel in two papers (1998, 1999) maintaining that to have a new life psychoanalysis must align itself with, and put itself at the service of, the findings of brain research, posing a dichotomy between a *scientific* view of psychoanalysis, namely those analysts contributing to a brain-led science of mind, and a *hermeneutic* view, where it turns into a philosophy of mind, to be read, he says, as philosophical or poetic texts. The great absentees are clinical method and clinical thinking, shuffled out despite his conceding that in the neurosciences 'we do not yet have an intellectually satisfactory biological understanding of any complex mental process' (Kandel, 1999, p. 508).

To illustrate how neurobiology can teach about unconscious mental processes, Kandel brings in the dichotomy of *declarative (explicit) memory*, a conscious memory for people, objects, and places, and *procedural or implicit memory*, which is wholly unconscious and evident only in performance, not in conscious recall: thereupon he construes a *procedural unconscious* akin to implicit memory, avowing that many changes in the psychoanalytic process belong not to conscious insight but to 'unconscious procedural (nonverbal) knowledge and behavior' (1999, p. 509). He then demands that psychoanalysts shift from Freud to Pavlov – 'from an emphasis on introspection to an objective analysis of stimuli and responses' (1999, p. 510) – in order to arrive at 'the elementary mechanisms of psychic processes' (1999, p. 511), which does nothing but postulate such assumed 'elementary mechanisms'. He takes it as given that 'during the first 2–3 years of life, when the infant's interaction with his mother is particularly important, the infant relies primarily on its procedural memory systems. Both in humans and in experimental animals, declarative memory develops later' (1999, p. 513). Now, that for Kandel the infant in the first 2–3 years has no conscious memory for individuals, objects, or places illustrates well the distortions that experimentalism introduces in the realm of the psychic: similarly – as is argued in chapter 6 – Bateson had already shown that Pavlovian stimulus–response psychology was an artefact.

To give the lie to the supposition that in the first 2–3 years memory is just procedural, my witness is a 7½-month-old baby left late in the evening at his grandparents' house. Uncomfortable at being there at, for him, such an unusual time of day, he showed dull eyes and a lack of vitality. Striving to make him feel at home, his grandmother showed him a photograph of his father, smiling: recognizing him, the baby exploded in a burst of excited laughter and kicking; seconds later, seemingly realizing that this was just a photograph, he lost interest but was attentive to incoming telephone calls, signalling his parents' arrival. That the baby often brought the pacifier (dummy) to his mouth the wrong way round, took it out, examined it, and put it in correctly is procedural, but it involves recognition and *thinking*; that on observing his grandfather biting his pipe he took his pacifier out of his mouth, attentively examined it, and then eagerly looked again at the pipe, shows a relational *inference*. Moreover, that on going to sleep furnished with two pacifiers, he would put one into his mouth and give the other to the teddy-bear he hugged while he slept evidences his *thinking* that his partner needed or enjoyed it, just as he did: thus, at 7½ months of age, in addition to showing an explicit memory for people, objects, and places, this boy evidenced, as concerns his partner the bear, the inklings of a 'theory of mind'. Explicit memory and, most importantly, *thinking* are there long before the baby can *verbally* identify people, objects, and places, and long before experimental approaches notice them. A baby who does not, by the age of a few months, show acute attention to and an ability to discriminate between individuals, objects, and places is in severe trouble. Our baby is witness to the fact that in the realm of the psyche experimentation pushes much process observation aside. It is much too early, then, for psychoanalysis to forego insight as its tool, tying itself to the chariot of the neurosciences.

★★★

This introduction can only provide signposts to the road ahead: events must be 'shown' before they can be 'explained', and such 'showing' happens in the book itself. The reader is asked to read it keeping in mind his clinical experiences. As Voltaire put it: 'the most useful books are those in which the readers themselves provide half the meaning' (Cronk, 1994, p. xxiv). Written over the span of some 15 years, it is the end result of readings on Gregory Bateson's work, starting in the 1960s and 1970s, so that in my own clinical development Bateson was coetaneous with Freud. Exploring Bateson's main intellectual roots in Darwin and Russell led to an interest in logic and in the ins and outs of the theory of science. The book highlights the central role of insight in psychoanalytic knowing and in scientific thinking, as well as in everyday life.

The first chapter opens on a main conceptual theme: the centrality of paradox in relation to insight. Entitled 'Logical Types and Ostensive Insight', it studies Strachey's classic contribution to insight in terms of the distinction between descriptive insights, obtainable from grasping the analyst's verbalized interpretations, and ostensive insights, gained directly from one's experience. In order to be effective, insight must attain ostension. What to my mind is his core finding – that, paradoxically, to the analysand *the analyst is/is not the archaic object* – emphasizes the role of the analyst's neutrality, which allows the analysand to discern both terms of the paradox, thereby modifying his up to then unknown 'unconscious theories', which generally come up as enacted meaning frames rather than verbally. While 'mutative', 'true' transference interpretation is usually deemed to be Strachey's main contribution to technique, my emphasis is on the centrality of paradox in the dynamics of insight and on his hint about 'implicit transference interpretation', the technical implications of which are developed in chapter 8. Given that in its clinical and technical dimensions the whole book builds on this first chapter, perhaps at this point the reader might take a break, leave the book aside for a while, reread this initial chapter, and then go on.

The next chapter should, hopefully, be easier going: my emphasis on the enacted (pragmatic) meaning frames implies a naturalistic frame of interaction, upon which chapter 2, 'Interpretation and Creationism', posits a critique of the hermeneutic and narrative approaches to psychoanalysis, which requires a first approach to a recurring theme: that of induction. The hermeneutic dichotomy of 'sciences of nature', derived from physicalistic notions of 'natural law', and 'sciences of the spirit', which study the singular fact on the basis of history, remove from the realm of science the observational sciences, and as concerns the psyche, it erases its bodily, enacted levels, which are at the core of psychic reality, while raising to centre stage language as 'text'.

The following chapter, chapter 3, 'What is a Clinical Fact? Clinical Psychoanalysis as Inductive Method' addresses the epistemic status of psychoanalytic evidence. Based on two clinical vignettes, it argues that the analyst chooses his interpretations guided by how he intuits he is 'used' by the analysand and how the analysand feels 'used' by him. Here the unconscious is conceived as a tautology of mainly enacted propositional 'forms' or 'theories' applied 'deductively' by the analysand to the universe of his factual objects, the analyst included. Interpretations as tentative 'verbal mappings' lead the analysand to 'descriptive insights'. But only through *his own* observational inductive refutation, once psychic facts have accessed some representability, does the analysand come to refute or modify his 'unconscious theories' – that is, he arrives at counterinduction, opening the way to new enquiries and new insights. The notion of a one-member class (the Class-Object) where the individual and the unconscious class coincide, is introduced in the second clinical vignette.

Again some respite is offered in the next two chapters. Chapter 4, 'Body, Meaning and Language' discusses how Wittgensteinian linguistic philosophy involves the demise of embodied psychism, while to psychoanalytic theories of language, following Ella Sharpe and Matte-Blanco, language is a metaphor of the bodily psyche.

Chapter 5, 'Fact, Context, Image, Narrative: A Bio-logical Approach', in its unfolding of a wide Darwinian–Freudian naturalistic framework, exemplifies extensive areas of experience that are beyond the descriptive grasp of mechanistic approaches and are simply dropped by hermeneutic–linguistic ones; as there illustrated, a wide naturalistic framework relies on 'open' concepts rather than on clear, distinct, undoubted ones.

Together with chapters 1 and 3, chapters 6, 7, and 8 provide, in their different ways, the conceptual epistemic kernel of the book. Chapters 6 and 7 engage in the epistemic wars waged on the part of scientism, addressing critiques of psychoanalysis made by Adolf Grünbaum's strict inductivism and Karl Popper's formalistic falsificationism. Chapter 6, 'Toward the Epistemology of Clinical Psychoanalysis', sorts out the meaning of induction and causality in the exact, 'theoretical' sciences and in the descriptive sciences, showing how Grünbaum's criteria of cause, evidence, warrant, and natural history of neuroses enclose the domain of mind within that of mechanics. Two versions of the Tally Argument are contrasted – Grünbaum's, where the analysand must excavate the real event causing the neurosis, and Freud's, in which interpretation must fit the analysand's unconscious psychic reality. It then clinically exemplifies how the Freudian *Deutung* involves interactions on two logical levels: an ostensive level of pointing to facts and events, and a metainterpretive level, a conjecture on the analysand's unconscious ways of piecing together his facts or events.

Passing on to chapter 7, 'Disclosures and Refutations: Clinical Psychoanalysis as a Logic of Enquiry', the reader must be warned that even though Popper presents himself again and again as a trial-and-error fallibilist, the fact is that an unremitting demand for formalization rules his epistemic logicism: his 'bold conjectures' must be part of *formal* systems, and only what operates fully deductively is deemed by him to be verifiable and therefore scientific. In a 'top-down' strategy purportedly leading from formal theory to facts, as opposed to Grünbaum's 'bottom-up' strategy supposedly rising from facts to theory, Popperian falsificationism similarly makes of 'hard', 'theoretical' sciences an organon for all science. Here we meet the gap between the practical scientist and the philosopher of science: after Feyerabend, it is argued that scientists develop a *practical logic*, allowing them to get results amid chaos and incoherence, built mostly *ad hoc*, which cannot be turned into an organon of research. The wide gap between the deductivistic 'rational reconstructions' of the philosophy of science and the practical logic that the scientist develops when faced with concrete issues backs Lakatos' claim that the huge differences between inductive and deductive logic make the term logic, used for both, a misnomer. Lakatos' method of 'proofs and refutations' (counterpoised to Popper's method of '[formal] conjectures and refutations') proceeds by evolving counter-examples in order to explore one's assumptions or lemmas, seeking hitherto undetected sub-conjectures: here 'proof' means simply a lack of available counter-examples. My view of the psychoanalytic method as a method of 'disclosures and refutations' follows rather closely upon this line of thought, except that working in pure geometry Lakatos underlines theoretical anticipation as a key to new facts, while my approach relies on the role of ostension and surprise, clinical psychoanalysis being an observational extension of everyday practical logic. Bion describes in everyday discernment a *psychoanalytic function of the personality* highlighting the painful nature of change towards mental maturity. Being multi-levelled, insight often involves traversing paradoxes – as is illustrated clinically.

Further clinical and technical detail on how interpretation helps the analysand to attain insight by ostensive refutation and redressing (counterinduction) of his until then unconscious 'theories' on relationship comes up in chapter 8, 'Counterinduction in Psychoanalytic Practice: Epistemic and Technical Aspects' evincing how he obtains, by multiple comparisons, an *experiential* correlation between the descriptive 'mapping' interpretation purveys and how he unconsciously colligates his events. Inasmuch as the analyst's attempts at interpretation threaten to actualize what he tries to describe, the situation has the formal qualities of a paradox. It is clinically illustrated how in the attempt to articulate multiple vertices of observation, effective interpretations often need to conjoin extra-transference and transference dimensions, which gives a due technical place to the notion of 'implicit transference interpretation'.

The clinical material in Betty Joseph's classic paper 'Transference, the Total Situation' (1985) gives the chance in chapter 9, 'Logical and Communicational Levels and Transference', to put to further use Matte-Blanco's notion of the unconscious as propositional functions, and especially Bateson's ideas on the logical levels of 'relationship' with its two sets of hierarchical levels: *metalinguistic*, referring to the language itself, and *metacommunicative*, with hierarchical 'frames' for the action and the emotion (analogical) relationship of the interlocutors. Chapter 10, 'The Double Work on the Clinical Evidences, and the Nature and Limits of Symbolization', develops clinically, in a series of transformational cycles, how psychic evolutions traverse various paradoxes. Then, based on the work of the Russian linguist Natalia Avtonomova, it reviews the term symbolization as used from Kant to the structuralist notion of a symbolic system and then to Lacan's Symbolic Order, striving to clarify the difference between the way symbolization is employed in philosophy and the social sciences, and its meaning in psychoanalysis, where it is ancillary to insight. The analysand's 'unconscious theories' can only be mapped as they evolve through particular concrete instances through which ostensive insights are gained; this, in turn, allows the analysand to traverse his conflict-ridden ongoing paradoxes. Though his psychic splits operate as powerful instruments of *un*knowing, at each step in the double work on the evidences, the analysand remains the epistemic arbiter.

Attempting to reassess the issues, chapter 11 'The Analytic Mind at Work: Counterinductive Knowledge and the Blunders of so-called "Theory of Science"' argues that the epistemic stance here employed follows upon and expands Freud's epistemic views. An extended clinical example illustrates the mingling of pre-genital and genital anxieties the analysand meets in traversing his paradoxes. Current views on the unitary 'theory of science' are re-evaluated, focusing on Popper's deductivist formalism. Such a restrictive view is contrasted with Whewell's broad notion of induction upon joint evolution of 'Facts' and 'Theory', a notion that suits the needs of clinical psychoanalysis.

Finally, the Postscript briefly considers the fate of insight in media culture.

As masterfully stated by Dale Boesky in his book *Psychoanalytic Disagreements in Context*, he relies, as do I, on 'the epistemological assumption that there is an imperfectly knowable real world' (2008, p. 27). This follows upon the fact that, as the historian Barbara Tuchman puts it, 'Contradictions . . . are part of life, not merely a matter of conflicting evidence' (1978, p. xvii). Enquiry on the multi-levelled, contradictory facts in the session focusing on a counter-inductive strategy of ostensive access to dysanalogies and emerging analogies recaptures and further specifies how Freud's method, keeping close to the facts of observation and removed as far as is feasible from philosophical apriorism, understood the modus operandi of our fallible reality-testing.

Fallibilism in the sciences extends, however, far beyond the multi-levelled contradictoriness apparent in the study of the psyche. It shines, prominently, in Einstein's lashing overall comment that 'Whoever undertakes to set himself up as judge in the field of Truth and Knowledge is shipwrecked by the laughter of the gods' (1954, p. 28).

1

Logical types and ostensive insight

It was Freud's opinion in 'Analysis Terminable and Interminable' (1937) that the way in which analytic cure comes about was well enough known, and that only the obstacles to it required further study. But while ink was still wet on his paper, Otto Fenichel challenged this assumption in a privately circulated manuscript (published in 1974). In fact, the process of psychic change in psychoanalytic therapy remains a main field of enquiry, in which a leading role, paving the way to the primacy of insight, was played by James Strachey's 'The nature of the therapeutic action of psychoanalysis' (1934) and his Marienbad paper (1937). This role is attested by the many papers written, even today, to evaluate his stress on 'true' transference interpretation, which he considers the mainspring to structural psychic change.

My enquiry addresses the process of insight. I shall argue that Strachey posits as background to insight a pragmatic paradox evolving towards a map–territory discrimination – that is, *an evolution in logical typing.* I shall then attempt to show that the analysand's 'judgement of reality' of his analyst's interpretations takes place through the evolution of this pragmatic paradox.

The theory of logical types, introduced in 1903 by Bertrand Russell and developed in Whitehead and Russell's *Principia Mathematica* in 1912, deals with mathematical paradox; it was expanded on later by Russell, Carnap and Reichenbach into a theory of logical levels in language. Little if any explicit use has been made of it in psychoanalysis, but what it postulates has relevance to our science: Freud's distinction, from the *Traumdeutung* (1900) on, of a thing-presentation (*Dingvorstellung*) different from, and previous to, the word-presentation (*Wortvorstellung*), comes from a recognition, *avant* Russell, of a fundamental difference in what are now called logical levels. Early on Freud linked to the word-presentation the possibility of a thought becoming conscious: 'Thus, as early as the "Project for a Scientific Psychology" (1950a [1895]), we encounter the idea that the memory-image, by becoming associated with a verbal image, can acquire that "indication of quality" which is the specific mark of consciousness' (Laplanche & Pontalis, 1967, p. 448).

In 'An analysis of the concept of insight' Jerome Richfield (1954) has taken up Strachey's work in terms of Russell's distinction of descriptive and ostensive knowledge. After examining Strachey's and Richfield's views on insight, I shall turn to Bateson's (1973, 1979) studies of analogic and digital codes and the role of paradox in evolution, and then to the implications of Matte-Blanco's (1975, 1988) idea that the unconscious can only recognize propositional functions and not individuals as such.[1] My intention is to use these ideas to approach the clinical paradox on which, in my view, Strachey bases the process of insight.

Strachey's contribution to the dynamics of insight

Strachey speaks of 'becoming conscious', not of insight, but he traced the line between suggestion and the structural psychic changes coming through interpretation (Etchegoyen, 1983). On his cognizance of the substantial difference between an intellectual awareness of unconscious processes and becoming 'really' conscious of them, the pivot of the analytic process turns to true transference or *mutative* interpretation, pointing to an actual id-impulse towards the analyst. Two phases, successive or simultaneous, characterize it: in the first, the analysand becomes aware of an id-impulse addressed to the analyst as archaic object, while in the second the analyst manages to establish the difference between how the patient sees him as his archaic object and his functioning as a real object. This contrast is possible only if the analyst rigorously maintains his setting.

As Strachey puts it, in words whose concreteness has led to misunderstandings, mutative interpretation attempts an 'introjection of the analyst'. By this he means that the analyst becomes the nucleus of 'a separate and new superego':

> his one endeavour from the very beginning is to differentiate himself from the patient's archaic objects and to contrive, as far as

> he possibly can, that the patient shall introject him not as one more archaic imago added to the rest of the primitive superego, but as the nucleus of a separate and new superego.
>
> (1937, p. 144)

This introjection, described as specific, gradual, and linked to reality, will occur at the time of transference interpretations. These are, he says, unique in the patient's experience, because the object of his unconscious impulses is both clearly aware of their nature and is feeling neither anxiety nor anger on their account. The unique quality of this introjection – contrasted with the 'benign' or 'vicious' circle of introjection–projection of the 'good' or 'bad' fantasy object – will prevent its absorption into the original superego and be a step towards structural psychic change. (This is so, in my opinion, because it has the characteristics – 'specific', 'gradual', and 'linked to reality' – of the emergence of a new logical type.)

But, while he sets apart true transference interpretations, Strachey knows that many extratransference interpretations are indeed necessary, and he introduces at this point a to my mind crucial hint on 'implicit transference interpretation':

> It must not be supposed that because I am attributing these special qualities to transference interpretations, I am therefore maintaining that no others should be made. On the contrary, it is probable that a large majority of our interpretations are outside the transference – though it should be added that *it often happens that when one is ostensibly giving an extratransference interpretation one is implicitly giving a transference one* . . . though it is true that extra-transference interpretations are not for the most part mutative, and do not bring about the crucial results that involve a permanent change in the patient's mind, they are none the less essential.
>
> (1934, p. 158, emphasis added)

On descriptive and ostensive insights

As mentioned, Richfield (1954) re-orders Strachey's work on insight on the basis of a distinction made by Bertrand Russell (1911). In *knowledge by acquaintance* we are directly aware of the object itself – that is, knowledge is gained without logical dependence on any inferential process. *Knowledge by description* transcends the private experience in the cognitive relation of acquaintance. Here, knowledge takes the form of judgements about an object; the judgement, and not the object itself, is what is known, and it is known by analogy and by inference.

Knowledge by description and knowledge by acquaintance in no way exclude each other, but no amount of discourse or description *about* something can be equivalent to the knowledge gained from direct experience. If a patient gains knowledge only by descriptions of his unconscious processes, these remain ego-alien and have no effect upon his symptoms, and so, says Richfield, 'the cognitions that achieve insight must result from the direct relation between the knower and his feelings' (p. 402). Something is, he says, defined *ostensively* when the thing defined is actually exhibited, and he quotes Russell (1948) to the effect that

> every word that you can understand must either have a nominal definition in terms of words having an ostensive definition, or must itself have an ostensive definition, and *ostensive definitions*, as appears from the process by which they are effected, are only possible in relation to *events that have occurred to you*.
>
> (p. 87, emphasis added)

On this basis Richfield sets apart *descriptive insights*, which provide the patient with truths about himself by making use of his capacity to comprehend the words used in any interpretation, and *ostensive insights*, which incorporate the actual, conscious experience of their referents – which involve, that is, an acquisition of knowledge by acquaintance with unconscious processes. He concludes that effective insight may be achieved by the proper timing of both types of insight, in an appropriate order:

> Without ostensive insights, the referent of interpretations made to the patient will never be known in any efficacious way. And without descriptive insights, the patient will never be adequately prepared to 'face' the necessary emotional contents which must be handled by his conscious personality, nor to understand enough of the facts and relations of his hitherto repressed drives to sustain . . . personality modifications.
>
> (p. 407)

To Russell verbal definitions about facts derive, ultimately, from direct acquaintance. This coincides with Freud's (1891) opinion that a word acquires its *meaning* by being linked to a thing-presentation – which is made up of the unconscious traces of innumerable single impressions of the object (Freud, 1917a, p. 256). In any case, we should try to learn more about how a patient comes to a genuine experience – that is, to a knowledge by acquaintance of his unconscious processes.

Analogic and digital codes: logical levels in the epistemology of relationship

Let me now introduce some notions about the characteristics of analogic and digital codes that to Bateson (1973, 1979) are essential to the epistemology of relationship: suffice it to say here that gestures and tones of voice are partly intelligible across cultural barriers, while verbal codes are unintelligible.

Analogic codes of relationship imply *actions*: the size of the gesture, the intensity of the voice, the tension of the muscle, or the length of the pause, says Bateson, are measurements of the relationship itself. Analogic codes are *continuous*, and they relate precisely to matters of relationship. They constitute a hierarchy equivalent to the logical levels of language: this includes mood-signs, iconic signals in which action messages operate on a part-for-whole basis, 'psychological frames' delimiting 'context', and highly abstract 'contexts of contexts', enabling the occurrence of pragmatic paradoxes.

As they employ arbitrary *names*, which are at the same time both discrete (i.e. discontinuous, though of course not numerative) and ordered as positions in a matrix, verbal codes can be said to be partly digitalized, and they belong to *a different logical type from the thing named*. They are not quite suitable for 'mapping' emotional events: they are superimposed on, but in no way replace, the analogical emotional codes. They make two crucial developments possible: to refer to things other than relationship, and to de-centre the subject in propositional forms.

In analogic codes the message-giver is necessarily the subject of the relational proposition, and the receiver – for whom the message is the 'context' of his own response – must always be present. Illustrating this point, Bateson (1973, p. 246) says that when a cat tries to get us to give her food, she will make the same gestures a kitten makes to a mother cat: her message is not 'give me milk' but 'be my mother'. While the analogic relational message is an enacted proposal in which emitter and receiver must be present, the partial digitalization of verbal messages allows its emitter to become the third party to the proposition. But, as verbal codes are superimposed on analogic ones, it is not feasible for a verbal proposition – an interpretation – to refrain from referring at an analogic (unconscious) level to the relationship between emitter and receiver.

On paradox in logic and in human communication

To logicians, paradoxes or antinomies, be they mathematical or logical, are simply anomalies. The most famous of these, the Epimenides or Cretan paradox – if a Cretan says: 'All Cretans lie', does he lie or does he speak the truth? – has puzzled mankind's best minds from antiquity on. At the simplest level it can be said: 'This sentence is false'. If the sentence is true, then it is false; and if it is false, then it is true' (Carnap, 1937, p. 213): but the sentence is meaningless, because the word 'this', which refers to the sentence in which it occurs, is at the same logical level as its referent. The rule of formation states that a sign-combination denoting any object must be one logical level higher than the object it denotes (Reichenbach, 1947, p. 224).

Reichenbach readily acknowledges (p. 2) that logicians deal not with processes of thought but with their rational reconstructions, necessarily bound to linguistic forms; they deal, that is, with the 'context of justification' of verbal propositions: language, as seen by the logician, restricts itself to its *cognitive* use: that is, for expressing true statements. *Instrumental* uses of language, even *communicative* use that attempts not only to convey a meaning but to make the listener believe the sentence uttered – and to Reichenbach every report by one person to another is of this kind – relates to pragmatics, to which the logical predicates 'true' or 'false' do not apply. Since logic deals perforce with written verbal propositions, it takes no account of the wide terrain of analogic emotional codes and their hierarchy of more abstract 'frames'.

In contrast to this rationalized world of logic, human communication operates on many different levels of abstraction simultaneously. Taking as a starting point what Reichenbach calls the 'zero level' of *object-language*, the seemingly simple denotative level ('the cat is on the mat'), Bateson (1955, p. 150) suggests that two quite distinct sets of hierarchical levels – that is, two different sets of metalevels – must be taken into account: the *metalinguistic*, whose object is the language itself, and the *metacommunicative*, setting the enacted contextual and metacontextual frames for the relationship of the interlocutors.

Metacommunicative 'frames' – that is, the higher level frames setting the 'contexts' and 'metacontexts' of relationship – are usually implicit, gestural, or situational rather than verbal. Any analyst who is attentive to gestural and tonal clues from his patient on coming into a session will, I believe, confirm that they frequently signal an unconscious 'frame' setting the 'context' for the session – a 'context' often quite split off from a verbal narrative of a different logical type, usually closer to consciousness. In the study of mammalian evolution it has generally been found that attempts to discriminate between categories of different logical types produce paradoxes: these *paradoxes are, to Bateson, intrinsic to an evolving communication* that, without them, would come to a halt.

The paradoxical 'reality' of the analyst

To André Green (1984), in the analytic situation word-presentations come closer to thing-presentations, and so language in analysis is closer to the unconscious – which to Freud (1915b) is a build-up of thing-presentations. It can be said that this is true too of the analysand's experience of his analyst (and, unfortunately, also of his experience of relevant people in his current life).

Strachey (1934), in describing how insight comes to the analysand by perceiving his analyst in two antinomic perspectives – one with the characteristics his id-impulses (projectively) give him and the other as someone who is aware of these impulses and is nevertheless able to 'map' them by verbal intervention while feeling neither anxiety nor anger – is positing a pragmatic paradox, which in cognitive language can be stated thus: *the analyst 'is/is not' the archaic object.* In Freudian terms, the paradox involves the 'reality' of the unconscious thing-presentation, on the one hand, and conscious thought linked to word-presentations on the other.

Strachey knows that this paradox is fragile and that the analytic situation threatens to degenerate into a 'real' situation: 'the patient is all the time on the brink of turning the real external object (the analyst) into an archaic one'. That is why, he says, 'the analyst must avoid any real behaviour that is likely to confirm the patient's view of him as a "bad" or "good" fantasy object' (1934, p. 146). Pleading for analytic neutrality, he acknowledges that it involves a paradox:

> It is a paradoxical fact that the best way of ensuring that his ego shall be able to distinguish between phantasy and reality is *to withhold reality from him* as much as possible. But it is true. His ego is so weak – so much at the mercy of his id and his superego, that he can only cope with reality if it is administered in minimal doses.
>
> (1934, p. 147, emphasis added)

The structure of paradox appears, too, in his use of the terms *real* and *reality*, which involves different logical levels: (a) the 'psychic reality' of the unconscious processes of introjection and projection of the archaic object, pertaining to the analogic codes of relationship ('action' and 'emotion' propositions), and (b) the apprehension of a 'factual reality', which in logical terms is a metalevel to 'psychic reality'.

The distinction between these two levels and the emergence of conscious thought about the 'psychic reality' come to be called 'insight'. Interpretation – the analyst's verbal 'mapping' or 'explanation' – aims to develop this (conscious) metalevel[2]: to this purpose his *withholding (analogic) reality* is a prime condition.

Here, in the epistemology of insight in the analytic situation, we may find proof of what is perhaps Bateson's most general assertion: that 'the relationship comes first: it *precedes*' (1979, p. 143). To Freud (1933b) the unconscious level of 'psychic reality' is the true mental reality; and in it, to paraphrase Bateson, 'the reality of the unconscious object-relationship comes first, it *precedes*'.

At the level of mainly unconscious analogic communication, patient and analyst are both subjects of the relational propositions they posit, this being the level of the point of urgency – addressed to the analyst as actual interlocutor. As any intervention by the analyst takes place within an unconscious transference 'context' set by the patient and determining his implicit relational role, he must be able to intuit it in order to formulate an interpretation, carrying towards greater explicitness the unconscious role whereby the patient sets a 'context' to his interventions. Otherwise he risks enacting either the role the patient is attributing him or his defence against it – that is, his projective counteridentification (Grinberg, 1956). In this way, he validates the projection and adds to its 'reality'; therein lies the risk, firmly stressed by Strachey, of precipitating massive projection of the impulse.

Hic, nunc, mecum?

We can now, I hope, better describe when an interpretation is transferential and when it is not. Following current usage, Strachey sorts out transference and extratransference interpretations on their overt formulation: that is, upon whether they do – or do not – explicitly refer the ongoing unconscious processes to the person of the analyst. But then he introduces 'implicit mutative interpretation'. Why? – we may ask.

As patient and analyst are present, it is a truism to say that the analytic situation is *hic, nunc, mecum*. In extratransference interpretation the *hic, nunc, mecum* is not alluded to, while in true transference interpretation it is directly referred to. 'Implicit transference interpretation' does refer to the *hic, nunc, mecum*, but not directly: it refers to an *unconscious propositional form*[3]: that is, to a 'property' or 'quality' shared – in whatever way – by an outside situation – in practice, one that is the focus of the patient's verbal discourse – and the present link to the analyst. So, while extra-transferential in its overt formulation, it is transferential as concerns the ongoing unconscious process. It is not the final formulation, but that, says Strachey, does not make it any less essential.

An interpretation that deals adequately with the urgent material addressed to the analyst is in substance transferential; but often it cannot be explicitly so, as it must modulate the emergence of its archaic emitter – that is, the patient's 'psychic reality', which is subject to the all-or-none laws of primary process. The point is that the analyst must avoid *being – to the analysand's unconscious – what he interprets*: therein lies the need for 'withholding (analogic) reality', and the technical need for implicit mutative interpretations.

Interpretation in psychoanalysis, though in essence communicative, attempts a 'pure' cognitive use of language to express true statements, as opposed to its instrumental use (which includes the attempt to convince). And, according to Reichenbach (1947), the predicates 'true' or 'false' apply only to cognitive use. This is similar to Strachey's 'withholding reality', which appears, then, as a requisite for the evolution towards semantization of the enacted pragmatic paradox. The 'neutrality' of the analyst includes his choice of models and his choice of words, the criteria here being *explicitness in 'mapping' plus enough distance between message and messenger.*

André Green (1984) has pointed out that the analysand's language is a hypercondensed content to be decondensed by analytic work. In practice, this is also to some extent valid for the analyst's language: because of this, it must be tactfully gradual as it unavoidably 'incarnates', in the process of making it explicit, the all-or-nothing archaic object projected on the analyst. Gradualness as to the *mecum* (as in 'implicit transference interpretation') avoids blurring this distinction; otherwise the concreteness of the archaic object's 'psychic reality', analogic and relational, may swamp the emerging difference in logical typing between the process level and the metalevel, in which the analyst can be listened to by the analysand as third party to the content of his interpretation – to what he is making explicit.

Transference, present and past, in ostensive insight

In his discussion of Strachey's paper, Rosenfeld (1972) takes the stand that, in addition to detailed verbal interpretation and working-through of the transference, it is necessary to establish, in a systematic way, links with the analysand's past and his present life situation. Matte-Blanco's (1978) proposal that the unconscious does not recognize individuals as such, but only propositional functions with no temporal ordering, lends a rigorous grounding to this indeed classical stand.

From this perspective, the actuality of repetition in the transference, the past as actualized in remembrance, and the actuality of the analysand's present life events come to be seen as areas for the appearance of the same a-temporal analogic and relational unconscious propositional functions – that is, unconscious 'action' and 'emotion' proposals. It is fitting, then, that attaining a new logical level requires an interpretive approach providing 'mapping' or 'explanation' in each of these different areas.

It would seem, too, that with the concept of the unconscious as propositional forms, the opposition between transference and extra-transference interpretations becomes less clear-cut. Indeed, in practice they are often tied together as parts of an interpretive formulation, and there is, I believe, some agreement that interpretations providing multiple 'mapping' by tying together the unconscious ways of 'action' and 'emotion' in the patient's past, in his actual life circumstance and in his link to the analyst, are, if adequate, most effective. This is a particular instance of a general finding in evolution: that the emergence of new logical levels occurs by 'double (or multiple) description' – that is, by correlation of descriptions from different vertices and different codes (Bateson, 1979).

Some comments on transference and extratransference interpretation

Wherein lies, then, the primacy – if any – of 'true' transference interpretation? This has been discussed for decades, and there is no simple answer.

From my own standpoint the problem seems largely tactical: I see 'true' transference interpretation as the keystone of an interpretive cycle of 'implicit' transference interpretations that gradually further the patient's acquaintance with the 'action' and 'emotion' relational propositions of his unconscious psychic reality and bring into the *here, now, mecum* an awareness of conflict.

In fairness, ostensive insights are not restricted to 'true' transference interpretations, a point argued by Harold Stewart (1990) and held decades before in unpublished conferences by Melanie Klein, who was of the opinion that transference interpretations were incomplete unless they linked the here and now of the session to the phantasies and, if possible, to the realities of the remembered past (Spillius, 2007, p. 187). Ostensive insights *may* and *do* come out of memories, dreams, current life interactions, and waking fantasies, each of which can function as a 'screen' or 'matrix' where instinctual derivatives attain representability. But it is no less true that, in principle, actualization of analogic relational codes tends to occur in the presence of emitter and receiver. This seems particularly true of the *early* conflict, arising from preverbal levels of the early Oedipus complex of which there are no preconscious memories, and coming into the analysis through repetition (Etchegoyen, 1982). And, last but not least, an adequate handling of the transference is essential for the giving of adequate overtly extra-transferential interpretations, which must, in my view, be implicitly transferential as to the process.

On the analysand's 'reality judgement' of his analyst's interpretive mapping

In the paradoxical situation between the pragmatic priority of unconscious 'psychic reality' and an evolving 'conscious reality' sustained upon the analyst's interpretive 'mapping', how does the patient come to attribute 'reality' to this verbal mapping?

In the actual relation to the analyst, the paradox is sustained simultaneously by relational unconscious repetition and a 'frame' where repetition is contrasted with the (relative) neutrality of an actual living being, who provides essential interpretive verbal 'mapping' and responds by *withholding the validation of archaic unconscious relational 'reality'*. The analysand's 'reality judgement' would seem to require an ostensive knowledge, 'in terms of events that occur', by way of a 'withholding' of the analogic 'action' and 'emotion' propositional forms of the archaic object. Perceived as 'clearly aware of his id-impulses and feeling on their account neither anxiety nor anger', the analyst introduces by his abstinence a dimension of pragmatic refutability to the primacy of unconscious 'psychic reality', allowing for its consistent resolution – 'specific', 'gradual' and 'linked to (factual) reality'.

If this is so, while the verbal coding of interpretations provides essential coordinates for 'mapping' unconscious psychic events, the *reality judgement* giving substance to this 'mapping' is the *patient*'s 'mapping' – unconscious as well as conscious, verbalized or not – at the analogic 'process' level, and *not* solely the analyst's verbal interpretive 'mapping'. In this way, analytic psychic change through ostensive insight can be seen to operate scientifically through refutability of archaic 'reality', rigorously *per via di levare*, in a manner totally opposite to suggestion. It takes up, to a present analyst, the mechanism of emergence of thought in the absence of the (archaic) object.

In this light, what Strachey calls the 'introjection' of the analyst comes to be seen as an 'insight on the projection' and not an introjection as such (in fact, Strachey himself distinguished it quite well from the 'vicious' or 'benign' circle of introjection–projection). In this area much if not most is still to be studied. But it can be said with some confidence that ostensive insight – that is, knowledge by acquaintance with unconscious processes – evolves through a tolerance of pragmatic paradox, and that the emergence of a distinction between an 'inside' and an 'outside' is part and parcel of the discrimination between psychic and factual reality.

2

Interpretation and creationism

The query about the nature of psychoanalytic knowledge confronts *Weltanschauungen* rooted in the mainstreams of Western thought, those of philosophy and science. Far from being merely academic, it determines how our method is to be used. From an empirical standpoint, the analyst's interpretation is part and parcel of an inductive method in which both analysand and analyst play a part, while to hermeneutic disciplines, in their current 'linguistic turn', the role of interpretation in the analytic situation shifts to the creation of meaning – to a *verbal creationism*. My argument will unfold as follows:

1 The oft-expressed view that psychoanalysis must discard its claims to be an empirical science ignores the differences between exact and observational science and hence is based on a straw-man conception of science.
2 The rift between 'human' and 'natural' or 'empirical' science, stemming from the religious idea of man's partaking of God and of the omnipotence of his Word, is old, dangerous and misleading, and it impinges crucially on the role language is seen to play.
3 Psychoanalysis is an observational science; its clinical method is inductive on the part of both analysand and analyst, and it rests on a pragmatic theory of observation.
4 The *Geisteswissenschaft* outlook of psychoanalysis eschews psychic reality; on the basis of such a dismissal, and on its rhetorical view of truth, it leads to a verbal creationism.

On exact and observational sciences: the nature of scientific induction

In the midst of the confusion over the nature of induction prevalent at the turn of the century and aiming to place historical experience in consonance with the methods of science, Dilthey and his followers construed a duality: that of *explicative* or nomothetic sciences, the *Naturwissenschaften* or sciences of nature, of which the model is physics, and *interpretive* or ideographic sciences, the *Geisteswissenschaften* or 'cultural' sciences, which pursue an empathic understanding of the motives of the singular fact, of which the model is history. This proposal has been backed by those coming into our field from idealistic philosophies, or lately from narrative backgrounds, who do not wish the study of man to be subject to scientific strictures, and it is helped along indirectly by such philosophers of science as Braithwaite (1953) and Ernest Nagel (1959), to whom the exact sciences are paradigmatic for all science. Out of the mutual upholding of that unlikely alliance come such manifestos on the status of psychoanalysis as that of Duncan in his Amsterdam Congress pre-published paper:

> Psychoanalysis has now fully outgrown its first unquestioned assumption that it belonged to the natural sciences. With this presumption has gone the corollary *that its theories must work in precisely the same mode as did those of physics and chemistry* in their attempts at illuminating and focusing quantifiable attributes of physical objects and their relationships.
>
> (1993, p. 25, emphasis added)

Equating the natural and exact sciences, Duncan and others, such as Home (1966), Steele (1979) and Holland (1990), impute to empirical stances in psychoanalysis the conceptual structure of physics or chemistry, and after thus setting up their straw-man they have no qualms in branding empirical approaches 'reductionistic'. Before we put that misconstrual right by attending to the differences between 'exact' and 'observational' sciences, those differences between 'formal' and 'empirical' sciences must first be explained.

Mathematical or logical systems are independent of factual constituents;[1] such purely formal sciences are *deductive tautologies* with no direct empirical bearing, and on that basis can always be true. Some influential conceptions of science do mimic formal sciences. For example, Braithwaite (1953) defines scientific systems as a set of hypotheses forming a *deductive system*, so that from some of them being taken as premises *all* others follow logically as conclusions, induction being the method for the establishment of hypotheses within such deductive systems. Holding that every scientific proposition is of the form 'All A is B', he avows that the purpose of empirical science is to establish such nomothetic, that is, general laws, as does Nagel too (1961). This being so, Black (1961) quips that Braithwaite's ideal of science is built on Euclid's *Elements*.

But the fact is that only the 'exact' sciences, such as physics and chemistry, which deal with variables assumed to be *homogeneous*, such as 'length' or 'mass', and rely on measurement or experimental manipulation of such variables (Waelder, 1962), can mimic deductive systems. Even in the case of physics, argues Frank (1959) after Bridgman, the operations that define 'length' or 'temperature', let alone those defining 'energy' or similar concepts, apply only in extremely 'smooth' conditions in which there are no abrupt changes in temperature or density of matter, so these terms have no global meaning (p. 304). The sciences of living forms – that is, the biological and social sciences dealing with *complex*, non-homogeneous events – rely on systematic *observations* and their *interpretation*; such is the case with Darwinian evolution, which is accepted for its fitting together of a wide array of unrelated data from multiple sources, not for any crucial experiment. H. Joseph (1916, p. 4) notes that the purpose of all science is the tracing of *forms* – that is, patterns – and to this purpose it is interested in the *singular fact*, in diverse instances or fresh details, not in mere repetitions. It cannot be stressed too strongly that the varied logics of the forms or patterns studied by the sciences of living beings are far more complex than Braithwaite's formula 'all A is B' allows. Even the simple buzzer, says Bateson, follows a quite contradictory logic: 'if contact is made, then contact is broken' (1979, pp. 62–63), that is, 'if P, then not P'. It is the repetitious circle in time of such logic that keeps the buzzer ringing.

The rampant deductivism tingeing the ideas of empirical science derives from the fact that since Hume's time induction has been seen by many as a 'failed deduction', as an unjustifiable jump from particular premises to universal conclusions. It is a scientist's dream, says Susanne Langer (1953), to formulate his facts in a completely deductive system: that is, to make empirical knowledge deductive in the manner of the 'formal' sciences. The pursuit of deductive *certainties* is out of place in the inductive systems of the empirical sciences, where, holds Langer, a wide array of non-inferable facts must be 'given' by experience. By 1874 Jevons had already recognized that inductive propositions, of which the consequences are to be deduced and tested, are *hypotheses* for which certainty in the philosophers' sense is not attainable (von Wright, 1957). As highlighted in the Introduction, Freud, a staid inductivist, knew full well that science 'lacks the attributes of definiteness, immutability and infallibility for which the human spirit so deeply longs' (1926, p. 191).

A lack of access to certainties is taken for granted by scientists, if not usually by philosophers of science. Scientific concepts are, to put it in Pap's (1958) terms, 'open concepts', ever subject to redefinition or rejection by findings emerging in new experiences or contexts. This ensues from the way in which scientific concepts are defined. In the actual process of knowledge, says Reichenbach (1947, p. 22), abstract statements are always verified by verification of statements about directly observable things; such definitions – for example, those defining 'metabolism' in reference to biological variables – he calls 'definitions in use'. Such a stand on 'open concepts' is also Freud's own, as shown – among many other instances – by his well-known avowal in the *Autobiographical Study*:

> The basic ideas or most general concepts in any of the disciplines of science are always left indeterminate at first and *are only explained to begin with by reference to the realm of phenomena from which they were derived*; it is only by means of a progressive analysis *of the material of observation* that they can be made clear and can find a significant and consistent meaning.
>
> (1925, p. 58, emphasis added)

This shows the gap in method between the Cartesian approach, grounded in aprioristic 'indisputable, clear and distinct concepts', and Freud's, which puts the convergence of seemingly unrelated findings to the forefront in trying to free as far as possible the description of phenomena from the overruling apriorisms of the enquirer. The futility of a search for empirical certainties, an idea that, in its postmodern revolt against its own quest for metaphysical certainties, has today been vindicated by philosophy, is plain to scientists, whose search for valid, provisional and limited 'open' knowledge is not spun in the yarn of the philosopher's quest for certainty.

Coming from the philosophy of history, Dilthey and his followers put up a straw-man idea of science built to the measure of Galilean mechanics – notwithstanding that, under the influence of geology, botany and Darwinian biology, science had by Dilthey's time already acquired a strong historical bent (see Kermode, 1985). Home is explicit enough: 'Science in origin and essence is the mechanic's mode of enquiry' (1966, p. 45). The Diltheyan duality is dichotomous in that every discipline falls to either one side of the division or the other, and on it rests the dichotomy between *causes* and *motives* (or *meanings*). Their straw-man 'natural' sciences they assume to be nomothetic, ahistorical and context-free, and hence linear and *univocal*; on the basis of such an assumed univocity of empirical science, Spence (1993) questions what he calls the 'psychoanalytic right' not to find a home for the 'Rashomon effect' – that is, the fact that almost everything worth looking at has at least two sides to it – forgetting that under the impact of quantum theory even twentieth-century physics is a mammoth case of the 'Rashomon effect'.

Once empirical science is made, as stated, nomothetic, context-free, ahistorical, linear and univocal, hermeneutists feel free to co-opt for purely 'cultural' disciplines the study of the singular fact. In this way, Habermas (1959, p. 271) invokes the opposition of the invariance of natural laws and the spontaneity of life history as grounds enough for putting 'causes' and 'motives' apart. But this basic hermeneutic tenet ignores the fact that from Baconian *interpretatio naturae* onwards interpretation has been part and parcel of empirical science, be it 'exact' or 'observational' – a point Grünbaum (1984) argues with his usual vigour. On such a false assumption of the univocity of empirical science, Steele forcefully alleges: 'Interpretation is hermeneutics' (1979, p. 398).

I shall close this short discussion on induction with a reference to Peirce, who, in what Russell (1959a, p. 277) considers a major contribution to inductive logic, took, against Mill, the discovery and verification of inductive propositions to be sharply diverse and gave distinct names to the 'context of discovery' and the 'context of justification': an hypothesis arises by *abduction* and its consequences are then to be obtained by *deduction*, to be in their turn tested empirically by *induction*, which Peirce restricts to the empirical proof of the hypothesis. Only through abductions do new ideas appear. Peirce calls it '*il lume naturale*', a peculiar instinct for conjecture, which he compares with the chick's ability to choose the right pickings as soon as he breaks out of the egg-shell (Sebeok & Umiker-Sebeok, 1980). However, as will unfold throughout the book, such separating of the contexts of discovery and verification loses its force in the observational sciences.

The theocentric gulf between 'natural' and 'human' sciences: the place of language

Decrying that 'human sciences' exist in a state of dependence on natural ones, having 'all the characteristics of a psychopathological condition' (p. 134), and that 'scientific' is used as a criterion of self-evident validity, Holland (1990) has recently argued that the disputes in our field bear witness to the 'nascent conceptions of a *human science*' (p. 147). But it was on such an idea of a 'human science' alien to nature that Dilthey had built up the *Geisteswissenschaften* – quite literally, the *'sciences of the spirit'.*

The idea of a rift between man and nature is traceable to our myth of creation, in the Book of Genesis, where after giving form to beasts God creates man *in His image*, the act of creation resting on the Word man shares: *In principio erat Verbum*. At the medieval debate of the *universals* (Rougier, 1960), Thomas Aquinas, Abelard and Duns Scotus maintained the *adequatio rei et intellectus*: on man's partaking of the Creator, words and concepts are deemed equivalent to reality (*unum nomen, unum nominatum*), enabling the discursive mind to use concepts in the manner of realities – the hermeneutic ideas that the discursive mind constitutes nature and of rhetoric as truth roundly follow this creationist stance. (By contrast, for the Oxford and Paris nominalists after William of Ockham, concepts were deemed generalizations of experiences: from this the empirical tradition of modern science derives.)

Upon such roots those who maintain the idea of a gulf between man and animal will hypostatize into a *human essence* that which comes to be taken as our 'specific difference'. In the case of Descartes, it was reason or soul, the *res cogitans* man shares with God, which is alien to the blind, purely mechanical nature that animals – and our bodies – share with the inanimate. His best-known statement, *Cogito ergo sum*, shows that only the thinking, *res cogitans*, but not the body, is identified with the self (Eisenbud, 1978, p. 288); animals do not *speak* and therefore lack reason; hence, for Descartes, they are automata devoid of soul. This theocentric assumption goes together with a dismissal of observational data coming through bodily senses and an overvaluation of apriorisms, our *res cogitans*' 'clear and distinct concepts', the truth of which God is deemed the warranter.

This creationist epistemology shines in new ways in Hegel's and Dilthey's main source, a Naples professor of rhetoric named Giambattista Vico, who argued that only God, having created it, can have perfect knowledge of the world, while man, himself created, knows it only imperfectly. For Vico, says Russell (1959a, p. 207), we know what we do, *verum factum*: the 'new science', at once knowable and real, is history, co-created by God and man. By his mien of man as creator, Vico, says Croce (1910, p. 129), turns man into a demigod, and this leads in Hegel to an idealization of the mind as the Universal Spirit or Absolute Idea, turning the Vician demigod into a deity. From Hegel, Habermas will take the central hermeneutic concept of 'self-reflection' in which he grounds the analysand's 'self-emancipatory process', assumed to transcend the causality of nature. To Hegel, too, who considered Descartes a hero, Rorty (1975) traces the daunting novelty that *discourse, becoming autonomous, by itself constitutes human knowledge.*

The gulf between nature and man leads to differing ideas of truth in psychoanalysis, as taken up by Hanly (1990) in his Rome paper. In the idea of *truth as concordance*, held by Freud and generally by scientists, truth pertains to the degree of correspondence between an object and its description, on the idea that the human mind can gain, through observation and its experimental refinement, a valid knowledge of objects. In the idea of *truth as coherence*, with reference to idealistic philosophies and hermeneutic psychoanalysis, facts are constituted by theories, which, they hold, rule over observation. In this outlook, mind constitutes nature, and self-consciousness abrogates causality; motives cease to be causes and become reasons at the disposal of consciousness; for Habermas (1959), psychoanalytic self-reflection transcends psychic causality, and where causality was, there a-causal choice shall be. The idea of truth as coherence, of the indefiniteness of persons as objects of knowledge and of voluntarism, is, for Hanly, logically interconnected. The premise is that one cannot verify theories, only increase their coherence.

The pretence of 'human science' to self-sufficiency also leads to two quite distinct conceptions of language. In the empiricist camp, language is considered an instrument for the *mapping of extra-linguistic facts*, as held by Russell and the logical positivists of the Vienna Circle; while in the *Geisteswissenschaft* camp it becomes *an autonomous linguistic reality*, after Sapir and Whorf, Saussure and the later Wittgenstein. Distinct outlooks on determinism are involved too: a *psychic determinism* in which meanings pertain primarily to mental facts outside language, and a *linguistic* one wherein meanings are deemed intrinsic to the linguistic code and independent of referents – the fundamental hermeneutic tenet is that there is neither meaning nor mind outside language.

In the Freudian idea, however, the psychic unconscious underlies language and has a communicatory function, 'everyone possesses in his own unconscious an instrument with which he can interpret the utterances of the unconscious in other people' (1913, p. 320), and on this basis the analyst's operational correlate to free association is his ability 'to catch the drift of the patient's unconscious with his own unconscious' (1923b, p. 239). The Freudian distinction of two levels of communication – the unconscious one of drives and thing-presentations having, as stated, the function of conveying *messages*, and the linguistic verbal one – agrees most precisely with Bateson's independent findings of two types of codes in the evolution of mammalian communication: on one side, relational analogic action–emotion codes playing a major role in intraspecies messages, and, on the other, digitally coded languages found in cetaceans and man, which use arbitrary 'names' to refer to a universe external to intraspecies relationship.

Freud's bodily experienced 'thing-presentations' forming the unconscious fit in closely with what Russell (1911) would come to call a 'knowledge by acquaintance', from which words derive their meanings; it is not necessary to remind the reader that to Freud from 1891 onwards it is out of thing-presentations that all meanings – including verbal ones – ultimately arise.

A brief explanation of language, consciousness and the unconscious in terms of logical levels would now seem necessary. Verbal languages use 'names' that are discrete – that is, separate from one another – their discontinuity matching that of consciousness, which, Matte-Blanco holds, grasps one thing at a time, separating each fact from the next while the unconscious '*does not know individuals but only classes and propositional functions*[2] *which define the class*' (1975, p. 139) and equates, thereby, class and individual. Conscious description, he affirms, strives to grasp 'in terms of discrete entities – a reality which has no discrete entities or parts, and which, as such, cannot enter consciousness unless it is translated into discrete entities, i.e. entities separable from one another' (1975, p. 278).

Consciousness can take the class into account in either of two ways: by considering at an intellectual level that which distinguishes it from other classes, or by contacting it through its individual members.

The two modes of operation of consciousness that Matte-Blanco points to merit closer scrutiny. It is only from the starting-point of the nomination of a factual object and a description of its perceived attributes that a construal of conceptual 'logical classes', which are distinct in discursive verbal definition, becomes possible (if these are privileged, we enter the terrain of nominal and conceptual realism). However, this ostensive contact 'in presence' may or may not allow the emergence in consciousness, as *attributes* of individuals, of primarily unconscious relational action-and-emotion propositional forms that do not in themselves become conscious. But they can, and do, crystallize in those nominable discrete entities that Bion (1962, p. 65ff; 1963, p. 90) called 'constant conjunctions': for example, *this* [with such and such action–emotion qualities] *is daddy*. The brackets mark here a difference in logical levels, 'daddy' being a single factual (and linguistic) object, to which correspond at the different levels of unconscious mind unfolding in the analytic process a multiplicity of usually polarly dissimilar 'psychic' objects. In our psychoanalytic work we keep in mind the distinction between the verbally nominable *factual* object and its consciously ostensive attributes from the multiple and contradictory action-and-emotion pragmatic qualities attributed to it as a *psychic* object, which are 'known by acquaintance' in an unconscious, not in a consciously ostensive, way.

From an empirical stance, interpretive formulations in verbal terms attempt in the analytic situation a 'mapping' of 'psychic objects'; as both everyday and analytic experience attest, this 'mapping' by consciousness and verbal language is indeed difficult, this being the basis for the idea of the indefiniteness of persons as objects of knowledge that Hanly finds in an ontologized form in coherence theories of truth. But the precise aim of our clinical method, I will now argue, is to attain a definiteness of description in the analytic session.

Psychoanalysis as observational science

Freud is specific enough on the groundings of psychoanalysis; as in any empirical science, 'that foundation is observation alone' (1914b, p. 77). Its concepts, he says, which are unavoidably nebulous and which it hopes to apprehend more clearly in the course of its development, are not the bottom but the top of its structure and can be replaced and discarded without damaging it. In psychoanalysis, method rather than theory is at the base of the structure; by making orderly observation possible, it allows an empirical science of the unconscious to be construed. For Freud, not only does psychoanalysis find its place in the frame of science, but the session itself puts scientific method into practice: as he states in a letter to Arnold Zweig of 13 June 1935, a proper analysis 'is a scientific undertaking rather than an easy therapeutic operation' (Leupold-Löwenthal, 1987, p. 66). Here we must thank Laplanche (1992) for noting that the German term *Deutung* is more ostensive, and much less hermeneutic, than our term 'interpretation': *deuten auf* means to point with the fingers or indicate with the eyes.

Chapter 3 illustrates how clinical facts evolve from the intuitable to the observable for both analysand and analyst, showing that the analysand's free associations are often to be taken as *unconscious abductions* giving form in verbal terms to aspects of the analysand's phantasmic action-and-emotion 'presences' enacted in his unconscious relationship to the analyst as an 'external phantasy object'; they are then part of the analysand's inductive processes in the session on his ongoing enacted (i.e. pragmatic) psychic reality. I will restrict myself here mainly to the role of interpretation as a 'mapping' of psychic 'facts' in the analysand's mind, and to the analysand's inductive re-evaluations or refutations of his unconscious 'theories'. In the evolution of the pragmatic paradox towards insight, analytic neutrality plays a necessary role. After the intellectual 'mapping' gained from interpretive description, the analysand is in a position to attain, within the experiential context of the analyst's neutrality, a 'judgement of reality' – that is, *a conscious ostensive re-evaluation and/or refutation* of his hitherto unconscious 'psychic reality'. The analytic session, then, gives the analysand an opportunity to put into practice the scientific method and to accede to a reformulation and/or refutation of his unconscious propositional forms and thereby to attain by 'double description' a jump in logical level.

This view of the role of interpretation in the analytic process as a 'mapping' of unconscious pragmatic paradoxes (a 'mapping' in which the semantic and syntactic offshoots of these pragmatic paradoxes serve often enough as guideposts) demands an interpretive approach relying heavily on the description of experiential evidences of the evolutions of the unconscious 'psychic realities' enacted transferentially in the here and now of the session. The analyst's task is here intuitional and observational (including the use of his unconscious as an instrument) and descriptive, and what is or is not to be his 'psychic truth' is left to the analysand to decide on the basis of his evolving ostensive insights. Historical material comes up here in the main as a secondary stage once the transference has been clarified, mostly as further associations aiming more often than not at evincing in the 'screens' of memory, in the manner of 'multiple descriptions', whether the transference findings hold rather than seeking an 'historical truth' – one that would be apt to change anew on further transference insights.

As chapter 3 argues, the appeal to ostensive knowledge – ostensive description on the part of the analyst and ostensive redefinition and/or refutation on that of the analysand – to which even an hermeneutist like Gadamer accords 'the univocity of that which one has seen by himself' (1960, p. 275), is the hub of my differences with 'cultural science' approaches to psychoanalysis, which assume that words have no referents and theories are not refutable. In my opinion, *an analytic process exists to the extent that, in the analytic session, these particular 'pragmatic theories'* that the analysand holds – his unconscious phantasies (Klein), his unconscious misconceptions (Money-Kyrle) or his unconscious propositional functions (Matte-Blanco) – can *accede to ostensive reassessing or refutation.* As Freud says, the unconscious knows 'no negation, no doubts, no degrees of certainty' (1915b, p. 186) – ostensive refutation, when attained, brings unconscious processes to the *Pcs.–Cs.* domain of the 'no'.

Verbal creationism in the *Geisteswissenschaft* outlook

In the current postmodernist vogue, language has the dubious role of undoing the Darwinian blow to human narcissism (Freud, 1917b, p. 140), reinstating the rupture between man and his animal nature. Here the terms 'psychoanalytic dialogue' and 'psychoanalytic discourse' frame psychoanalysis within what is purported to be a purely linguistic context where language becomes a *self-sufficient tautology* freed from empirical referents. In the purported methodological gulf between 'natural' and 'human' (i.e. linguistic) science, the Freudian triad of the dynamic unconscious, infantile sexuality and transference, being of a nature other than linguistic, will slip into the background.

It was Dilthey's conviction that 'self-knowing spirit' is achieved in historical consciousness. In the philological tradition of hermeneutics he took to the *text*, to the deciphering of the writing as a form of the 'spirit' which, in his opinion, gives the spiritual scientist as congenial a comprehension as can be attained between an 'I' and a 'you' in life; for Dilthey, history is a text in need of deciphering. But, argues Gadamer (1960, p. 304), his effort leads to an a-methodical induction incapable of verification – an appraisal indeed valid for 'cultural' psychoanalysis. In postmodernist hermeneutics, states Vattimo (1985), 'the being that can be understood is language (and nothing but language)' (p. 153); from Nietzsche on, he holds, 'rhetoric completely replaces logic' (p. 25) and natural sciences become a threat to philosophy, against which it must defend irreducible human values: liberty, freedom of choice, unforeseeableness of behaviour. Forsaking empirical observation, such a posture leads to the creation of meaning by interpretation: hermeneutic truth, says Vattimo, 'is essentially rhetoric' (p. 119), rhetoric being the art of persuasion through discourse.

On the *a priori* of man's uniqueness by a language that comes to take the pivotal role in experience our method is drastically redefined. Lacan holds that 'psychoanalysis is a dialectical experience' (1951, p. 38), and Steele (1979) maintains that our method as an interpretive science follows on from that of hermeneutics, which

> is simple – it is dialogue. We come to understanding, we establish *meaning – mutual co-understanding* – by the age-old dialectic method of question and answer. Meaning . . . is established through language in relation to people, to their products, and to the world. Dialectic as the art of conducting a conversation is an ongoing process of questioning and answering. It leads to the formation of concepts through *the working out of a common meaning.*
>
> (pp. 391–2, emphasis added)

It is plain that, in contrast to free association, hermeneutic 'agreement' restricts meaning to the preconscious. Restricting meaning to language, it leaves scant space for unconscious repetition and early transference.

The *Geisteswissenschaften* explicitly oppose their method to that of science. Steele takes, after Gadamer (1960), the objectifying methods of science to be techniques of domination forcing man and nature into repetitive patterns; in his view, verification implies a repeatability that undermines history by distracting us from the constant changes of experience (Steele, 1979, p. 391). In such Vician and Hegelian visions of man as demigod, the basic psychic determinisms of his animal inheritance – his dependencies, his lusts and his hates, in short, his unconscious drives – are rejected as unwarranted restrictions on the sovereignty of his freedom of choice; no wonder, then, that theories of truth as coherence leave instinctual drives aside (Hanly, 1990) and instrumental use of the analyst's unconscious is renounced. But then psychoanalytic method as revised by the *Geisteswissenschaft* perspective lapses into a rhetorical creationism: coming from Saussure and Lévi-Strauss, as in the case of Lacan (1954–55), from Habermas and Gadamer, as in the case of Steele (1979), or from Wittgenstein and Davidson, as in the case of Cavell (1991), *only language is deemed psychic.* 'They do not know what they talk about, they who speak of a psychic reality. I should not call anything by that term' avows Lacan in his rhetorical style (RSI, unpublished Seminar of 15 April 1975, quoted by Julien, 1985, p. 5, my translation).

On the idea of language as a *complete set of signifiers*, Eco (1973) considers a main advantage of such a self-contained system of *semantic units of meaning to be explained solely in terms of other semantic units* that residues of mentalism or intuitionism built on 'unobservable entities', such as ideas, concepts or states of consciousness (not to speak of unconscious ones), are abolished. Likewise, from the Wittgensteinian standpoint, Davidson derides those who would think a statement relates to something it states (Rorty, 1975). On such premises – on their shared upholding that 'meaning' rests on articulations intrinsic to the linguistic code, which can be deemed *syntacticist* (Klimovsky, 1984) – with no acknowledged dependencies whatsoever on psychic or external facts, the self-sufficient linguistic machinery ticks, like Cartesian reason, all by itself.

It was stated above that, for an empirical stance, psychoanalytic interpretation relies on the description of experiential evidences –

intuited through the instrumental use of the analyst's unconscious or grasped observationally – of the evolutions of unconscious psychic realities enacted in the here and now of the session. As clinically illustrated by Tuckett (1983), it is our biological sensitivity to the whole range of semiotic systems our senses can grasp, often without our consciously knowing how, that permits us to respond to our patients' unconscious and partly share in their transference enactments. Understanding in terms of an hermeneutic text not only rejects flatly the idea that psychoanalysis is observational on the grounds that it requires a partner in dialogue (Steele, 1979, p. 408), it also heeds textual findings to the neglect of pragmatic ones; hence it discards description of the here-and-now transference enactments, tilting towards a verbal creationism in the form of 'pattern-making' and to an historical construction of a 'psychic truth' in which 'interpretation creates a coherent meaning, one analyst and analysand can *agree* on' (Steele, 1979, p. 400, emphasis added) in line with rhetorical truth. This entails the risk, says Kernberg (1993), of an intellectualized construction of the past on the basis of conscious memories, bypassing unconscious phantasies and meanings in the transference. In the hermeneutic search for 'agreements' it is mainly the *negative* transference that gets bypassed.

When language is granted autonomy from psychic and factual referents, the dismissal of unconscious meanings becomes inescapable. On the premises of 'ordinary language' philosophy, Cavell holds, after Wittgenstein, that 'language is the condition of the mental in general' (1991, p. 150). On such grounds, she states, 'there is nothing we can speak of as subjective experience prior to language' (p. 150), thereby deeming inadmissible the Freudian account of 'a primary non-rational mental order'. Cavell proposes:

> Giving up its theories about the infant's subjective world would deliver psychoanalysis from a primary source of theoretical disagreement, while leaving analysts free to use whatever images and metaphors they find clinically useful.
>
> (1991, p. 151)

As the 'theories about the infant's subjective world' generalize clinical findings in both children and adults, she would willingly throw away the child's unconscious psychism and the 'child in the adult' for the sake of an a-methodical spontaneity.

It must be said that in *Truth and Method* (1960) Gadamer seeks to preserve ordinary and philosophical experience in the face of the advances of technology, but he does *not* presume that hermeneutics can give dictates to empirical science – as his followers and those of other philosophers, as in the case of Cavell, certainly do. We can agree with Gadamer (1992) that one cannot establish once and forever a system of true statements, this being why he keeps to Platonic dialogue as a road to mutual agreement; but that is a poor observational field vis-à-vis the psychoanalytic situation. On matching psychoanalytic method and hermeneutic dialogue, the discord of science and philosophy is plain: philosophy assumes that ordinary life data are grounds enough for a reflection able to transcend them, whereas science seeks for each field suitable methods and instruments, from Galileo's telescope to Freud's analytic setting, in order to widen its observational stance and gain access to data unavailable in ordinary life.

At this point some sobering thoughts occur concerning Wallerstein's (1988) idea of clinical method as our 'common ground': when method is limited to dialogue and meaning narrowed to a language freed from referents, the creation of meaning falls upon the analyst's *Verbum*, and then his task passes from observation (including countertransference scrutiny), description and interpretive hypothesis to 'pattern-making'. In the case of Lacan, who alone in the 'cultural science' field accords a primary role to unconscious repetition, pattern-making pertains to the analyst's action as 'scansion' of the analysand's 'text', be it by the 'letter' or by his ending of the session, deemed to have a 'subjectifying effect' (*effet de sujet*), 'authentification of that point of cut, of that drawing of a border, by a *punctuation* marking the text: end of session . . . period!' (Julien, 1986, pp. 139–40, my translation).[3]

Psychoanalysis thus turns, in accord with rhetorical voluntarism, into verbal or enacted persuasion, *per via di porre* – a posture pushed to its extreme when it is encompassed in the purportedly all-inclusive frame of that epitome of postmodernism, Foucault's *discursivité*, wherein Freud – and each analyst at work – is taken to be the founder of a discourse. Viderman's (1970) belief that the analyst's interpretation 'does not reproduce a phantasy pre-existent in the patient's unconscious but causes it to exist by telling it' is an example of such a primacy of discourse. Where words take on such a Promethean role, no proper place is left for analytic neutrality, and on such a basic contrast in method the actuality of a clinical 'common ground' is, at the least, dubious. It is not a moot point that while the so-called 'hermeneutic left' cloaks itself as 'progressive' or even, as does Bruner, as 'a prelude to revolution' (1993, p. 11) against a purportedly reactionary empirical psychoanalysis, in these 'sciences of the spirit' the interpreting analyst's *Word* comes to partake so transparently of that of the Creator.

There is in these complex affairs no place for dichotomies. For Modell (1978, p. 651), psychoanalysis encompasses both types of knowledge, scientific and hermeneutic, this being the central paradox in its epistemology, a tenable idea springing from a more restrictive view of empirical science than that of Freud. Cheshire and Thomä (1991) hold that Freud leans heavily on the confirmatory (or perhaps merely rhetorical) power of the 'convergence' or 'coherence' of recurrent patterns of observation, as opposed to relying on the crucial experiments to which Popper's positivism single-mindedly adheres. But this is precisely the difference between the methods of 'observational' and 'exact' science, and there is nothing rhetorical about it – as long as the propositions that converge do actually rest on legitimate observations. In fact, for Reichenbach (1947, p. 22), it is out of 'definition by co-ordination of propositions' issuing from inductions that 'open concepts' are defined and redefined, and for such a stringent member of the Vienna Circle as Otto Neurath, the strength of Freud's theories is – like Darwin's – their putting together of observations of quite divergent sorts of facts (see Frank, 1959, p. 308). It must be said, too, that, just as is the case of psychoanalysis, so the Darwinian theory of evolution is not seriously predictive (Demos, 1959, p. 331).

This runs directly counter to the primacy of theory postulated by the *Geisteswissenschaft* stances. It is true, as commented on by Parsons (1992), that, as Einstein told the young Heisenberg, theory decides – that is, both makes possible and limits – what we can observe. But it is also true that being 'open concepts', our theoretical constructs result from attempts to explain previous experiences and are, in turn, subject to redefinition or rejection by new findings. In the same way they are, like the analysand's 'unconscious theories' that psychoanalysis attempts to open up to experience, themselves open to inductive reformulation.

Philosophical 'cultural science' advocates may, though timidly, be moderating some claims. Spence (1991a) agrees that hermeneutic or deconstructivist critiques can trace how theoretical models reflect an author's personal situations or cultural metaphors, but they *cannot* correct faulty concepts or provide better ways of describing clinical facts. Deploring the excesses of rhetoric that have gone hand in hand with primacy of language and the view of the analyst's role as 'pattern-making', Spence has now come (1991b, p. 283) to avow that 'pattern-matching' is the essential clinical activity: an inductive idea – indeed, in fact, one guiding clinical judgement in medicine since antiquity and, as cited above, one already argued by H. Joseph (1916) for all the sciences some eight decades ago. Hamilton's allowance that 'coherence works because there is sufficient correspondence at the edges' (1993, p. 67) is of more dubious stock. It is to be commended if it is a cognisance, half-hearted though it may be, that language does not, after all, tick by itself; but, of course, it can be meant otherwise, as a vindication of a belief in a pre-established harmony between language and objects in the manner of the Scholastics – a form of omnipotence of the Word. Holland, for his part, acknowledges that 'it will be necessary to notice the continuities between recursive processes in the animal world and reflexive processes in the human world' (1990, p. 155) – good news indeed, though tempered by his premise of a 'principle of reflexivity' as the *defining condition* of human existence, evincing the philosopher's penchant for thinking in terms of *essences* (that which is *uniquely* human) rather than in terms of processes – a way of thought leading to 'principles' that, like the Cartesian *Cogito*, are a royal road to unbridgeable dichotomies.

A 'human science' construed upon what comes to be thought of as *uniquely human* is, by its defining condition, brazenly dichotomous. It was Freud's fate and merit to enquire into the ways in which we are less uniquely human than we like to think.

3

WHAT IS A CLINICAL FACT?

Clinical psychoanalysis as inductive method

Clinical facts are part of a process, and our main question today, 'what does the analyst attend to in the clinical situation?', is of a piece with an equally cardinal question: 'what does the analysand attend to, consciously and unconsciously?', or, in wider terms, 'how does *he* operate inductively?'

As we are aware, not all analysts allow even a modest degree of independence to clinical facts: it is a premise of the 'creative–hermeneutic' stance that there are no facts, and then no clinical ones; hence it holds that what matters is that the analyst constructs a coherent whole, which does not reproduce a phantasy pre-existent in the subject's unconscious, but causes it to exist by telling it (Viderman, 1970). Facts thus become radically theory-dependent and 'language-dependent', inasmuch as the analyst's words are deemed to cause psychic facts. A quite different matter is to allow that our approach to facts is not 'assumption-free', as did that eminent empiricist, Sigmund Freud:

> Even at the stage of description it is not possible to avoid applying certain abstract ideas to the material at hand, ideas derived from somewhere or other but certainly not from the new observations alone.
>
> (1915a, p. 117)

Assumptions and theories, following Freud, have no claim to primacy, being 'scaffoldings ready to be discarded' (1914b, p. 77) as soon as new clinical facts require. While I can agree with Spence (1994) that much of what we listen to is not ostensive by any stretch of the imagination, I hold that it is our task to arrive, and help the analysand arrive, at an ostensiveness of 'facts', which, as Quinodoz (1994) emphasizes, are both relational and subjective.

The emergence of 'facts' in a given clinical situation depends less on the analyst's theories than on his ability to build an intuitional and observational field for the patient and for himself, on his keeping to his neutrality, on his intuitive and observational capacities, and on whatever countertransference insights he is capable of. A 'happy guess', an act of invention of a conception not previously apparent, the finding, that is, of 'one supposition that succeeds in binding together the Facts' (Whewell, 1858, p. 136) allowing description from a new and more adequate standpoint, is necessary for successful induction. While a framework of conceptions or theories is the background to the emergence of such happy conjectures, these do not derive from theory in any direct way. Against the primacy of theory, Bion (1977, p. 18) quotes Darwin: 'it is fatal to reason whilst observing, though so necessary beforehand and so useful afterwards'; deeming the psychoanalytic domain intuitable, Bion holds that memory, desire and understanding hinder intuition (1992, p. 315).

Psychoanalytic facts must, in my view, evolve, for both analyst and analysand, from the intuitable to the observable; in Peirce's terms, from 'abduction' to 'induction': from the emergence of an hypothesis to its experiential, observational testing. Intuition is not enough. From Aristotle on, induction has depended on observation, and our field is no exception: effective insights are, as we have learnt from Richfield (1954), *ostensive* ones, built on a direct observational grasp of psychic facts. We can usually expect these first to be consciously available to the analyst on the basis of whatever intuitional and observational grasp of the analysand's (and of his own!) psychic reality he can muster, and, with the help of his descriptive verbal mappings – the interpretations – eventually to the patient.

My purpose here is to enquire how in the analytic situation *the analysand operates within the frame of a system of inductive testing of his unconscious 'theories'*; here ostensive 'facts' will come up mainly *against* the analysand's unconscious-driven conscious 'theories' and assumptions, and often against ours too – that is, *counterinductively*. To this end, I offer two clinical vignettes: the first on the protracted struggles of a post-autistic adolescent for and against awareness of 'clinical facts', that is, of his psychic reality in the frame of an unremitting negative transference; the second approaches in logical terms an aspect of the process of distinguishing between *psychic* and *factual* reality.

Ostensive, says Susanne Langer (1953), is that which may be pointed to by saying 'this', such also being her definition of *individual* – be it a person, event or thing. Against the current 'flight into hermeneutics' in the appraisal of the interpretive method, Cheshire and Thomä (1991, p. 429) hold that, from the Project onwards, Freud, the former neuropathologist, struggled for a way of 'staining' (i.e. making observable) the unconscious states and processes inaccessible even to introspection – a way he found, they state, in free association and dream-interpretation. To these, the setting, transference and analytic neutrality must also be added. As mentioned in chapter 1, Freud's *Deutung* is much less hermeneutic than our term 'interpretation', so in Freud's usage it is an ostensive term. Not that I think that a hard-and-fast line divides intuition and observation; much if not all of our intuition is, I surmise, dimly observational in ways we are not conscious of: a favourite term of Bion's was *adumbrate*. William Blake puts it more poetically: *'wise men see outlines'*. Let us turn now to our first clinical example.

First clinical example

John, a 13-year-old boy, was brought to consultation because he was withdrawn and indeed lethargic at school; on vacations he was livelier, but aloof and cold to adults. His parents had divorced when he was 4, at which time his mother had gone through a depressive episode. His father, an emotionally isolated man working abroad, saw or phoned him quite randomly. The mother, an overly dedicated teacher prone to feelings of failure, volunteered that she felt the strain of being both mother and father to John. A brother one year younger was subject to sporadic immoderate bouts of rage. John was usually compliant and non-committal, but he gave way to grotesque grimaces in public or in front of mirrors, which infuriated his mother. At school and doing homework, his attention span was nil; he attended a special school.

In step with the diagnostic impression of secondary encapsulated autism (Tustin, 1986), in his four-times-weekly sessions John resorted to a 'deadly serious' silence, save for bouts of grimacing, at once mocking and self-demeaning; his few isolated comments he did not follow up. He answered questions telegraphically, if at all: if, for example, at the start of a session I asked him, 'How are you, John?', he would just say 'Very well.' It was pointed out to him in many ways that he didn't think talking about himself to me – or to anyone else, for that matter – could be of help; in fact, he had little use for words. However, he would listen to my attempts at guessing what was going on, and often he would nod when he felt I was right; then he would curl up on the sofa and fall sound asleep. He would not draw and, more generally, he refused to play what he felt to be the analyst's game: that is, to be a collaborator. But as the months went by, on growing more confident, he played repetitive games with objects he brought along, such as coins or a steel ball-bearing that he would balance on his drawing board, or else grab one of my pipes and gently play with it while looking sideways at my reaction. As long as he kept moving at his games and I kept quiet, he would be lively; if I imposed my 'game' by interpreting, he would listen eagerly but soon become lethargic and fall asleep.

Of his scant utterances, which came out of the blue, I will single out one on *poor little toads run over by trucks* on country roads. This seemed to be a type of clinical 'fact' that was different from those coming from observations such as John's silences or lethargy or his 'deadly serious' demeanour. I take it to be an *unconscious abduction* – a conjecture that in this case is not known to its beholder and refers to the here and now. There can be few doubts that to John the conscious referent of this statement is unrelated to the clinical situation, but can be taken as a verbal model of a central dimension of his enacted unconscious relationship to me as an *external phantasy object* – that is, as a verbal 'diagnosis' of the way in which I, as an external object, have come to 'incarnate' his unconscious internal one. However, it is useful to introduce at this point a logical distinction between the two levels of the analyst's role: as a transference *'object'*, having some degree of conscious ostensiveness, and as a transference-relational *'frame'*, which is not consciously observable to the patient and must be intuited or inferred by the analyst. Such a distinction is implicit in Betty Joseph's (1985) consideration of transference as a 'total situation'. Quoting Klein (1952, p. 55) to the effect that 'it is essential to think in terms of *total situations* transferred from the past to the present', Joseph adds:

> She [Klein] went on to describe how for many years transference had been understood in terms of *direct references* to the analyst . . . It seems to me that the notion of *total situations* is fundamental . . . What he [the analysand] brings in can best be gauged by focusing our attention on what goes on in the relationship, how he *uses* the analyst, alongside and beyond what he is saying.
>
> (1985, p. 447, emphasis added)

So, transference can be understood restrictively, as direct cognitive references to the analyst, or in a wider, more unconscious sense, as a pragmatic level of 'use': John's comment points to this wider, 'frame' level of the relationship. The remark about poor little toads run over by trucks alludes to the projected covert murderous rivalry and its denial, which very much lead the process; it puts into words his attitude in the session and in his games. What it *alludes to* can be described as *the pragmatic enactment of a relational proposition*: I, his analyst (but more generally, adults), am to poor little John as trucks are to little toads (Analyst = overbearing truck; John = run-over toad). This free association is then John's unknown interpretive modellization mapping of an aspect of his ongoing unconscious link to me; having no immediate effect on his over-riding denial of his psychic reality, it does not bring him nearer to an insight. It must be noted that it was essential that neither of us overtly act out this rivalry. Once, he started making small paper bullets, which, in a lively, increasingly manic mood he would shoot in seemingly random fashion, in a kind of Russian roulette, aimed at hitting/not hitting me; when a 'bullet' did hit the cushion close to my face and he thought he had scored a hit, he froze into the state of *unmitigated terror,* which Tustin (1991) puts at the core of autism. He gave up his shooting game forever, interpretation proving ineffectual.

While looking at a Cape Horn clipper's lamp that lights my office, its vent-holes abruptly reminded him of the Bermuda Triangle. Work on this led to some inroads in his denial of psychic reality: he grasped my saying that both the session and his inner world are to him a sort of Bermuda Triangle where emotional contents are felt to vanish without trace. (It helped that we had already explored how, for example, those that were his playmates, while on vacations, will vanish in town.) Shortly thereafter he recounted a nightmare *in which he was falling in front of a tall building, and then the scene changed and he was looking with no feelings or anxieties at his badly torn, dead body after hitting the pavement.* As he brought no associations to the dream, I asked him to draw it, which to my surprise he did, in four scenes of a free fall from the top of an obelisk-shaped high-rise building. These depicted what I take to be his main transference defence: his devitalization in front of the oversized and overbearing phallic analyst (in contrast, he drew himself as a minimal stick puppet) as well as the main transference conflict, an overarching unconscious phallic rivalry. Let me underline that there was no overt anxiety or hostility addressed to me: unconscious hostility leads to *autotomy* (Ferenczi, 1924), to a *dematerialization* illustrated by the lizard's sacrifice of its tail to the predator. The dream, and then its drawing, are steps in the 'staining' process that, for Cheshire and Thomä (1991), is at the core of Freud's method; his devitalization in the frame of unconscious rivalry attains representability in the passage from an enacted and until then unrepresentable and unthinkable 'concrete representation by identification', in Money-Kyrle's terms,[1] to a visual 'ideographic representation'.

In-session sleeping went on for months; interpretations, even when agreed to subtly by John and leading to such changes in his liveliness and his relationships with his peers and family (but not, at this time, in his studies) that friends and relatives would say, 'this is a different child', did not make a dent in his lethargy in the session – so much so that I had to shake him firmly in order to wake him up when time ran out. After watching a film on TV about the discovery of the sunken remains of the *Titanic*, he *dreamt it hit a big iceberg and slowly sank into the deep in utter silence.*

This was interpreted both ways: as his hitting what he unconsciously felt to be my 'wall' of icy coldness towards his enthusiasms, and, increasingly, as his having made my therapeutic enthusiasm hit the wall of his cold aloofness. Disappointments were, I surmise, a component of the 'wall', and hence he would evade enthusiasms or needs. In a third *dream he had come in a run-down bus to a service station; on his asking for some water, the attendant got angry and chased him as he fled up a thorny hill.*

While, as far as I can gather, he feels no discernible anger or depression on listening to me, and admits he may be quite interested in what I was saying, it is a clinical fact that my voice is by itself enough to turn the overriding, annihilating phallic-rivalry 'frame' on and hence to turn him off, the devitalization and collapse into sleep (into the pavement in the first dream, into the deep in the second) being the unconsciously chosen alternative to an annihilating collision. Covert explosive rivalry and intolerance of need and disillusion are interrelated unconscious relational 'frames', which, while *not* ostensively seen by John as my *individual* attributes, act as a pragmatic 'frame' – that is, as a metalevel to most of his verbalizations and to the content of my interpretations. Thus, while John regards me consciously as 'fairly good', the same as his uncles and his grandfather, or even 'quite good', as he has volunteered to his mother sometimes, unconsciously the *general relational 'frame'* – annihilating phallic analyst/truck, John/little toad – holds, my voice being a 'realization', in Bion's sense, of the truck's noise.

As explained in chapter 1, the antinomy between John's unconscious relational perception of me as 'annihilating [phallic] truck' and his conscious perception of me as 'fairly good' amounts to a pragmatic paradox: *the analyst is/is not the archaic object*. A necessary step for the resolution of the paradox is the disproving of the unconscious relational proposition, and a requisite for this is the achievement of representability: only what comes to be 'shown' can be inductively refuted. The attainment of representability demands adequate descriptions: such is the task not only of interpretations but also, as noted in the case of the remark on the poor little toads, of free associations working as indications, as *deuten auf*, of as-yet 'unthought' unconscious relational levels. The analyst's interpretations can often receive privileged support from such verbal associations.

In any case, as John gained some tolerance towards his psychic reality and me, he came to speak in the sessions of his explosive games at home, in which he emptied shotgun cartridges to procure powder and, relying more on my neutrality – that is, that I should not murderously collide with him – he would spend sessions on end watching his drawing sheets burn in all kinds of ways: proclaiming himself a researcher, which in a sense he was, as long as he did not feel impinged on by intruding adults or their allotted tasks. Close to New Year's Eve, and as a dire test of that which I would consider my neutrality but to John's unconscious is my being a 'wall', he exploded a small rocket while carefully gauging my reaction. It was after this pragmatic test that he brought in, on my questioning, his first ever explicit comment on his intentionality in a session: he had wanted me to be scared. We came to understand that in his 'dematerializing' burning games he *becomes* the 'Big Prick' by burning rival pricks. In fact, he exclaimed jubilantly at the charred remains of a rolled sheet he was holding, 'a prick' – perhaps the charred remains of the interpretive analyst's prick. In such a way he himself came to act what some time before he had brought up in an expansive and even manic mood as the narrative of a film, *Home Alone*, in which a child lost to his parents wages an utterly mocking war against malevolent intruding adults. Such games, while they lasted, put an end to his lethargy. He did keep some boundaries as far as soiling my office was concerned – he would, for example, deftly build paper trays to keep the ashes in, if only then to start penetrating the trays with spots of fire. While protesting loudly at home about having to come to his sessions, he would come in punctually in an unacknowledged show of enthusiasm for his therapy.

Indefiniteness and ostensiveness of clinical facts: pragmatics and cognition

Even a lengthy report is bound to select a few from among a myriad of facts. To quote Eric Rayner:

> At the start of any session the analyst gives his free-floating attention; he *tunes in* and resonates with affects and ideas from the patient *until an underlying theme* is distinguishable. He can then begin to think about verbal interpretation. Resonances and unfolding sequences early in an analysis are likely to be sporadic and *undefined*. However, later in treatment sequences are likely to have vital and *distinctive* features so that deep resonances often occur between patient and analyst and interpretative verbalization is richer.
>
> (1992, p. 39, emphasis added)

Resonances and unfolding sequences evolve thus from being undefined – *intuitable* – to acquiring distinctive – that is, *observable or ostensive* – features, a process in which a 'psychic reality' that has no distinct geometry evolves 'in' or 'through' factual persons – the analyst among them. That such pragmatic 'facts' (i.e. unconscious action-and-emotion relational proposals) are at the same time both concrete and immaterial makes their inductive knowledge – which, I would remind the reader, depends from Aristotle onward on observation – difficult and peculiar indeed.

The idea underlying my account of the psychoanalytic method as an inductive system – that conscious cognitions of psychic 'facts' come out of and are construed upon a background of unconscious, that is, consciously unknown, action-and-emotion meanings – finds support within psychoanalysis, for example, in Freud's ideas of unconscious *Triebe* and 'thing-presentations' as the 'psychic reality' from which all verbal meanings derive, or in Sharpe (1940), for whom verbal meanings come from unconscious bodily ones; and in a wide array of logicians, such as Bertrand Russell's (1948) conception of 'animal inferences' as the basis of all knowledge, and of object-language as bound to pragmatic component; as well as in the field of ethology, in Bateson's (1973, 1979) evolutionary studies of the pragmatics of mammalian communication, from which the semantic universe evolves.

Reichenbach explains, in his *Elements of Symbolic Logic* (1947), that in statements made in the flesh by one person to another the pragmatic component supersedes the semantic one, so they cannot be considered purely cognitive, and the logic–semantic categories of 'true' or 'false' do not apply. Renunciation (partial) of this pragmatic component will establish the analyst's neutrality, this being a requisite for the inductive operation of the analytic situation as cognitive context. Reichenbach holds that, contrary to Aristotelian–scholastic definitions in terms of *genus et differentia*, which define one element in terms of other more abstract ones, empirical 'definitions in use' are not purely verbal and define their elements in terms of concrete observational ones: in such a way we define metabolism, says Reichenbach, in terms of observational measures of biological variables, not in purely verbal terms. In the actual process of knowledge a verification of abstract statements is always given by verification of statements about directly observable things. For Rougier (1960), these *indicative* or *ostensive* definitions can be highly complex, as they must include the theory of the instruments validating the observation. Concepts so defined, which remain open to redefinition in new contexts, Pap calls 'open concepts' (1958).

My first clinical example has striven to show how a verbal allusion, a series of dreams and a drawing represent and make explicit a transference-relational 'frame' of which the analysand is not consciously aware, but whose detectable effects, such as John's deadly serious demeanour, give the analyst a basis for his analogies and help him select those relevant from the wide spectrum of the patient's verbal associations. Pragmatic enactments are unconscious 'definitions in use' the patient makes of the analyst – both of how he uses him, as Joseph (1985) emphasizes, and of how he feels 'used' by him. These, and the *deuten auf* coming up in free associations, are the grounds for the intuitions and observations the analyst will verbalize in interpretations, which can lead the analysand to 'descriptive insights'; but only through observational refutation of his psychic facts will these evolve into structural psychic change.

The second clinical example represents in logical terms a structural psychic change, in the achievement of seriation as a map-territory distinction between psychic and factual reality – this being an instance of the 'work of the negative' (Green, 1993).

Second clinical example

Andrew, a gifted, schizoid young man in his mid-twenties who had achieved joint degrees in quite separate sciences, had long known that his intellect provides continuity to his sense of an identity. He consulted me at his girlfriend's prompting about troubles with his sexuality; he feared losing her, and having just found out his brother was homosexual he dreaded also becoming one. Quite wary of treatment, at first he said he could come for just a year – he would then leave to do a Ph.D. abroad – and that for financial reasons – his father was paying my fees – it would have to be just thrice weekly.[2] Fears of the analyst–father and of the homosexual transference played a role in this reticence, but we came in due course to understand that it was mostly due to a dread of an annihilating fusional dependency on the analyst as oral mother.

During his whole second year of treatment Andrew was enmeshed in the turmoil of the break-up of his first love affair, in an at times extreme replay of his early symbiotic link to the primary Object.[3] The three-year affair was not his first 'crush': at school he had been in love from afar, waiting for hours on end just to see a certain girl pass by; later on he had gone out with another girl for a short time, never daring bodily contact – a timidity for which he would later harshly blame himself. So, prior to his current affair, he had had no physical contacts; Sylvia, his girlfriend, took the initiative in the relationship and soon after hustled him, in spite of his evasiveness, into his first sexual relations. He spaced them out as much as possible ('not more than once a week'), did not have an orgasm for some time, and was much disturbed during and after. This clear-cut 'clinical fact', *impotentia ejaculandi*, led me to point out, on the basis of his behaviour in that relationship and on his dread of the analyst's violence in the session, his fear of what he felt to be an explosive component of himself. At first this did not make sense to him, but then he brought up a 'fact' from his early childhood, the start of which he had no conscious memories of: at the age of 2, on the birth of a sibling, he had gone into an outright hyperkinetic syndrome, furniture-climbing and all. He did remember later examples of his impulsivity, one of them being that at the age of 7 he had gone through a glass door, getting deep gashes in his arms and face – a memory that still made him shudder. He now came to realize how afraid he had been all along of his impulses, and that his motor hyperkinesis was the reason for his intellectual one, intellect being the sole domain in which he had felt comfortable.

A fear of damaging Sylvia with what he unconsciously felt to be his highly intrusive, explosive penis shaped up as a motive for his ejaculatory troubles; later on we were able to understand that he felt coitus to involve violent clashes with father's penis-inside-the-mother (as shown in some illustrative dreams) and a catastrophic loss of the idealized oral mother. Dread of the father's penis and the oral-mother transference jointly led to a pleading needy 'good-boy' attitude to the mother–analyst, weekend breaks becoming quite disorganizing; dread of the annihilating analyst–father showed in his fearfulness and in passive homosexual dreams, which he recognized as referring to the analyst and, indeed, were meant to appease me. To win Sylvia's heart, he appeased her, too, with his endearing 'good-boy' demeanour, which he relied upon to a nearly delusional degree; alternatively, he would try to guess and tend in a motherly way to her every wish, cooking special foods, buying her sweets and chocolates, or surprising her with gifts. When these tricks failed, as they did more and more as time went by, he would stay befuddled at her reproaches and dismissals with no known anger on his part; but when quarrels came up while driving, he would suddenly enact the dreaded father–penis and go up to 100 miles an hour, which scared her out of her wits.

To cut a long story short, he found himself more and more 'passed from the cunt to the ass', as they say in some parts of Latin America – that is, losing his place at the good side of Sylvia's affects and becoming increasingly subject to her expelling, demeaning outbursts. The day came when she told him of her infidelity with a fellow student; in a panic that she might notice his anger and chastise him by departing, he repressed his jealous fury and thoroughly forgave her – and went on to tell the boy involved that he was not angry with him either! But some time later, when she left her diary open at his home, where she recounted what she had felt during another affair, he did become angry. From then on, things went from bad to worse. Unable now to mask his reproachfulness, he found himself accused, and he duly accused himself, both of not being manly and not being caring enough – that is, not being maternal enough. Again he resorted to his enticing submissiveness, which enraged her, making things worse; this he knew, but he could not stop himself. The failure of his 'good-boy' appeasements led to feelings of annihilation, of a 'black void' vivid enough for him to feel that *on looking at himself in a mirror, he would see nobody* – a feeling liable to appear during analytic breaks, when, in the context of the loss of the analyst as primal Object, rifts with his girlfriend would push him to the brink of non-existence. He was unable to feel – or, later, to sustain – anger or hate either at her or at me, hate and love felt at this level as one and the same, as he came to recognize; so he would come out of his 'black void' by massive denial in nearly delusional phantasies of regaining her love, even if it were to take years.

During this long process he thought at times of seeking other girls, but this he felt to be impossible because *at a feelings-level there were just no other girls*. At the time of the session we shall now go into, he strove, as he said, 'to fortify my self-esteem' for what, against all odds, he felt as a decisive meeting with a by now estranged love who, he knew, was prone to fly into a rage at any approach; this he denied, to avoid the 'black void'. He wanted to take her by surprise with his unconditional love, in what amounted to a magical 'if-I-am-yours-then-you-are-mine' equation, as she was leaving a concert to which they used to go together – and this magical character of his approach was duly pointed out to him. At the end of the previous session he had brought up a dream, which, he said, he remembered poorly, that he was anxious about snipers, which earlier I had linked to his dread of the analyst's phallic rivalry at any assertive attitude of his. To his surprise, on waking he felt no anxieties; this time, he said, there were no snipers: which he thought important, but did not know why. As a closing comment, I said in passing that it was not unusual that when a psychic situation starts being dreamt, waking life is relieved of it.

On taking to the couch, he told me smilingly that he was under what economists would call an 'external shock' due to a variable not pertaining to the model studied. It happened that he had found on his answering machine a message from an unknown girl – let's call her Van – saying, 'what a nice voice you have'; after making other pleasing comments, she had said she would phone again. At that he underwent a complete change, and that was why, he said, 'you never saw me so happy'. He felt it important to be aware that his mood change had to do with a quite phantasmic girl, whose chance of being satisfactory he rated as remote. Thereafter he felt in better shape to meet Sylvia and take whatever response she might give. He now realized, he said, how true was that which we had worked at for so many months: his extreme dependency on a deified maternal object projected into Sylvia. He knew that the phone message had its impact at the level of this primary Object felt as a deity; he was aware all along both of its massive 'reality' and of the illusory quality of his enthusiasm for someone unknown. He added, as having somehow something to do with this, that he had felt well after the previous day's session, feeling my comment on closing as an acknowledgement of his efforts to progress in his analysis.

I told him that he seemed indeed surprised that the way his self-esteem followed upon his relation to his female 'Deity' – that is, to a primary Object – had suddenly become, in such a chance manner, a neat observable, and that, as far as I could gather, he had put to joint use two vertices of observation: that of what has gone on in his relationship to Sylvia, and also to me, with its sharp swings from ecstatic recognition to annihilating rejection; and that of an attention to the impact of Van's voice and her message as an acknowledged phantasmic 'apparition' of the said female deified Object, recognizing him and fortifying him against annihilation by rejection. I also told him that what he felt as my recognizing his efforts by my comment yesterday seemed to have played a role, and that a main part of his joy stemmed from the fact that on visualizing this primary link, he felt disentangled.

He agreed and then went on rather manically to assert that he planned to meet this girl Van after his meeting with Sylvia, so that 'my balloon does not burst before that'; in this way, he said, 'I'll be able to meet Sylvia with a higher self-esteem; my problem is that I have a much too low self-esteem'. I told him that while this was true in a way, it seemed to me that the trouble with his thinking of his predicament in terms of self-esteem was that it lead him to a solipsistic 'theory' of himself, blotting out what he has just had the opportunity to observe: his self-esteem's extreme dependency on feeling acknowledged by a phantasmic female Deity. In this way he ended up trying to pull himself up by his own bootstraps – until the time came for some traumatic rejection by his 'Deity'. After a silence he acknowledged this, but, he said, in trying to think in those terms, he has to bear feeling like the people in the cave in Plato's dialogue, who see only shadows and do not know it; only on getting out of the cave do they come to realize these are shadows. Then, and perhaps sensing that the session was drawing to a close, at which time he brings in his dreams as a way of retaining me, he said he had had a dream, one he could not remember well either. *It had to do with a trip and someone who had taught him to fish; this man was doing some repairs at his home, repairs my patient was not sure he was satisfied with; but he did know he'd helped him by teaching him to fish.*

He added that he thought this man was me, but he did not know what the fishing meant. I volunteered that 'fishing' in our slang often means 'becoming aware of'; he answered that it could be that, but he would rather think he was asking me to help him 'fish' for a girl.

Unsurprisingly, the following day, after meeting Sylvia, he said 'I come all bruised up.' She had accepted his invitation to dinner, but in the midst of it she had left, furious. Bruised and sad as he was, he said he was glad that throughout Sylvia's outburst he had kept feeling very much himself; also, he had grasped that there was no human reason to stand such mistreatment. And he said, too, that – sorrowful but relieved – he realized for once that his rupture with Sylvia was, indeed, final. (But, as at the unconscious level in which the relationship enacts the symbiotic link to the primary Object, 'the finding of an object is always a re-finding' [Freud, 1905, p. 222], things can never be final). What opens up at this point – and this I consider a structural psychic change – is what may be called the *seriation of the unconscious 'class'* in diverse *individuals*; indeed, this material was selected for the purpose of showing this 'clinical fact' in concrete terms. I shall presently go into this.

Andrew had come to analysis to extricate himself from the anxieties raised by the annihilating vicissitudes of an archaic link enacted in the amorous relationship to Sylvia, who is concretely his archaic

Object actualizing the up-to-then split-off 'class' of 'sexual women' – a 'class' equated to a relationship with what Matte-Blanco (1975) calls 'the power of the class'. In such a *Class-Object* with no map-territory distinction the archaic oral and genital Object and a given individual coincide fully.

Factual seriation – that is, the 'class' of 'sexual women' that come to be *felt* as a series encompassing diverse individuals as distinct from being plural only in conscious thought – is, to put it briefly, part-and-parcel of a renunciation of the Class-Object's actuality in a given individual. (It is likely that the enactments in the transference link to the analyst are steps towards this seriation of the unconscious class into separate individuals.) As the days passed, and much to his surprise, a veritable series of females came to be *felt as sexual*: apart from Sylvia and Van, with whom he took some initiatives, there was Margaret – 'who I realize is the first girl whom I have asked for a phone number' – and others, too, in a passage to activity towards females (though I will not go into this, what I am describing is in some ways coincident with what Klein assigns to early obsessive mechanisms). This access to genital strivings seems quite distinct from the impulsiveness of the motor and intellectual hyperkinesis concomitant with expulsion from the fusional oral–genital maternal Object: at this primitive level the impulsive-penetrating component is felt as destroying the oral mother, this being a main deterrent to the access to genitality.

It must be noted that Andrew's access to a renunciation of his 'Class-Object in Sylvia' came out of an ostensive, correlational grasp of how he put forward – by projective mechanisms – this Unique Object, and that this in turn resulted from his ability to attain what Bion (1959) called 'binocular vision' and Bateson (1979) called a 'double description' of his psychic reality – that is, of his psychic 'facts'. This 'double description' uses findings on a *mnemic* screen (the remembrance of the vicissitudes of what he felt and what I had interpreted in the link both to Sylvia and to me) and those on a *perceptual* screen (his grasp of the impact on his mood of Van's phantasmic call). Ostensive 'double description' on the screens of memory and perception allows multiple correlations, and thus a grasp of the 'psychic reality' he puts into play. After this ostensive cognisance, the plenitude of the 'sexual (oral–genital) class in Sylvia' was renounced, and seriation of the sexual 'class' in diverse individuals came through.

The operation of the method

My argument can be summarized by saying that psychoanalytic method aims at *disproving, by consciously ostensive refutation in individual concrete instances*, unconscious pragmatic *general propositions* that have been left out of inductive operation and function not as hypotheses but as unconscious-driven certainties.

As it operates only in *specific* – that is, *individual* – instances, ostensive refutation requires that unconscious general propositions be 'objectified' in concrete individuals; this Strachey (1934) discerns in masterly fashion, speaking of the analyst as *external phantasy object* in which unconscious phantasy becomes 'objectified', analytic neutrality being the 'frame' that allows descriptive insights purveyed by transference interpretations to give rise to ostensive insights. As Andrew's vignette shows, analytic neutrality not only plays a role in the 'judgement of reality' of transference interpretations, but also serves as a 'frame' to insights outside the transference proper.

Unconscious pragmatic relations (and their semantic components) are 'known' by the analysand through *unconscious acquaintance*, but, not being known in *consciously* ostensive ways, they are not 'open' to refutation or redefinition. On this basis we can consider *the unconscious as a tautology of pragmatic propositional forms (or enacted 'theories)' applied 'deductively' by the analysand to the universe of his external factual objects*.

His 'deductive' applications of such tautology are interpreted by the analyst: (a) in intention, at the level of the intrinsic meaning of verbal statements as such, that is, as 'sentences'; and mainly, (b) in extension, describing the ways both verbal and nonverbal statements are pragmatically enacted, especially, but not at all exclusively, in the link to the analyst.

In other words, our enquiry into the analysand's nonverbal and verbal utterances is mainly in search of the operation of 'closed' patterns or concepts 'deduced' from unconscious 'theories' that have not attained inductive re-evaluation in his everyday life and which he applies with various degrees of rigidity to his external objects, the analyst included. But these unconscious relational 'theories' are in themselves partly a product of early failed inductions, of 'misconceptions' (Money-Kyrle, 1978b), and they certainly do keep some degree of dependence on relational contexts that can increase or reduce their closedness. In 'Remembering, Repeating and Working-through',

Freud (1914a) says that the repetition compulsion is rendered harmless, and indeed useful, when we admit it into the *transference as a playground*, in which it is allowed to expand in almost complete freedom, the transference thus *creating an intermediate region* between illness and real life. It is a piece of real experience, but one made possible by special conditions and having a provisional character (p. 154). May I add that the analyst's pragmatic – and semantic – neutrality allows an attenuation of annihilatory phenomena: in Andrew's case, a lessening both of the annihilating expulsive anxieties of the early maternal transference and of the dreaded phallic rivalry projected into the analyst.

Within the pragmatic context given by his neutrality, it is the role of the analyst to purvey a 'mapping' through interpretations leading to descriptive insights, in an attempt to 'open' these closed 'deductive' unconscious pragmatic levels, which will, in turn, contribute to their re-evaluation and/or refutation by the analysand, which will, in my opinion, be unavoidably ostensive: ostensive refutation, when attained, brings unconscious processes to the *Pcs.–Cs.* domain of the 'no'.

4

Body, meaning and language

Thomas Kuhn argues in *The Structure of Scientific Revolutions* (1962) that scientific disciplines start in a pre-paradigmatic period when its practitioners are grouped in competing 'schools', claiming each as its own a field they approach from a different direction. The post-paradigmatic period ensues after some notable scientific achievement unifies the field under a shared paradigm.

Kuhn restricts this thesis to physico–mathematical disciplines, and later on (1974) he further delineates and refines the plural meanings of the term paradigm. Events in our psychoanalytic discipline are, in any case, at variance with such a scheme. Emerging from Freud's genius as an evolving conceptual net with some cohesion, it later scattered into diverging schools of thought. From a Galilean stance, Grünbaum (1984) takes its plurality to be proof enough of the empirical shortcomings of our clinical findings, while to others, such as Feyerabend (1981), the coexistence of conceptual frames and theories in a discipline shows its vitality, an idea introduced by Mill. Plurality of theories gave its title to Wallerstein's (1988) address in Montreal, 'One Psychoanalysis or Many?', holding that our diverse theoretical stances share a common clinical ground, a thesis discussed from both sides at the Rome Congress. While the clinical field provides a common ground, I am inclined to think that divergences in conceptual frames and the use of clinical method are such that a clinical common ground is a goal rather than a finding.

Freud's psychoanalytic theory came out of his findings in an attempt to meet clinical obstacles. And since the dawn of psychoanalysis, technical problems – that is, the obstacles found on using the method – have led to theoretical divergences. Ferenczi's 'active technique' from 1919 on, then Rank's attempts at focal analysis of the 'birth trauma', and again Ferenczi's 'technique of neocatharsis' in the 1930s, pioneered substantial shifts. In the same way in the 1950s Lacan traces to the technique the source of his theoretical discrepancies.

That today psychoanalysis is fragmented into various conceptual stances is obvious enough. Moreover, a watershed in basic epistemology adds to theoretical and technical discrepancies. Two paradigmatic stances can be discerned with some ease: the empirical stance advocated by Freud and, flourishing since it was posited by Lacan in France, by Schafer and Spence in the United States, and by Lorenzer in Germany, what despite its disparities can go under the label of linguistic–narrative–hermeneutic stance. Its force partly reflects an 'external change', given that our discipline and its practitioners got uprooted from its initial medical soil which fostered a respect for observational findings, be it in anamnesis or by direct observation in the semiology of disease. People bred on verbal argument rather than observation, coming to psychoanalysis from philosophy or literature, often ascribe it to such prior conceptual and methodological frames; besides, academic teaching of psychology at universities often advantages 'theory' – that is, verbalism – over an ability to observe. Additionally, the force of the linguistic paradigm in psychoanalysis reflects a wider happenstance: the 'linguistic turn' in philosophy. Following the later Wittgenstein, an Oxford philosopher, Simon Blackburn (1984) affirms:

> it has become natural to give the nature of language considerable autonomy, and even sovereignty. . . . An individual's psychology becomes whatever is needed to enable him to understand the language which stands revealed, and the world becomes whatever is necessary to make true the true statements made with that language. This is the 'linguistic turn', for better or worse, of most of the important philosophy this century . . . people find it hard to see how there can be any enquiry except into the relations of speakers and their language.
>
> (pp. 5–6)

Paul Feyerabend (1969), on his part, warns that belief in linguistic arguments as eliminative instruments, applied before a theory has reached the point where empirical examination of it becomes feasible, is a two-edged sword that stumps scientific research. What would be the result for psychoanalysis if, as Blackburn attests, it were to restrict research to the relations between speakers and language? In terms of Lakatos' (1970) ideas on the methodology of research programmes, would the ensuing change in psychoanalysis' programme lead to an increase in the content of our knowledge, or, conversely, lead to a degenerative problem shift due to engulfment of the discipline in the maelstroms of philosophical apriorisms?

What concerns philosophy of language, says John Searle (1965), is to make explicit the semantics of a given language – which is different from what concerns psychoanalysis, and involves a triple restriction of meaning: a restriction to conscious meaning excluding unconscious ones; a restriction to its binding to rules, and a restriction to rules having to do with linguistic signs. Speech acts, notes Searle (p. 222), following Wittgenstein, are rule-governed acts, meaning public rules. Philosophy of language and psychoanalysis thus shape, I shall argue, different universes.

Dropping the Freudian empirical paradigm has effects beyond those of technical variants or emphases in different 'schools': it abandons the Freudian *via di levare*, the care for ostensiveness of psychic reality as enacted in the session. Freud liked to say, after his teacher, Charcot, that 'it is necessary to let facts speak', that they show up, this being cardinal to the method; thus, linguistic–narrative stances turn method-less in core clinical dimensions. My main point in this chapter is that linguistic–narrative abandonment of ostensiveness jettisons Freud's bodily unconscious.

The bodily unconscious in Freud's work

'The ego' – says Freud (1923a, p. 26) – 'is first and foremost a bodily ego': it comes about in perceptual interplay, as a differentiation of the id. The ego 'is continued inwards, without any sharp delimitation, into an unconscious mental entity which we designate as the id and for which it serves as a kind of façade' (1930, p. 66), and he argues soon afterward that 'the ego is in its very essence a subject' (1933a, p. 58). Bodily rooting of unconscious and subject are not isolated statements of the Viennese master: a bodily, unconscious psychism is for him the basis of meaning. The unconscious' basic components, the *Triebe* – the instincts or drives – are of the body both on their emerging from erogenous zones and on their object, the other's body, or eventually one's own body:[1] such a position between psyche and soma does not pose an antithesis: it shows the bodily nature of psychism in Freud's conception. This applies also, and mainly, to unconscious 'thing-presentations', traces of early life experiences invested, says Valls (1995), by libido from each erogenous zone; from these the meaning of conscious verbal terms is derived: Freud holds that verbal meanings ultimately depend on the thing-presentation – that is, the invested unconscious experience – that words link to.

Of course the term 'body' has various meanings. Hysterical conversion showed that the topography of the erogenous body is not the same as anatomy: it fits, more generally, into the bodily nature of relationship; thus, Dora's cough and aphony condense bodily erotic feelings in her link to Mr K (and, on a deeper level, to father). In such a way, the erogenous body of psychoanalysis is representational as regards unconscious erotic linking.

The bodily nature of the primary emotional links is obvious enough in early childhood when, according to Freud (1923a), identification and object relationship cannot be distinguished: at the fusional level of erotism – oral, cutaneous, and visual – in the link to the breast–mother are primary meanings: 'the highest erotic bliss, which is never again attained' (1910, p. 129). Earlier (Ahumada, 1990), I stressed Freud's hints in Leonardo (1910) of the baby's passing from the link to the breast to acknowledging the mother as a whole person, which implies perhaps, says Freud, a felt loss of the link to the breast. In spite of this single but crucial statement, and in spite of his findings on symbolization and loss in the cotton-reel game, Freud does not unfold the genesis of symbol-formation, which Melanie Klein does, connecting it to weaning. Though it may be argued with André Green (1984) that Freud does not fully attain a theory of language, he prepares the ground for Ella Sharpe's (1940) and Ignacio Matte-Blanco's (1975) psychoanalytic notions of language, which closely link meaning to unconscious bodily linked experiences. As earlier explained, Money-Kyrle (1978b) distinguishes three levels of representation: first, image-less unconscious representation by identification;[2] second, representation in visual terms, which Freud studies in dreams; and, third, verbal representation in language, having, according to Freud, free access to a consciousness it dominates. These three distinct levels of meaning are co-opted by narrative–linguistic stances as internal to language.

To these three meanings of the bodily – the anatomical, the erogenous, the bodily emotional linking – a fourth sense may, after Bion, be added, somewhat ironically: the body in –K, a prevalent mode of unknowing, avoiding emotional experience by way of splitting. Here the body, felt along Cartesian lines as mechanical and alien to the psyche, usurps its place. Such splitting is promoted nowadays by a culture of fitness and sports, backed by commercial interests.

Two concepts of meaning in psychoanalysis

As I have said, for Freud and his empiricist followers the meaning of words resides in the unconscious traces of experiences that are, simultaneously, bodily and relational. Two intertwining levels are seen as continuously active: (a) a process motivational level of instinctual drives and thing-presentations, giving rise to a subject's main meanings, grounded in his early experiences, and (b) a level of 'mapping' of such meanings in conscious memories and on a linguistic apparatus of socially shared coded word-presentations; these – but not the unconscious meanings they are tied to – freely access consciousness and can function according to the laws of secondary process. The motivational process level is, in veiled and overt ways, strongly representational: the baby recognizes the mother's breast and her eyes on which early on he sets his gaze; recent work on amodal perception (see Rayner, 1992) shows his up-to-now unthought-of capabilities.

Conversely, in narrative–hermeneutic–linguistic stances meaning dwells in language, which puts it into action. To Austin (1962), at the core of philosophical 'linguistic turn', 'speech acts' have an illocutory aspect – what we do when we speak, such as threaten, promise or implore – and a perlocutory aspect, the effect of the 'speech act' on the other person. In the same way, in French postmodernist quarters, the terms "mean" or "signify" are used (in and out of session) in the sense of state or affirm: as meaning is seen as inherent in language, one grants or assigns it instead of finding or unveiling it. From Austin on, for linguistic stances to 'mean' is part of a speech act. This might do for common language and some functions of the analysand's language operating *per via di porre*, but not for an understanding of free association nor of the properly interpretative use, *per via di levare*, of the analyst's wordage.

Ella Sharpe's and Ignacio Matte-Blanco's psychoanalytic notions of language account for the bodily unconscious as it appears in common language and free association; let us compare them with the hermeneutic model of the 'text', and then study the analyst's interpretative use of language in both stances.

Ella Sharpe's classic 1940 paper, 'Psycho-physical Problems Revealed in Language: An Examination of Metaphor', holds that analytic experience shows that, in terms of Aristotle's definition of metaphor in his *Poetics* as 'a transference of a word to a sense different from its signification', displacement of meaning goes from bodily experience to the psychic, but not vice versa. Analytic understanding proceeds from metaphoric language to the bodily and experiential ground from which metaphors arise: examination of metaphor leads us to a psycho-physical experience – in my terms, to a relational, bodily experience – that has hitherto had no access to consciousness, or has been forgotten.

Illustrating her idea that language acquisition is a pre-requisite of and equivalent to control of urethral and anal sphincters, Sharpe proposes the following vignette: A father, whose young son was attempting sphincter control, and whose wife tended to explode when the child had an 'accident', told his wife: 'Of course you feel angry, that's natural, but don't let John see your anger. Think to yourself you must keep your anger in and hold it in until you get to another room, and then you can let it out.' Such is metaphor: the father speaks in words that refer to a sense-perceptible object, but they are used to denote a different order or category: namely, emotion. In time the child will come to a similar way of thinking as regards his actual urine and faeces: 'I must hold it, and hold it until I get to the other room' (p. 157). Discharge of a feeling of tension, no longer relieved by physical discharge, will find an outlet in speech, while words themselves substitute for bodily substances. In that sense, says Sharpe, speech is itself a metaphor of bodily and emotional discharge, and patients will use words to express: (a) feeling without thought, as in onomatopoeia; (b) thought without feeling (i.e. ideational), and (c) metaphor, which, like a symptom, is a compromise between ego, superego, and id. In other words, a model of relational, bodily meanings is articulated verbally at a different logical level.

To Ignacio Matte-Blanco (1975, 1988), every verbal reference to the psychic employs metaphors built on a comparison with a temporal and spatial phenomenon. In logical terms metaphor implies that *a* is to *b* as *c* is to *d*. So if, of a given situation, I say that 'a dog that barks does not bite', I apply to it the relationship of the first member, the dog's barking and biting. Metaphor involves an analogy relating to a general relationship, taken from one example when it seems to apply to another: metaphor accounts for classes of relationship. According to Matte-Blanco, the unconscious takes heed of open classes: the psychoanalytic 'breast' encompasses an infinite number of elements. Let me add, illustrating Matte-Blanco's statement on the infiniteness of the unconscious relationship to a 'breast', that when children who have just an initial grasp of linguistic codes give us an inkling of their primary relational universes where such open classes rule, we often get a surprise.

My example is a dialogue: a 5-year old boy, seeing a big jet plane take off, asks: 'Mum, where does that plane go?'; his sister, not yet 2, answers as if it were obvious: 'Goes after Mum'. Such use of language uncovers the differences of the logic of reference at the Freudian level of impulse, thing-presentation and primitive emotion, and at the verbal level of word-presentations that linguists inhabit, which gives us access to two distinct – indeed, representational and relational – universes, that of common understanding, which the philosophy of language studies, and that of the psychoanalytic grasp of the unconscious. What the philosophy of language finds relevant and tries to explain is the uses of language, how we come to understand and use words, and, more generally, the functioning, subject to rules, of language; the philosophy of language sets the issue of meaning within such constraints. The credibility of such a thesis requires undermining appurtenance of meaning to representational issues external to language and obviously previous to it. The fundamental premise of philosophies of language involves, to a greater or lesser extent, leaving aside the motivational bearing of affects, of sexuality and drives, as well as the evidence from ethology.[3]

This is honestly expressed by Simon Blackburn, a lucid expounder of the ideas of the Oxford Wittgensteinians. In his book *Spreading the Word* (1984), two long chapters entitled: 'How Is Meaning Possible?' show that restrictions on meaning by the philosophy of languages lead to a break with our animal nature, turning a pseudo-problem into a core task: to explain how meaning is possible. Having ironed out the bodily, the relational, and the sexual, meaning is not something one accedes to or unfolds: it needs being created by and through language.

The basic Wittgensteinian thesis, semantic externalism, maintains that no term can exist in any language as a function of terms present only in the mind of whoever understands the term. Blackburn (1984, p. 95) states that 'if we accept semantic externalism, we must revise our whole conception of the privacy of the mental, and our knowledge of the contents of our own minds'; as earlier cited, semantic externalism restricts individual psychology to how the individual understands language.

The central and obvious truth about words, argues Blackburn (1984, p. 40ff), is that we understand them: we confer their powers, know how to use them, make them work for us. But, he says, What kind of truth is it that I can use a word to mean something, or express a thought about something? The usual approach, he holds, has been to understand it in terms of a dog-legged theory, words being reinterpreted into another medium, that of Ideas, whose own powers explain the significance words take on. Classically, we would understand meaning by mapping words back onto ideas, which implies two stages. They are associated with elements of an interpreting medium (in this case, Ideas) having their own representative powers, their own 'lines of projection' onto the world, whereby they signify aspects of it. Such representational theory of knowledge coming from Aristotle and Locke brings forth, though, the idealist response exemplified by Berkeley, who holds that there is no guarantee that such ideas correspond to an external world, and thus the knowable world is restricted to ideas, private, occult, and personal; our words will only refer to this world of ideas.

The Cartesian requisite, univocity of 'clear and distinct concepts', shines, though, in the Wittgensteinian demand for warrants: that is, in the idea that to admit the highly visual representational model requires, he maintains, that its connection to the external world be transparent and not in need of additional interpretation in one sense or another. There must be a medium that carries its own interpretation with it, otherwise we fall into an infinite regress of interpretations. If its own connection with whatever it represents were mutable and contingent as that of words with things is – or, as Blackburn (p. 54) holds, in the way that scientific facts are mutable and contingent – we would need an additional medium to know how the interpretation is to be taken, which opens the way to infinite regression.[4] The problem of interpreting words to stand for aspects of the world becomes, absurdly, replaced by two problems: that of interpreting words to connect to the right aspects of one's mental scene, and that of interpreting aspects of one's mental scene to stand for aspects of the world, extending them – magically, affirms Blackburn – towards a world beyond themselves. What we need, he argues, is a more direct approach to meaning, trying to grasp what it is to use words in ways governed by rules. For genuine judgement demands faithfulness to a pre-existing rule: judging is something that is essentially capable of being correct or incorrect, and on this basis Wittgenstein rejects the idea that meaning be private, because in such a case it will not be possible to make a distinction between: (a) someone who is genuinely faithful to a pre-established rule, which determines correct and incorrect application, and (b) someone who is disposed to use the term under the illusion that he is following a rule that determines its application.

In any case, different authors, even within this stream, differ considerably in the idealism that permeates their 'semantic externalism' – that is, as concerns the rupture with perception and the conception of an external world. Thus Austin (1954) argues, against Strawson – and against Blackburn's avowal that ideas of a mental projection onto an external world are magical – that he does not think for a moment that 'facts' are pseudo-entities or that the idea of 'adequateness to facts' be a useless notion. In fact, as is expanded in chapter 6, arguing against Grünbaum, Darwinian evolution rests on meaning – that is, on what matters in some way or other – at a mental-representational level: the fox for whom the hare had no meaning and so was unable to find, confuse, and hunt its hare would die hungry, while the hare to whom the fox is not meaningful enough to anticipate and evade him is out of the game. This goes, too, for a baby for whom nipple and mother have not meaning enough and for the baby who is not meaningful to his mother. Needless to say, here 'meaning' again needs to renounce the Cartesian (and Wittgensteinian) demand for 'undeniable, clear and distinct concepts'.

The universe of 'Use of Rules' and the universe of the unconscious

Let us review now the dialogue between the two children cited above:

(Five year old boy): 'Mum, where does that plane go?'

(Two year old girl): 'Goes after Mum.'

In terms of Oxford linguistic philosophy – that is, of Wittgensteinian semantic externalism – our five year old boy's use of language holds to the pre-existing rule, while his sister would be someone who either: (a) holds to a bent rule establishing an idiolect, a private language, or (b) holds to no rule in a linguistically senseless universe.

Psychoanalytically we can agree that the boy's language poses a question that overtly holds to secondary processes, while her sister's answer, though she can recognize and appropriately name an aeroplane, evidences that her speech is at the service of primary processes. If, contrarily to Wittgensteinian assumptions, we assume that the girl's language aptly describes her relevant universe of meaning, distinct from that of adults and even more distinct from that of Oxford philosophers, and if we keep to Matte-Blanco's idea that the unconscious recognizes classes and classes of classes, we can, I believe, reach a more precise and detailed explanation of how both assertions differ in their logic of reference.

To the girl, but not to her brother (in what is conscious and expressed in language), the aeroplane pertains to a wide relational class of 'Mum-seeking-objects' that she herself belongs to. In other words, both she and the plane are members of a class that is simultaneously relational and bodily, 'going after Mum', this being why the plane's 'bodily' movement has such an obvious goal – a class that, though of dubious acceptance to Oxford philosophers, is active in less obvious ways in adult life. Examples from common language metaphors include Mother Earth, Mother Nature or Mother Church, mother countries, mother–planes and, now, motherboards.

Verbal metaphor takes in most linguistic stances a causal status, an idea on which the psychology of propaganda rightly rests. In Matte-Blanco's conception metaphor will allow 'mapping', a grasp of an analogy based on shared belonging to an unconscious class.

Common language, then, leaves out what that normative Golem of linguistic philosophies, the 'community of speakers' establishing shared rules, is not conscious of and has not nominated, being beyond existing social consciousness. From their own premises on, Wittgensteinian philosophies of language and psychoanalytic enquiry of the personal concreteness of unconscious emotional–bodily relationships form divergent universes.

The contexts of meaning

As a common clinical field between different analytical stances remains a goal rather than a fact, one can join Richards (1995) in that the road to solve our discrepancies, thorny as it may be, entails open discussion rather than evading or hiding the issues. The divergent universes of Wittgensteinian linguistic philosophy and psychoanalytic enquiry of unconscious affect impinge on the use of our method: where the meaning of what is enacted concretely in the session in bodily–relational–sexual ways is ignored or abandoned, technical cautions on the setting and analytic neutrality tend to go overboard.

Against the premise of linguistic philosophies that meaning results from language, to my mind the enacted 'contexts' in the session set the frame to verbal interchanges. Here I join Álvarez de Toledo (1954) and Betty Joseph (1985). Showing how our work in the session centres on what, standing on the rarefied heights of linguistic reflection, Blackburn deems absurd, how in the analytic session words recapture emotion and meaning by way of 'mapping' onto what we gain from an awareness on what is being enacted, Luisa Álvarez de Toledo holds:

> The act of speaking, the utterance of words, as a mode of contact, stands for, replaces and achieves the first form of contact with the object, namely sucking. . . . When 'associating' and 'interpreting' are analysed as such, the primitive identity of act, image and object arises and becomes a reality in the act of speaking and listening to the analyst. The repressed concrete somatic aspect of symbols becomes conscious and the verbal images take on the corresponding emotion and content.
>
> (1954, p. 294)

Which puts into their right places creativity on the one hand, and creationism on the other hand. Creativity, the analyst's ability to grasp events from a new point of view allowing new interpretative hypotheses, and the analysand's capability to generate his own hypotheses, to attend to those the analyst proposes, and to recognize the hitherto unknown patterns of his unconscious functioning, is a must for effective analysis. Meanings inescapably evolve as the work goes on: the lifting of repressions, and that the vast and never fully achieved rearrangement that Klein called the depressive position and Garma (1974) the integrative position, are ways in which meanings evolve. And here I go back to my core point, the effects of theoretical choices on the use of method. To empirical stances meanings evolve as a result of working through, of *Durcharbeitung*, as Álvarez de Toledo masterfully shows. To interpretative creationism, as proposed by authors like Viderman (1970), assignment of meaning rests, *per via di porre*, on the *parole analytique*, on the 'analytic word' leading to rhetoric voluntarism and suggestion. When in academia the 'analytic word' envisions a public 'transmissibility of psychoanalysis' foregoing the ostensiveness of psychic reality the session allows, we are squarely in the realm of the psychology of propaganda.

Linguistic philosophies share a scorn for ostensiveness. It took Gadamer (1986) a full quarter of a century to arrive – in the Supplement II to the sixth German edition of his monumental *Truth and Method* – at taking heed of extralinguistic meanings, while in *From Text to Action* Paul Ricoeur's (1991) 'militant hermeneutics' happily refuses meaning to any action that is not the action of the text. For his part Eco (1990) vigorously joins with rhetorical creationism, avowing that 'rather than being something that can be submitted to a verification test, language is a mechanism able to create belief and to impose a reality asserted in the context' (p. 253). Small wonder, then, that in his essay, 'A Portrait of the Elder as a Young Pliny', included in *The Limits of Interpretation* (1990), Eco bravely puts himself as reader in the shoes of the author creating a 'metanarrative' which replaces history. Such are the protagonistic gains, or if you will the narcissistic and megalomaniac satisfactions, afforded by the epistemic nihilism of the 'linguistic turn'. The reader's creationism is given free rein in the deconstruction of 'infinite semiosis'; vilifying, to no one's surprise, whatever be deemed 'descriptive'.

Blackburn and a major champion of the 'linguistic turn', Richard Rorty (1990), agree that its heyday is already past. But this would not seem to apply in our field, where method is freely revised upon linguistic premises: on Wittgensteinian grounds Cavell (1991) argues for theory-free spontaneity, while on narrative ones Spence (1994) restricts psychoanalytic material to the verbally enounced. Lacan's initial move, unlinking the ego from perception-consciousness, reiterates the epistemic rupture that characterizes idealisms, linguistic ones not exempted; a Cartesian rupture subtending also Wittgensteinian philosophy of language, as traced by Blackburn. Four decades under the aegis of the linguistic signifier, however, led Lacanianism, as testified by Lacan's biographer Elisabeth Roudinesco (1993) and everyday experience, to theoretical dogmatism and anarchy in method.

That, as Oxford linguists hold, we know words, we confer on them their power, we make them work for us, helps us to understand the impact on psychoanalysis of the philosophic 'linguistic turn' and the ensuing spread of linguistic postures. The linguistic turn allowed philosophy to escape a mainly epistemological role as handmaiden to the sciences, regaining its ancestral role as *regina scientiorum* where, set above the partial and contingent knowledge of the sciences, philosophical reflection purports to grasp the whole (Gadamer, 1976).

In the case of psychoanalysis, though, displacement of meaning from the bodily and the relational to language, from the unknown to what allows us – rightly or wrongly – to assign meanings amounts to a 'bottom-up' shift, from the unconscious to the intellectual – which evades the main obstacles that the psychoanalytic method confronts us with, at the cost, I am afraid, of shedding its virtues.

5

FACT, CONTEXT, IMAGE, NARRATIVE

A bio-logical approach

> But the psychologic rests on the biologic.
>
> W. R. Bion (1992, p. 363)

Let me start quoting a founder of modernity, the Franciscan monk William of Ockham, who died in the Black Death of 1349: 'Man thinks in two kind of ways: one, the natural way that we share with beasts; the other, the logic, enjoyed by man alone'. Which, being revolutionary six and a half centuries later, marks the pugnacity of a basic epistemic confusion in Western philosophical thought: the equation of psyche and consciousness.

This confusion, signalled by Freud (1917b, pp. 142–143) and whose epistemic pitfalls are illustrated in this chapter, is endorsed by Descartes in the *Discourse on the Method* in 1637: his methodical doubt radically doubts all certainties but comes back to them, given that *cogitatio* involves indisputable, clear, and distinct concepts. This establishes an ontic hiatus between the purely mechanical *res extensa* of beasts and the *cogitatio* where language consubstantiates man, the fallen angel, with the Deity, the *Verbum*. Bertrand Russell's (1897) comment that geometry is at the core of the theory of knowledge highlights the demand for certainties in Descartes' theory of knowledge and in Galilean science. Such demand for certainties grounds *contrario sensu* the pretence of autonomy of the hermeneutic postures of the 'end of metaphysics', holding with Nietzsche that 'there are no facts, only interpretations'.

That man thinks in two ways, one way shared with beasts and an alternative one linked to consciousness and language, has noticeable Freudian resonances, as Freud separates thing-presentations from word-presentations, and, more generally, an unconscious and a consciousness bound to language. From the *Studies on Hysteria* (Breuer & Freud, 1895) on, for Freud thought is originally unconscious, becomes conscious at times and partly, and encompasses much more than Cartesian 'indisputable, clear and distinct concepts', which helps adumbrate the obstacles to a neat distinction of 'fact', 'context', 'image' and 'narrative'.

Delimiting what, after Ockham, I understand as a bio-logic, the forms of thought we share with beasts, I will narrate an incident witnessed years ago while talking to friends near a forest. Pursued closely by three dogs, a hare appeared, losing distance and obviously tired. She/he shot right through our group and, noticing a disorderly pile of firewood, veered sharply, almost on my feet, and hid in the woodpile; the dogs eagerly went past along her/his previous path. After a few seconds, the hare came out, ears raised: detecting a trailing dog, she/he hid again, allowed the dog to pass by, and then escaped rapidly the way he/she had come. Though this short fragment might seem far removed from what goes on in psychoanalysis, let us delve into these 'facts'.

Facts

My narrative selects a few from a variety of events at noon on a summer day. Stylistic improvements would be irrelevant to what we can delimit and conjecture, but a different ontology may have led to a different story.

My epistemic stance of methodological fallibilism, following Lakatos, does not seek empirical certainties. I cannot, though, doubt what I witnessed, despite the fashionable threat of 'naive realism': I find it unlikely to think with Descartes that a wicked demon could have deceived me, leading me to see dogs and hare where there were none. Hare and dogs are 'facts' that, as other everyday ones, evoke no reasonable doubt. I shall also take as a 'fact', or if one prefers, as an event, that the hare deceived the dogs, though not knowing well enough what 'deceive' means in such context; to appeal to 'deception' as a level of 'facts' implies a first interpretive level. To suppose that the deception aimed, for the hare, at evading being eaten does not seem risky, as it joins myriad observations, others' and mine, in many contexts: Money-Kyrle (1955, p. 290) astutely said that for each organism other living beings are food, something one may be eaten by, or someone to unite with. Plainly, deception required a 'knowledge' on the part of the hare – though I do not consider what this consists of – about the dogs' likely course of action: she/he kept in mind that speeding dogs rely upon visual images and, after losing visual contact, they would return to track a smell – as indeed they did; such a 'fact' would explain her/his hurry in leaving the hideout (what I call 'fact' here, though arising from observation, is only my best conjecture on the conditions for the success of the hare's strategy).

While it is more difficult to sift here observation and interpretation, that is, conjecture based on the context, I assume that the hare and the dogs felt 'emotions' in the events: in the case of the dogs, this was made evident by their howling after they lost the hare. I don't have, though, 'clear and distinct concepts' on such emotional 'facts', which I conceive in human rather than doggy or hare-y terms. More conjectural yet – if not purely imaginative – is to make assumptions on the hare's feelings upon the sudden appearance of humans. Obviously, she/he did not avoid us, as would have happened were not the dogs after her/him: she/he shot into our group with no hesitation.

The dogs did hesitate before us, which may have favoured the hare. Was the hare's shooting right through us part of a strategy?[1] Evidently, the hare interpreted the 'fact' of the encounter with us upon her high-priority relational context, persecution by the dogs, 'interpreting' it at the level of a bio-logic, not at what puts us apart from beasts. That the hare interpreted our group in terms of the persecution context fits a wide observational background on hares' behaviour towards groups of humans: they flee, they do not push through. What here I call 'fact' is my interpretation of the hare's 'interpretation'.

At another level, upon the perceptual screen of my internal experiences (for Freud consciousness is a perceptual organ for psychic qualities; Russell concurs, adding ostension in mnemic screens to perceptual ostension) I regard as a 'fact', solely perceptible to me, my partisan identification in my terror of the dogs, were I put 'in the place of' the hare': I was quite relieved that the deception came out happily.

The term 'fact', far from being univocal, thus ranges from the directly observational to well-grounded conjectures, where 'well-grounded' means the absence of viable alternative hypotheses. This, additionally, underlines that terms are not univocal, including, as we shall soon see, that of 'image', and cannot, *stricto sensu*, be sharply defined: being 'open concepts', they are redefined in their different contexts of use. As happens in diffuse logics where 'reality value' lies anywhere between 0 and 1, the term 'fact' refers to multiple and diverse levels according to the realms and contexts to which it applies, and it accepts varied degrees of verisimilitude, ranging from quasi-certainty to the metaphoric.

Some readily observable events leave scant margin for doubt, but this does not apply to varying aspects of their interpretation. I cannot delimit observation and inference fully, as concerns my hare and myself: that the hare took to the firewood pile makes me surmise *prima facie* that she/he 'knew' dogs would follow the visual track; this a necessary condition of the deception, not something that I can fully affirm in particular instances. However, ethologic observation of prey–predator interaction provides a conceptual background for assuming that the hare has a 'theory' of the dogs' actions framing those other 'facts', her/his strategic choices. Certainly, such 'theory on dogs' is not a Galilean 'theory', nor does it sport Cartesian 'clear and distinct concepts'; it pertains to the levels of thinking we share with beasts, those of a bio-logic.

Where to locate those other 'facts', my 'placing' myself in the hare's skin, my terror 'from' the hare that she/he be caught, and my joy at the success of the stratagem? Again, the Cartesian paradigm does not help here, as this is not a *cogitatio* but something immediate: in psychoanalytic jargon, a projective identification of a part of my internal world, a putting into others a part of my self and my unconscious objects; here, an 'inter-species' projective identification in an event where annihilation anxieties were at the heart of the game, allowing highly emotional bonds to arise between distant species – something usual that arises strongly in small children.[2] This 'emotional experience', with its peculiar 'thought through identification', pertains in Ockham's terms to the 'natural way that we share with the beasts', which is different from the 'logic' exclusive to man. This 'natural way' of thought, a logic that is simultaneously emotional and relational, takes into account the logic of the conduct of the other, as my hare took account of the dogs: in this case, 'theory' on the behaviour of the 'other' belongs to conflict – quite far from the 'intersubjectivity' addressed by Gadamer's 'search for agreements' or Habermas's 'mutual understanding'.

All the above fits badly with the Cartesian ontic distinction, basic and unbridgeable, between a mechanical material *res extensa* allotted to beasts and an immaterial cognoscent *res cogitans* having man as a fallen angel and God as his warrantor. The hare's inferences on its pursuers' conduct do not fit the notion of mechanism, nor do my feelings on the scene fit that other side of the Cartesian ontology, the *cogitatio*. Deception is understandable, indeed unavoidable, in the conceptual frame of Darwinian prey–predator survival strategies.

However, some 140 years after it was enounced, the Darwinian paradigm does not permeate everyday understanding. Euclidian deductivism and its Galilean heirs, assuming a neat demarcation of formal 'theories' and 'facts' and seeking empirical certainties, rule what is deemed empirical.

Against the arrogant claim to generality of Galilean physicalism in its pretence at deductibility and certainty of all empirical facts, an eminent mathematician, physicist, and epistemologist, Henri Poincaré, argued in 1902, introducing his first book, *La Science et l'Hypothèse*:

> For the superficial observer scientific truth is beyond doubt: the logic of science is certain, and if scientists sometimes make mistakes, it is because they ignore its rules. Mathematical truths derive from a small number of evident propositions by means of a series of impeccable reasonings that they impose on us, and also on nature. They chain the Creator, so to say, who just chooses from a short list of options. A few experiments will be enough to know his choice, which gives place to numberless consequences by way of mathematical deductions, allowing each to know a corner of the Universe.
>
> This it is for many, and for high-school students in their first physics lessons, the origin of certainty in science. Such is the manner in which they understand the role of experiment and mathematics. In such way it was grasped also a century ago by many scientists, in their dream to build the Universe, taking from experience as little as possible.
>
> Later reflection took into account the role of hypotheses, because the mathematician and the experimenter cannot do

> without them. And then it was argued that such constructions were not solid, and it was thought that they could be turned down with a single blow. To be sceptical in such a way is also to be superficial. To doubt everything and to believe everything are equally comfortable forms to obviate reflection.
>
> (1902, p. 23, my translation)

Thus Poincaré ironizes at the notions of univocity, deductivity, and certainty of 'pure' scientific 'facts'; which, notwithstanding, still characterize the common man's idea of science, that of a major part of the scientific establishment, and our epistemic controversies. At about that same time, Russell (1903) maintained, advancing the position of methodological fallibilism, that empirical statements can be refuted but never proven, and that absence of contradictions and counterexamples never amounts to proof. The dispute, archaic and venerable, on the nature of scientific facts finds its roots, as already mentioned, in two main approaches to science in ancient Greece: the Pythagorean demonstrative tradition and the Aristotelian descriptive tradition in science built mainly on biology, based on observation and examination of the largest possible amount of 'exemplars', in search of characteristic analogies and 'forms'. The gulf between what both traditions understand as 'fact' is vast.

It is true that Pythagorean heirs felt triumphant in the seventeenth century – witness the Galilean outcry that 'the Book of the Universe is written in mathematical language'. Strict inductivism translocates to empiry a Euclidian deductivism that assumes that 'science' is what starts from a list of axioms, lemmas or definitions leading by deduction to a growing system of unalterable truths (Lakatos, 1976). Thus, for Tarski and Popper, only formalized systems are deemed scientific; on such criteria Darwinian biology, let alone psychoanalysis, is not an empirical science. An alliance of science and technology currently lends weight to the Pythagorean–Galilean redefinition of empiry upon the spell of number as certainty: thus, the president of the New York Academy of Sciences, Rodney Nichols, urges a return to Kelvin's injunction: 'When you cannot measure it, when you cannot express it in numbers . . . you have scarcely, in your thought, advanced to the stage of Science . . . whatever the matter be' (1996, p. 4). Such ideologization bred on the symbiosis of science and technology currently finances most sectors of the scientific establishment, where the realm of emotional phenomena, including psychoanalysis, is displaced by the neurobiological study of the molecular or genetic 'basis' of mind. Abrogation of the emotional at the scientific establishment agrees in the wider global milieu with the explosion of media 'visual power', pushing into social normality the attempt to evade emotional evolutions and to abolish the pain they involve.

The epistemic dream of building a Universe starting from 'certain, clear, indisputable concepts' along axiomatic tracks while taking from experience as little as possible ideologizes in the realm of science the search for the primitive omnipotence of thought. That science is the main supplier of technologies, which must indeed grasp the facts at the level of some 'mechanics', grants it full validity in the eyes of everyman. Here psychoanalysis is the loser: not only it does not give rise to technologies furthering the primal omnipotence of thought, it dares to question it. However, as pointed out by Poincaré, the basic ontology of this archaic form of deductivism known, curiously enough, as strict inductivism expired two centuries ago. Therefore the notion of 'facts' as certainties should play no role, for or against, in our epistemic discussions. The terms 'certainty' and 'truth', coming from philosophy, cannot be applied directly to the sciences.

Before addressing the issues of the image I will approach, in-between 'fact' and 'image', those of 'context'.

Context

That relational 'facts' are inevitably interpretive – that is, that they depend on the 'context' – is shown in our encounter with the hare in ways not easy to refute: only the persecution of the dogs as the dominant relational 'context' makes it conceivable that a hare can 'interpret' our presence as neutral – which is my minimal 'interpretation' – cutting at a run across a group of people.

This example of a hare's 'interpretation' being to practical ends unrepeatable, I turn now to an observation from an intraspecies 'context' – one closer to 'intersubjectivity' as agreement or mutual understanding. Take two male puppies from one litter, give one to a friend as a gift, and over an year later invite him back to where the second then puppy and now dog is entitled to territory. Should our friend come with his dog, we might witness a curious 'intersubjective' scene, arising from a double relational 'context': the newly arrived dog is both intruder and a sibling from the same litter. Face to face, the two dogs will oscillate between attack and paralysis, amid sniffs and grunts: each 'interprets' the other in the double relational context, observing how, meta-interpretatively, the other dog, in turn, 'interprets' the encounter in terms of 'fight' or in terms of 'recognition'; the signs of 'fight', piloerection and baring of the fangs might, if 'held' or 'contained' long enough, lead to forfeiting the fight.

If everything goes well – well for my example, well for the integrity of the dogs and well for their owners' friendship – then after some moments this tense wait gives way to a frantic fight/play, the dogs pursuing one another, flailing and fake-biting with no damage for several minutes, gradually becoming more play than fight, until the conflict pertaining to the territoriality-intrusion 'context' declines into 'play' and both dogs – after what may be compared, without assimilating it fully, to a successful Freudian *Durcharbeitung* – recognize, and feel recognized, as dogs of the same litter, veering into playful euphoria and then quietness. Such exercise of 'intersubjectivity' in a 'search for agreement' approaching its Gadamerian sense entails hints of an individuation, the mutual 'recognition' as blood brother; *pace* Gadamer, it has, however, no use for 'language' in any reasonable sense of this term. The main lesson, which perhaps not many will share, is that the realm of the session as 'playground' where transference unfolds and the repetition compulsion turns innocuous (Freud, 1914a), and humour, too, have longstanding antecedents in our animal inheritance. Before exhausting my reader's patience and, *homo sapiens sapiens* that he is, he bares his fangs, let us turn to the topic of the image.

Image

As the example of the hare shows, at the bio-logic (primary) level 'image' is inseparable from both 'facts' and 'contexts' or 'theories'. Narrative, belonging to a 'logic' exclusive to man, depends on the 'image', on a knowledge by acquaintance allowing a verbal description to be built from some point of view that does not exhaust the phenomena. It leans also on the reader's 'knowledge by acquaintance': bringing something new beyond mere data, it works counter-inductively, as a 'thought experiment' on the reader's notions.

Were we to start our enquiry on an image with its smell, the description would soon break down. To what extent is the scent of the hare, its 'smell' image, the hare itself? In some measure, if we consider the dogs' excitement on picking up a trail. However, the scent would be not that of one particular hare as an 'individual' but as 'member of a class of hares', in principle homogeneous; a presence lacking a spatial location; we miss, though, a 'geometry' within which to think it plausibly. It shows however that the *pars pro toto*, the part taking the place of the whole, is not an error, as happens in that highly exclusive human field, formal logic: it is bio-logically fundamental (and we meet the *pars pro toto* in the Freudian dynamics of the logic of the unconscious, condensation, displacement, and lack of contradiction). Whether the dogs' excitement is translatable in the image terms of a 'hare' or those of a 'context of food' cannot be distinguished.

The scent of the hare is, for the dog, somehow, the hare; whether or not it is an 'image', it might be surmised to be unlike the visual image of a given hare, and by no means to be that of the final hare, the taste of the flesh. We may assume that, starting from a smell image picked up by the dogs and the hare's picking up the auditory image of the dogs, the hare interprets the dogs as 'danger', while to the dogs the hare is 'food'. Interpretive thought, on which depend the mutual strategy and 'theory of conflict', starts from 'images' (not necessarily visual), working upon *pars pro toto* with the forcefulness of 'facts': for hare and dogs, as for Edison, nothing is as practical as a good theory.

Narrative

Going by hare and dogs, or by dog and dog, our referents – 'facts', 'contexts', 'images', 'strategies', and even 'theories' – pertain to a bio-logic: to what Ockham considers we share with beasts, and what for Freud pertains to *Dingvorstellungen* – to thing-presentations, not to 'word-presentations'. We witnessed how hare and dogs, on interpreting their facts, in a way follow the hermeneutical thesis that 'there are no facts, only interpretations': but these 'interpretations' do not belong to language nor to *cogitatio*, the 'clear and distinct' concepts that for Descartes reign outside pure mechanics. It is best to avoid dichotomies between 'fact' and 'interpretation': facts are accessed within contextual 'frames' and must – in my first example, as a life-and-death issue – be appropriately interpreted and 'meta-interpreted'. This makes it clear, far from the philosophies of the 'death of truth' and the 'death of values', that the term 'interpretation' does not remain with linguistic narrative but belongs in all bio-logical contexts, where what is at stake goes quite beyond 'truth as interpretation' or the philosopher's 'aesthetic model'.

What is at stake is what the nihilistic reflection on the 'death of truth' does away with: the concreteness of pain, fear, sexuality, and death itself, as well as issues of emotional growth that are at the axis of psychoanalysis. I said above that in order to bring in the new, narrative works mainly counterinductively, acceding to 'facts' about relationship – facts from our animal lineage, which are more clearly demonstrated close to childhood and to affects than in the ivory towers of philosophical reflection.

For example, when a 9-month-old infant wakes in his cradle, the alternatives are:

1 The baby wakes, plays with his voice, his hands, or a baby rattle, and then emits a stronger sound. The mother enters, they smile to each other, he is picked up and held in her arms and waits attentively but not anxiously, smiling at times, while mother prepares the bottle.
2 The baby wakes up, restless or whimpering, calls mother straight away, and when she comes, or perhaps on being lifted up in her arms, he calms down, and the scene goes as before.
3 The baby cries even while mother picks up and consoles him, but he calms down in face of the visual evidences as she prepares his bottle.
4 The whimpering, tearful baby calms down when mother brings in the bottle or, one step further, when she places its teat in his mouth.
5 The baby does not calm down; howling, he spits the milk out instead of swallowing it.

The ongoing anxieties and needs lead the preverbal baby to interpret in quite different ways the visual and corporal contact with both the mother and the bottle, mother's functional correlate. Verbalizations or, often, singing may accompany the scene, but the interaction is not linguistic in any proper sense. Little, then, could add on the baby's dynamics the 'radical interpreter' of the second Quine (1960, p. 31) deducing linguistic meanings from interaction with objects, nor will the interpreter *à la* Habermas (1959, p. 228), striving to recover an excommunicated language. 'Good-enough' mothers refute, as concerns their grasp of the preverbal baby's needs, the fundamental hermeneutic statement that 'the being that can be understood is language'. That meaning is internal to linguistic frames is but an *a priori* guiding Habermas' critique of the notion of instinctual impulse in psychoanalysis: 'We have only derived the impulse concept privately from language deformation and behavioural pathology. At the human level we never encounter any needs that are not already interpreted linguistically and symbolically affixed to potential actions' (1959, p. 285). In terms of hermeneutic fundamentals, the baby's feelings and anxieties (and those of hares and dogs), in departing from normative linguistic frames, lack meaning and must be ontically shoved off from the 'human level'.

Which restates the theology Descartes supported and is alive and well in today's philosophy of language: In the beginning was the Verb, and the Verb was in God, and the Verb was God. As Lifton indicates (1968, p. 64), all cultures enshrine the word as immortal as against the transience of individuals – and this Dilthey and the second Wittgenstein happily turn into basic ontology. So, for Dilthey, 'the 'grammar' of ordinary language does not merely lay down relations internal to language, but regulates the communicative structure of sentences, actions, and experiences as a whole; linguistic analysis also reveals the empirical content of indirectly communicated life experiences (Habermas, 1959, p. 172): in this way, it 'discovers the empirical content of individuated conditions of life while investigating grammatical structures' (p. 173, my translation). Consubstantiating man with the Deity, the Verb transmutes in and through language the impulses and anxieties of our animal heritage. On this assumption Heidegger leads Habermas and, among others, Vattimo (1985, p. 64) in maintaining that language is 'the relationship of all relationships'. Such a notion was at the back of the daring Wittgensteinian attempt at a social therapy of common language 'through the careful distinction of the diverse linguistic games and their specific rules' (Vattimo, 1994, p. 105, my translation).

Obviously enough, what in our baby's description can be deemed intersubjective is outside the Wittgensteinian norms of 'language games' and finds a place only as anxieties and conflicts allow. At the limit, when he spits the milk instead of sucking the bottle, anxieties overcome need.

Those who, with Lorenzer, maintain that 'psychoanalysis turns around an alteration of language' (1969, p. 46) also hold (1973, p. 26) that the baby's individual structures "can only be called 'subjective' after the introduction of language"; whatever has gone before will be mere 'prelinguistic accord to interaction forms' that, though not symbolic, responds in structure to language as the regulating system of praxis (pp. 29–30). This bears strongly on clinical tasks: focusing on language as *primum movens* of subjectivity discards the concreteness of unconscious impulses, anxieties, and emotions as motors of the psyche and subordinates observation to intellectualizing reflection.

Events in the case of our hare are more akin to our analytic tasks than seems at first sight, as recounted in a final work by Wilfred Bion:

> There is an inherent fear of giving an interpretation. If a psychoanalyst is doing proper analysis, then he is engaged on an activity that is indistinguishable from that of an animal that investigates what he is afraid of: it smells danger. An analyst is not doing his job if he investigates something because it is pleasurable or profitable. Patients do not come to him because they anticipate some agreeable imminent event; they come because they are ill at ease. The analyst must share the danger, and has, therefore, to share the 'smell' of the danger. If the hair at the back of your neck becomes erect your primitive, archaic senses indicate the presence of a danger. It is your job to be curious about that danger – not cowardly, not irresponsible. . . . Anyone who is not afraid when he is engaged on psycho-analysis is either not doing his job, or is unfitted for it.
>
> (1979, p. 83)

What I needed to be able to 'smell' was the danger that was shared by both – the danger of the tiger and the deer which approached close. . . . I could diagrammatize it thus:

> Something is going to be eaten up
> Tiger   Something is going to run away   Deer
> and leave nothing to eat
> That describes a shared fear.
>
> (1979, p. 85)

'Smelling' danger as an analytic task specifies the first phase of that peculiar narrative, psychoanalytic interpretation. As Bion puts it in *Attention and Interpretation* (1970), in the phase of patience the analyst approaches the unknown in the analysand and in himself, a state he should retain without 'irritable reaching after fact and reason' (p. 124) until a pattern emerges, a form leading to a state of security, with associated safety and diminished anxiety. Traversing both phases, he works his way to an interpretation implying no 'certainty' or 'truth' in the philosopher's sense, just what can be tentatively stated then and there.

Bion (1977, p. 18) calls patience the mental state rescuing naive observation, proposing his conditions for observation – or, as he calls it at other times, for intuition – to 'smell' shared fear: no memory, no desire, no understanding, so that the 'pattern' or 'form' of the shared fear can evolve. In any case, here – and contrary to my first example – analyst and analysand will each, at different times and in multiple immaterial ways, be dog and hare, making observation at once more difficult and more fruitful.

Working with a different ontology, the narrative might wish to select 'mechanical' 'elements' as its fundamental intellectual constructs – that is, elements conforming to an Euclidian–Galilean ontology – but it is unclear how the observations backing the narrative would come out. What would be the 'laws of nature' by which hare, dogs, baby, or mother abide, and what are the 'baselines' to such laws? Similarly for an attempt to restrict my observations to hermeneutic–linguistic outlooks with language as their basic ontology: even while stretching the term, as did the second Wittgenstein with his 'language games' and, after him, Quine and Davidson, it would require, in the manner of Aesop, La Fontaine, or Kipling, an anthropomorphic fable with hare, dogs, and preverbal baby as speaking subjects. The limits to linguistic ontologies that equate meaning and language stand out in *Word and Object* (1960), where Quine articulates two approaches, mechanical and linguistic, namely neurophysiological 'stimuli' and the socially endorsed linguistic elements investigated by the 'radical interpreter': he thus construes an epistemic 'black hole', flanked by Galilean science – here, neurophysiology – on the one side and ruled linguistic codes on the other. In turn, Habermas' methodological critique of psychoanalysis in *Knowledge and Human Interest* (1959) dichotomizes 'empirical sciences in a rigorous sense' (p. 247), so-called strict inductivism, and hermeneutics as inhering in language: small wonder that terms like sexuality or aggression find no place, despite his thesis that 'the achievements of the transcendental subject rest on the natural history of the human species' (p. 312). The same goes for Ricoeur in *Freud and Philosophy* (1970), while Gadamer in *Truth and Method* (1960) seeks in the truth of the aesthetic experience what language is unable to provide. Lorenzer (1973), in turn, recognizing that '*psychoanalysis overflows toward interaction forms*' (p. 10; the emphasis is Lorenzer's) expands hermeneutics from language towards a theatrical model. But this is not enough to raise the hermeneutic–linguistic view to clinical needs. As Etchegoyen argued (1986), psychoanalytical experience shows often, if not usually, a use of the language in –K, at the service of unknowing, and the same is valid for Klein's and Betty Joseph's (1985) idea of the transference as a 'total situation', where enacted 'use' in the session provides the general frame for verbal meanings. Whenever language takes over as fundamental ontology, the body, emotions, and primitive anxieties are minimized, and where method is concerned, the role of observation, on which from Aristotle on empirical content depends, is ignored. There are crucial differences in the notion of symbolization as employed in the hermeneutic–linguistic context, where a symbolic universe, grounded upon the normativity of the speaking community, exists by itself, outside conflict and psychic growth, and in the psychoanalytical context, where we properly speak of symbols only as they capture a contact with emotional meanings (Meltzer, 1993, p. 325).

Demise of the corporeal–emotional universe of the bio-logic of relationship marks linguistic currents both philosophical and psychoanalytic. What is more, most of the current scientific establishment excludes that emotional facts be explanatory, dealing with these issues in genetic or molecular Galilean variants: psychiatry replaces a psychopathology grounded in emotional dynamics by statistical listings of symptoms, tailored for commercial pharmacological empires: the DSM-IV and its likely successors. Worse still, a mechanical neojargon governs daily life, reflecting the deaffectivization of culture, the mechanization of the body, and the abolition in –K of emotional contact. Self-description of psychic facts turns mechanical or energetic: anxiety or overadaptation to it becomes 'stress', to get excited or just active is 'to put the batteries on', inability to pay attention and keep emotional contact is 'to unplug', to rest is 'to load the batteries'.

Within psychoanalysis proper, when 'biological' is taken as synonym for 'physiological' – in the Cartesian sense of mechanical and thus not psychic – such mechanistic language excises the multiple-levelled complexities of affect. The universe of an emotive-relational bio-logic is thereby degraded. This is not the case in the Darwinian conceptual frame, where Bion sets out the statement heading this chapter, and I like to think he would agree to his being paraphrased: 'But the psychologic rests on a bio-logic'. In that spirit, my narrative on interpretation sketches what I assume belongs in the Freudian area of *Dingvorstellungen* and unconscious thought: navigating between the Scylla of Galilean mechanics and the Charybdis of hermeneutic cogitation, it purports to exemplify a relational, emotional thinking to which physicalisms and linguisticisms do no justice.

The above describes an emotive thought, which, under the guidance of intuition and countertransference scrutiny, is accessed by psychoanalytical observation leading to interpretive work, to *Deutungsarbeit*: which, as Freud noted (1919, p. 160 ff) and we would do well to recall today, bears on the conjectural description of evolving unconscious processes, to the psychoanalysis making the unconscious conscious, while keeping away from attempts to determine the psycho-synthesis, the emergence of new syntheses of meanings.

Granted that the analyst's reverie is the initial step for interpreting, that he maintains an essential emotional 'holding', and that in an evolving psychoanalytical process insights will recontextualize meanings, giving place, often explosively, to new ones – however, that in the emotional evolutions of the analytic process new structures and mental spaces do emerge does not allow the analyst the novelist's licence to remodel emergent meanings, adding his own to the analysand's. As García Márquez points out, the reality of the novel maintains 'lies pure but likely' (1996, p. 6) such as the errant horseman facing lions in the plains of La Mancha or Gargantua urinating on cathedrals. Analytic credibility rests on keeping to the enquiry on a psychic reality that, as Moses before the Promised Land, we glimpse while building interpretations, discerning the contradictoriness of the multiple levels of psychic reality, from the enacted to the verbal.

It is valid that the analyst cannot be a 'spokesman for reality'. But he is even less entitled to an interpretive creationism seeking to govern the analysand's psycho-synthesis in the manner of a privileged poiesis, as Viderman (1970) proposed and as is maintained today by a good part of the hermeneutic–linguistic stances on 'intersubjectivity'. The genesis of new meanings belongs inalienably to the analysand.

Whether or not one agrees with the 'inaugural force' Heidegger lends to the poetic word, in the current context of secularization of culture, poetic mythology becomes a substitute for religion, inheriting, as Vattimo admits (1994, p. 108), 'the task and the contents of religion.' That the analyst provides – as does the philosopher, the ideologue, or the poet – his own meanings to the analysand is to Freud (1919, p. 165) 'after all only to use violence, even though it is overlaid by the most honourable motives'. He thus diverges fully from hermeneutic stances that, with the idea that language is 'the relationship of all relationships', ignore the distinction between psychoanalysis and a psycho-synthesis of meanings, assuming, on the contrary, that the analyst's rhetoric configures the truth of the analysand. It is a permanent temptation for the psychoanalyst: to exert the encantatory power of rhetorical fascination which, the Peruvian essayist and novelist Mario Vargas Llosa (1996), in a note entitled 'The song of the sirens', cautions against: the more persuasive a style, the more it engenders an engaging and seductive flow of images and concepts flowing in harmony, the more will the reader have the illusion of adhering to strict reality.

Good fiction, he warns, bribes the reader – and the analysand – suspending his critical spirit with the pull of verbal magic. The force of poiesis engenders or exacerbates confusion and deceit: joining Charcot and Freud (*'J'appelle un chat un chat'*), the analyst should stay away from demiurgic enchantments, enticing as they are, helping the analysand attain representability, *per via di levare*, for the multifarious and contradictory cats, dogs, hares, and babies of his internal world, so that he comes to recognize and acknowledge them as his own and to call each by its name.

6

Toward the epistemology of clinical psychoanalysis

> . . . it keeps close to the facts in its field of study, seeks to solve the immediate problems of observation, gropes its way forward by the help of experience, is always incomplete and always ready to correct or modify its theories.
>
> (Freud, 1923b, p. 253)

The empirical status of the clinical psychoanalytic method is under mounting challenges from two opposing stances which, I hold, disregard essential qualities of 'mind'. On one side the method's empirical cogency is dismissed by such 'hard science' stalwarts as Ernest Nagel (1959), Karl Popper (1963, 1983) and Adolf Grünbaum (1984, 1993), who hold that in spite of Freud's methodological sophistication its findings do not attain evidential, probative status. Such appraisals ascribe to all science the method of physical science; on an implicit requirement of a *reduction* to 'specific' variables fit for rigorous prediction, they reject as not probative explanations made in terms of the intrinsically complex variables of the clinical process. On the other side, those who hold that psychoanalysis is not a *Naturwissenschaft*, an empirical science of nature, but a *Geisteswissenschaft*, a hermeneutic 'human' or 'cultural' discipline close in its method to history and law, insist it has not empirical but *interpretive* value.

Both challenges miss the point. Mind is not an apt subject for the kind of reduction demanded by a Galilean science built on the regularities displayed by inanimate nature; as shown by ethology, here the organism's own inferential processes are central to the events studied. In its turn the *Geisteswissenschaften* concept of a purely human science relinquishes mind's animal nature, a position that leaves aside the fact, succinctly stated by Paracelsus, that 'only the acme of man is man'. This relinquishment is not without serious effects on the notion of psychoanalytic clinical method held by hermeneuticists.

Fittingly, replies to Grünbaum from hermeneutic quarters share his criteria for what counts as science. Defining science in Galilean terms and ascribing empirical certainty to it, hermeneuticists claim as their own the interpretive approach that emerged in clinical and observational sciences long before the current flourishing of hermeneutics in the academy: given that interpretation of 'other minds' (and of one's own) is no place for certainties, they come to deem it nonempirical and purely hermeneutic. André Green (1984) touches on a characteristic of hermeneutic approaches when he notes Lacan's backing away from Freud's remark that in the beginning there was action, to a formula hewing more closely to Saint John: 'In the beginning there was language' (p. 231). This 'linguistic turn' redresses what Freud called the second blow on the part of science to man's narcissism, the Darwinian continuities between man and animal at the level of mind. As argued in chapter 2, the hermeneutic model of the 'text' (Gadamer, 1960) sacrifices unconscious psychic reality and the pragmatics of its enactment in the here and now in favor of reconstructing the analysand's language. What is more, hermeneuticists lash out at precisely those aspects of our method that allow unconscious enactments to attain representability and ostension. Thus Bouchard (1995) would gladly do away with Freud's idea that our clinical method works *per via di levare*, which he deems a reversion to a 'naive' realism.

Among responses that reject the 'retreat to hermeneutics' (Blight, 1981) and endorse Freud's idea of psychoanalysis as empirical, those of Spruiell (1987), Edelson (1983, 1984, 1988), Wurmser (1989), and Wallace (1989) may be singled out. To Spruiell the resemblance of the analyst's work to that of the historian or sociologist is only superficial: the analyst is interested in the past mainly as it is repeated in the present, as it *is* the present, and in the internal, *psychic* reality of the individual; he appropriately holds that there is no consensus on the definition of science, that not even the so-called 'exact sciences' can meet Grünbaum's criteria, and that it is high time for the great scientific myth of the twentieth century, that physics is the model of all science, to be finally put to rest. Edelson tries to meet the challenge by refining the methodology of the single-case study; however, I must join Spruiell's opinion that Edelson accepts too readily Grünbaum's criteria of scientificity and evidence. Wurmser points to the 'either/or' quality and the notion of linear causality in Grünbaum's conception of psychoanalysis and posits, instead, a *conflict causality,* complex, many-layered, and discontinuous. Wallace, who regards Grünbaum's work as an important methodological contribution, singles out two bases for its major fallacies: unfamiliarity with the actual method of psychoanalysis and a positivist view of science with physics as its paradigm, which leads him to an atomistic testing of psychoanalytic hypotheses, whereby one or at best a few variables are teased out, to be tested longitudinally, statistically, or epidemiologically.

This cardinal point, I must add, was raised previously by Waelder (1962) in a response to Ernest Nagel (1959) at the 1958 New York University Symposium on Philosophy and Psychoanalysis. Waelder stressed that the validation of causal claims by prospective longitudinal studies employing experimental controls assumes discrete, simple variables not subject to qualitative changes during the lapse in which observations are collected, an assumption valid only in 'exact' sciences, in those parts of biology that can be reduced to the physicochemical frame, or in the experimental manipulation of single extraneous variables. Nagel's presumption of universal validity for this epistemic framework led a famed empiricist, Sidney Hook, to the remark that there are no hard-and-fast criteria of scientificity, and to the caveat that anyone denying scientific status to psychoanalysis on the ground that it is not like physics would then have to rule out the whole of biology as a science, which would be absurd (1959, p. 214).

Wurmser (1989) notes that nowhere does Grünbaum spell out clearly the philosophical basis of his critique. But, as his physicalism is the foundation for an indictment of clinical psychoanalysis that pivots on a demand for empirical 'warrants', the assumptions of that physicalism must be assessed in detail. I will argue that Grünbaum rejects the evidential value of psychoanalysis because the complex observational variables of its clinical method are neither homogeneous nor discrete and cannot be incorporated into formal deductive systems or subjected to John Stuart Mill's rules of experimental manipulation. They are therefore judged to lack predictive power. Though their general structure may be subject to repetition, this repetition is not linear; hence, being insufficiently 'specific', they are deemed neither 'cogent' nor 'probative'.

Given that Grünbaum's critique attacks a misconstrued version of the psychoanalytic method (Wallerstein, 1986; Wurmser, 1989) and willfully puts forward Mill's canons as valid for all natural sciences, what is to be gained by leaping into the fray? In an earlier chapter I have argued that clinical psychoanalysis operates with an inductive method in the domain of mind regarding both analyst and analysand, whose insights involve an inductive, ostensive refutation of a hitherto unconscious *psychic* reality; I shall examine Grünbaum's closely argued stance in order to situate by way of contrast the epistemological status of clinical psychoanalysis.

Empirical and Galilean science: varieties of induction

The terms *natural science* and *empirical science*, embracing fields as dissimilar as physics and ethology (or psychoanalysis), can lead the unwary to a belief that rules of inference work similarly in such unlike fields. The term *induction* has quite varied meanings: (a) As an overall term, induction is any inference from the known to the unknown; it encompasses the obscure and unformalized processes of the discovery of new conjectures or findings that Pascal brought under the *esprit de finesse* and Peirce called *abduction*, the processes of inductive generalization and counterinduction, and those of informal verification of hypotheses. (b) In the sense of inductive generalization, it refers within hypothetico–deductivist frames to the inference from particular cases to general laws. (c) As inductive testing, it covers the process by which hypotheses are validated. Similarly, the term causal, Russell has noted (1950, p. 233), has a diversity of meanings. A brief excursion into the history of science is pertinent at this point.

As recounted in the Introduction, in ancient Greece two main scientific currents are discernible: the Pythagoreans founded mathematics, geometry, cosmology and mechanics on the idea of *number* as the ontological basis of reality, while Aristotelian science rested on an *informal logic,* which relied on systematic, unaided observations and correlations of complex natural, mainly biological, phenomena. From Aristotle on, says von Wright (1957), induction depended upon observation, and the major premise of a syllogism was to be grounded on a wide induction. In the seventeenth century, with the rise of a new mathematics, a new instrument (the telescope), and the Galilean method, as well as the momentous discovery of Newtonian celestial mechanics, phenomena as diverse as the behavior of falling bodies, the movements of the planets and the moon, and the movement of tides came to be subsumed under a single explanatory concept, that of gravity, and a simple mathematical formula. This led to a new, restrictive concept of induction in what would later be called the positive sciences; the new cosmology, says Pierre Duhem (1906), became paradigmatic for scientific method, and only 'exact' sciences attaining *theoretical* concepts – that is, those susceptible to reduction to variables fit for measurement, and then allowing rigorous deduction and prediction – came to fully merit the name of science.

Both a restrictive, hypothetico–deductivist, and a broad, ampliative view of induction can be found in the work of William Whewell (1858), mathematician, geologist, and historian of science, an eminent contemporary of Mill and consultant to Faraday and Darwin. In the restrictive (Galilean) view he states that only the ability to decompose complex facts, reducing them to elementary facts, which enables us to justify by deduction and calculation what induction has guessed, truly marks scientific induction. Similarly, advancing what would a century and a half later be the basis of Grünbaum's dismissal of the evidential value of clinical (observational) psychoanalysis, Mill (1852) stated that 'Observation . . . without experiment . . . can ascertain uniformities, but cannot prove causation' (p. 221); using this distinction, he posited a gulf between 'Sciences of Experimentation' and 'Sciences of mere Observation'. While, on the model of Newtonian cosmology, Mill holds to a conception of 'empirical laws' and of causality as invariable, unconditional, and based on the regularities of very simple elements (a conception in which knowledge of the effect of each separate cause allows deductive, a priori prediction of conjoint effects), he honestly concedes that this 'Composition of [simple] Causes' (p. 211) can be put into practice only in the realm of mechanics. In other fields, such as the study of organized living bodies, he concedes, 'we have not, properly speaking, as yet ascertained a single cause, a single unconditional uniformity' (p. 222). Physics thus became the epistemological model for a standard hypothetico–deductive stance that assumed well-behaved, projectible variables (Blackburn, 1994) on which rigorous deduction and prediction could be based: Galilean science accepts only Humean causes logically unrelated to one another, just as space and mass were thought of as independent. Already at the turn of the last century Henri Poincaré (1902) warned, however, that while in mathematical physics the complex phenomena observed are due to the superposition of similar elementary phenomena bound by the same simple law, in the natural sciences homogeneity of variables, relative independence of distant parts, and simplicity of elementary facts are not to be found (pp. 171–172).

Primacy of observation as the basic level of all scientific systems is perhaps best expressed by Bertrand Russell (1950): 'When we are considering empirical knowledge, the earliest propositions in the hierarchy, *which give the grounds for all the others,* are not deduced from other propositions, and yet are not mere arbitrary assumptions. They have grounds, though their grounds are not propositions, but observed occurrences' (p. 20; emphasis added).

Recourse to ethology – the observational science of animal behavior in natural contexts, as contrasted to its experimental manipulation – highlights the pros and cons of the scientificity appropriate to psychoanalysis as against the standard scientificity insisted on by physical science ideologues. Though explicit in the Cartesian idea that the stuff of life is fully resolvable in terms of mechanics, and in Carnap's thesis (1932–33) that laws of psychology are special cases of physical laws, the demand that all science be patterned after physics is usually disavowed. Grünbaum (1984, p. 85) is no exception, but his criteria of cause, evidence, warrant, well-attested baselines, and natural history (of neuroses) introduce unacknowledged physicalistic requirements.

Causality of mind in mechanical terms

Let us examine the attempt to define causality in the domain of mind in terms of mechanics. Asking whether *intra*subject validations authorize using a given analysand to test *intra*clinically 'the causal assertions made by the long-term etiologic hypotheses of psychoanalytic theory', Grünbaum (1993, p. 230) seeks situations in physics where a *probative equivalent* of controlled experiments is furnished by other means. The astronomer's causal claims, like the time-honored example of the billiard ball gaining momentum on being hit by another ball, depend on *attested background knowledge*. Newton's well-attested law of conservation of linear momentum gives background knowledge on the natural history of objects at rest and unexposed to external forces: such objects will remain at rest. This allows us, says Grünbaum, to identify the moving second billiard ball as furnishing the *cause* of the change in the momentum of the first. On that simplest of events in that simplest field of physics, mechanics, he issues his rule for evidence in the domain of mind to be deemed empirical or cogent: intraclinical validation in psychoanalysis, he argues, cannot exhibit a well-attested baseline and so has no basis for a cogent evaluation of therapeutic response. Here Grünbaum ignores what Poincaré was aware of in 1902: the differences in the nature of the objects of study, and thus in method, of mathematical physics and empirical natural science; his version of causality is valid for closed systems like those of mechanics, not the open, adaptive ones of living organisms (von Wright, 1971). Similarly, Bateson (1973) warns that billiard balls do not 'behave' and that living beings do not fit under the epistemic rule of the law of conservation of linear momentum: 'If I kick a stone, the movement of the stone is energized by the act, but if I kick a dog, the behavior of the dog may indeed be partly conservative – he may travel along a Newtonian trajectory if kicked hard enough, but this is mere physics. What is important is that he may exhibit responses which are energized not by the kick but by his metabolism: he may turn and bite' (p. 200). The dog may also dodge the kick, flee, throw himself on the ground whimpering, or do myriad other things, depending on his character and history (as difficult to specify as these are) and on his relationship to the kicker – who may be, for example, owner or intruder. And it is crucial to note that, as is not the case with billiard balls, the dog's response to a second kick will differ from the first: his inferences on the basis of the first kick will modify his response to the second, a point that should put to rest attempts at identifying in the realm of mind an equivalent of well-behaved variables and baselines displaying a Galilean–Newtonian regularity, simplicity, and homogeneity.

Whereas Aristotelian science, built mainly on comparative biology, strove to put together a complex set of causal categories – material, formal, efficient, and final – in Galilean physics only the efficient cause, that which actually sets off the change, just as pulling the trigger sets off the rifle, is deemed causal (Russell, 1959a,

p. 88ff). The material cause and the formal cause (i.e. the configuration) become necessary conditions for the causal situation, and the final cause is abolished. But, he notes (1948, pp. 214–216), physical laws need only account for matter and motion, and they assume the homogeneity of matter and the independence of efficient causes. It is, however, illustrative of the Cartesian snares even the best minds are apt to fall into that Russell (1959a, p. 89), writing that it was from Aristotle's biological interests that the notion of final cause arose, holds in the same stroke of the pen that teleology is ultimately anthropomorphic or theological, since only human beings pursue ends. The snare is that he (and most everyone) throws out the baby – the capacity for purposeful inferences as a central quality of animal mind (instanced by prey–predator interaction) – along with the bathwater, the metaphysical final causes.

To turn now to my test case, drawn from ethology, it is plain that animal inferential systems support diversity of response. The ubiquitous case of prey–predator interaction makes clear how evolutionary pressures place a premium on variety and anticipation of response: the fox not clever enough to outmaneuver the hare goes hungry; the hare that does not outguess the fox is out of the game. In a broad and certainly not Galilean sense, fox and hare are here 'causal' to one another. But, given that their anticipatory, highly context-sensitive inferential responses will lack a baseline such as Newton's first law provides for billiard balls, statements on the fox's, the hare's, the aforementioned dog's, or the analysand's responses will not be deemed cogent according to Galilean criteria. However, we may safely hold that the evaluation of responses in psychoanalytic therapy, while more complex, is closer to the assessment of these organisms' inferential responses than to explaining the movement of billiard balls. Thus, recourse to physical 'probative equivalents' is shown to be vacuous.

I have scant hope, however, that this argument will impress those holding the Galilean view, given that Grünbaum (1993, p. 14) maintains that the context-dependence of magnetic particles amounts to a historicity similar to that of psychic processes, and that it is a banal fact that Freud's narratives are psychological while his examples of context-dependence are avowedly physical. The inferences, then, that organisms are capable of drawing are irrelevant to Galilean science.

Let us take a closer look at the consequences. Point-by-point induction being requisite, manipulation of discrete extraneous stimuli takes the role of the not-to-be-found specific intrinsic variables. Citing the case of a head-banging autistic boy of 7 who underwent a punishment procedure involving a series of one-second electric shocks that led shortly to a dramatic diminution of the unwanted behavior, Grünbaum (1993) notes approvingly that this change can be attributed to the shocks, the use of control groups being unnecessary since the operation of other causal agencies seems to him very unlikely. In his view 'the *paradigmatic* example of an *intra*subject clinical validation of the causal efficacy of a given intervention is furnished by the following *variant* of using the patient as his own 'historical' control: (a) The natural history of the disorder is presumably otherwise well known; *or* (b) the therapist intervenes only in on–off fashion, and this intermittent intervention is found to yield alternating remissions and relapses with dramatic rapidity' (p. 231). The lapse is glaring enough: deeming them irrelevant, he leaves out the intrinsic dynamics of the autistic boy's affective–inferential ways. Grünbaum's method and his idea of causality leave room only for simple, quasi-mechanical entities extraneous to each other: head-banging rate as an enumerable target symptom and electric shocks as discrete stimuli able to be manipulated on–off at will. Intelligibility of intrinsic processes is deemed merely heuristic, and he hence accepts clinical psychoanalysis as heuristic as well, while dismissing the evidential value and causal cogency of the intrinsic processes it studies.

Grünbaum, in extolling the experimental method, ignores its pitfalls. These are, however, blatant when we compare experimental animal psychology with ethologic observation of animal behavior in its natural social milieu. Experiment, through its isolation of extraneous variables, destroys the context in which behavior occurs. A distorted, artificial, 'experimentalist' reality is thereby constructed and 'validated.' [See, for example, Bateson's (1979, p. 127ff) criticism of Pavlovian psychology as an experimentally constructed artifact that misconceives as 'conditioned reflexes' the inferences the dog makes within and through his relationship to the experimenter, a criticism with which Griffin (1992, p. 7) agrees; see also Goodall's response (1986) to De Waal (1983) on the conditions for ethological observation.] When looked at from this angle, Freud's reliance on free association and analytic neutrality are ways to keep the analyst–observer from distorting the contexts of the field of observation.

Having built his epistemic straitjacket, Grünbaum (1993) cries out: 'The natural history of a person *not* subjected to the experiences deemed pathogenic by Freudian theory is *notoriously* unknown!' (p. 231). But unlike the mechanical causality displayed by billiard balls, a person's 'natural history' has no formal baselines and cannot be rigorously predicted; indeed, the very idea of a natural history of neuroses ignores their dependence on both internal and external contexts and restricts the concept of causality to what complies with projectible linearities. Hook was astute enough to grasp that on such premises biology – and, in fact, every observational science – is to be found guilty of ad hoc operation, the exception being, of course, classical cosmology, which though purely observational allows for rigorous prediction through the homogeneity of its variables and their clock-like regularity.

A note on a Darwinian epistemology

After so much physicalistic reductionism passing for epistemology, it is refreshing indeed to turn next to an epistemic consideration on psychoanalysis based not on cosmology and physics but on the study of Darwinian evolution of mammalian communication: Bateson (1973, 1979) argues that most of the premises of mammalian interaction are inaccessible to conscious inspection and that an epistemological turnabout takes as its start Freud's introduction of the unconscious. At that time,

> thinkers regarded conscious reason as normal and self-explanatory while the unconscious was regarded as mysterious, needing proof and needing explanation. Repression was the explanation, and the unconscious was filled with thoughts which could have been conscious but which repression and dream work had distorted. Today we think of consciousness as the mysterious, and of the computational methods of the unconscious, e.g., primary process, as continually active, necessary and all-embracing.
>
> (1973, p. 108)

Conscious reason and logic being indeed to Grünbaum normal and self-explanatory, he flatly rejects unconscious psychic functionings as 'illogical'. In a Darwinian epistemology, however, logic and consciousness are merely final evolutionary levels of mind superimposed on (and structurally different from) a phylogenetically antecedent affective–relational mental life relying primarily on the computational methods of the unconscious. When applied to the domain of mind, physicalistic epistemologies are, in their disregard of the manifold inferential processes occurring during biologic evolution, starkly pre-Darwinian and also precybernetic.

For an epistemology making use of both Darwinian evolution and information theory, 'mind' turns out to involve not linear causalities but circular chains of determinism that are far more complex. The transformational rules of mind, though more stable than its contents, are themselves subject to transformations, and these processes of transformation involve a hierarchy of logical types inherent in the phenomena (Bateson, 1979, p. 98). While a rock resists change (and ideal billiard balls linearly transmit it), living beings escape change by correcting it, by changing to meet the challenge, or by incorporating continual change into their beings (p. 110) – processes readily recognizable as phylogenetically (and ontogenetically) previous to the emergence of consciousness or logic.

Processes of change are active throughout the animal kingdom, from bacteria on up (e.g. their rapid development of resistance to antibiotics). Affects, an example that interests us directly, can be thought to exist from reptilians on up (Levin, 1991). Certainly affects play a major role in the dynamics of mammals, where a whole universe of instinctual–affective intraspecies relationships is at the service of reproduction and of that harshest issue of survival, care of the brood. From the standpoint of evolutionary endurance, affects are causes. The emotive pragmatic universe of instinctual–affective responses is the background, as Bateson details, to the extremely complex analogic–iconic codes of mammalian communication, which are previous to, and independent of, digitally coded languages such as our own.

Instinctual relations are, as Russell (1948, p. 526) recognizes, both inferential and requisite to biological survival, which renders unremittingly banal any Humean causal requirement that variables be independent. This complex universe, in which not only is the seed causal for the tree, but group and maternal affects and care are causal for the brood, is being charted by the labors of ethologists, foremost among them Goodall (1986). This work supports the Freudian idea that 'the psychoanalytic study of phantasy patterns is the study of instinct in man (Money-Kyrle, 1978b, p. 278).[1]

Grünbaum's wider critique

Grünbaum's critique of clinical psychoanalysis (1984) rests on the futile hunt for 'specific' causalities, the kind of simple variables that suit his method. This is accompanied by the outspokenly deductivistic demand for 'justificatory criteria in advance for weaving *particular* associations together' (p. 235) and, presumably to avoid the charge of ad hoc, nonscientific functioning, for specificity, discreteness, and linearity regarding 'types' of associations. Such is the background of his 'epistemic' dismissal of Freud's 'causal inferences': 'the inability of the psychoanalytic method of clinical investigation by free association to *warrant causal inferences* leaves the major pillars of the clinical theory of repression ill supported' (1993, p. 3; emphasis added).

Let us say first that to speak here of a warrant of causal inference is simply rhetorical, the brandishing of a specious demand for infallibility (Laor, 1985); empirical knowledge is, of its nature, uncertain, inexact, and partial, unlike the posits of logic and mathematics (Russell, 1948). Second, as with Mill, for Grünbaum 'causes' are Humean causes, logically independent of one another, while the psychic 'causes' dealt with by psychoanalysis are part and parcel of the actors' system of inferences and thus *cannot* be rigorously independent. (While on his Galilean idea of causality Mill argues that the seed is not to be considered a cause of the tree, Darwin was acutely aware that the tree was causally dependent on both the seed and the conditions for its growth, and that the hare and the fox are causally dependent on each other.) Third, for Grünbaum psychic normality is self-explanatory (perhaps, as for Descartes and Malebranche, in the manner of a reliable clock), not the outcome of complex, conflictive, and largely unconscious developmental processes. The problem of neurosogenesis, as he calls it, is therefore for him that of proving a 'causal' archeological anomaly, an 'original specific real-event pathogen'. Thus, he misconstrues the causal issue as that of the linear relation of real events in infancy to the present neurosis, a point that Wallace (1989) explores in depth.

In his hunt for specificity, Grünbaum construes his model of the causality of neuroses on that of Koch's microbiology co-opted from medicine, a field where the ages-long work of Darwinian evolution indeed supplies specific pathogens.[2] Grünbaum notes that early on, Freud (1896, p. 209) draws an analogy between neurosis and tuberculosis; but Kochian pathogens are of a different sort than psychic ones: they are extraneous species of organisms, whereas psychic pathogens are relational events with affectively relevant *intra*specific others impinging on one's psychic reality; they are cumulative and repetitious intrasubjectively and often also in terms of the dynamics of the immediate milieu and lack the specificity of natural history that germ–host interaction to some point displays and that Grünbaum requires for causal events to be deemed cogent. The question of the relation of 'real' events to pathology, while significant, is not central for psychoanalysis, whereas that of its inductive functioning vis-à-vis psychic reality is crucial; the latter, however, is beyond Grünbaum's observational and conceptual grasp. Here Mill's apt caveat (1852) fits: 'Not only what man can know, but what he can conceive, depends upon what he has experienced' (p. 338).

Ignorance of the epistemic differences of data in the exact and the observational sciences, and an inability to conceive the complexities of causality at the level of mind sketched in Bateson's work, not to speak of those of psychic reality, authorize Grünbaum (1984) to tongue-lash psychoanalysis for a putatively major epistemic fault: its 'flouting the elementary safeguards of causal inference familiar since the days of Francis Bacon, not to speak of J. S. Mill' (p. 254). Such safeguards are elementary only in the sense of being reductive to assumedly simple 'elements': as we saw, Mill honestly grants he has been unable to put to use such elementary safeguards in the realm of life. Indeed, an outdated *Weltanschauung* underlies Grünbaum's idea of causal inference; as von Wright (1957) puts it, 'the view . . . that it is possible to reduce the phenomena of the Universe to combinations of a limited number of simple elements is the central point of Bacon's whole system' (p. 203). The same is also true of Mill (1852), whose idea of cause is tied to the metaphysical belief that 'the prodigiously complex Facts of Life may all be deducible from comparatively simple laws', which he deems likely to hold also for 'the phenomena of mind' (p. 213). In embracing this idea of 'specificity', Grünbaum loses sight of the limits to linear predictionism and the applicability of experiment; these are not lost on von Wright, however, who warns (1957, p. 201) that Mill's method of Agreement and Difference, used in experimental setups and the *only* method Grünbaum accepts as 'probatory', while able to deal with Plurality of Causes is unable to deal with Complexity of Causes. So the criticism lodged by Demos (1959) against Ernest Nagel at the NYU symposium mentioned earlier applies here as well: that, by assuming 'that there is a universal *essence* of science applying equally and in the same manner to all enquiries which claim the name of science' (p. 331), Nagel was putting psychoanalysis to the test of a nonexistent Platonic science.

Grünbaum's core critique: the Tally Argument

In his core critique of psychoanalytic clinical method, Grünbaum (1984, p. 138) constructs his famous Tally Argument on Freud's contention (1916–17) that the analysand's 'conflicts will only be successfully solved and his resistances overcome if the anticipatory ideas [i.e. the interpretations] tally with what is real in him. Whatever in the doctor's conjectures is inaccurate drops out in the course of the analysis; it has to be withdrawn and replaced by something more correct' (Freud, 1916–17, p. 452).

Breuer and Freud's 1895 finding – that the undoing of repressions involves cathartic episodes in which the surfacing of pent-up affects and details of memories of specific real events results in a seemingly durable demise of specific, separate symptoms – is taken by Grünbaum as tenable, point-by-point inductive grounds on which we can '*certify* an original pathogen', the repressed affect linked to a specific real event that can be deemed to be causing a specific symptom. But, Grünbaum adds (1993, p. 27), the whole argument collapsed when Freud recognized that the pattern of symptom relapses and remissions was highly correlated with the analysand's personal relation to the analyst; this, in Freud's words, 'proved that the personal emotional relation between doctor and patient was after all stronger than the whole cathartic process' (1925, p. 27). Failure of point-by-point induction from real events to specific, separate symptoms leaves, says Grünbaum, the repression etiology bereft of support; this, and the weight of the emotional relation to the analyst, leads him to the view that the link to the analyst institutes an 'epistemic contamination' by suggestion or placebo effect, which will make a shambles of any attempt at clinical validation.

There are then two versions of the Tally Argument, Freud's and Grünbaum's. For Freud, interpretations must tally with the analysand's unconscious psychic reality, while for Grünbaum (1993) they must disentangle the neurosogenesis, the excavated real-event causes of neurosis, on the idea that to document insight requires an authentication of actual 'neurosogenic' events (p. 233). It would, he holds, beg the etiological question to retort, as analysts have, that the unconscious operates dynamically in 'allusive, *illogical* ways' (p. 126); here, against the massive weight of ethologic evidence, Grünbaum attempts the feat of postulating logic as a primary mental functioning. Off-handedly dismissing the illogical ways of the unconscious (and thus of psychic reality and transference), misunderstanding insight as 'engendered as a result of using Freud's *etiologies* in the analysis of their transference and resistance' (1993, p. 69, emphasis added), and convinced of 'the *poverty* of the introspective access to the *causal dynamics* of our mental processes' (1993, p. 204) he comes out frontally against what he considers the 'bold assumption of the causal indispensability of psychoanalytic insight' (1984, p. 139). This, and the idea of the supremacy of the analyst's interventions in the clinical field, will lead Grünbaum to assume that whatever knowledge emerges in the session will have in common 'a *shared* contaminant, the analyst's influence' rendering it 'empirically flawed' (1984, p. 248). In the belief, then, that 'the patient's childlike doctrinal compliance with his therapist is *itself* formally part and parcel of the targets of the resolution of the "transference neurosis" ', he issues his verdict: 'I cannot emphasize strongly enough that such invocations of the analysis of the transference to rebut the charge of self-validation is logically a vicious circular bootstrap operation' (1984, p. 144).

It should be noted, however, that this indictment rests not on formal logical defects in Freud's argument but on a difference of opinion as to what counts as empirical: for analysts transference is an observational fact; for Grünbaum it is not. This discrepancy may be accounted for by a difference in their observational fields: the clinical session for analysts, everyday life for Grünbaum. And we can note here how in the case of the observational sciences the privilege of the philosopher of science, his remaining alien to the observational field, may easily backfire into an argument from ignorance, into what Mill chastises as the foremost fallacy, that of nonobservation. The ubiquity of emotive pragmatics in the psychoanalytic session, misconstrued as 'suggestion' or 'placebo effect', pushes Grünbaum into a rush to judgment in which the Tally Argument is ruled untenable, clinical validation indefensible (1984, p. 248), and inductive consilience between different pieces of clinical evidence valueless.

Given that the ubiquity of pragmatics is not confined to the analytic situation, Grünbaum must be advised that in his *Elements of Symbolic Logic* (1947) Hans Reichenbach pointed out that the statements of one person to another pertain to pragmatics, an idea endorsed by Russell (1948) and supported by the primacy of pragmatics over the entire range of ethologic evidence. All statements made in the flesh by one person to another will entail such 'shared contaminant', not just those the analyst as participant–observer makes to a supposedly submissive patient. In relational affairs of the sort dealt with by psychoanalysis, cognition emerges from an interactional field, and it is ludicrous to ask that it be 'uncontaminated'.

The contradictory structure of the analysand's inductions

Let us now consider the most elementary of clinical examples of transference analysis, my best try at billiard-ball simplicity. I will attempt to show how in the clinical session cognition emerges inductively from pragmatic–affective transference enactments, at the level that Grünbaum considers an 'epistemic contamination'. The patient, now several years into analysis, has shown a compliance that before treatment took the form of an impulse to suck the penis of important men he met in the course of his duties. Though this compliance has retarded his career advancement, he is at present going through a period of success in his work, which we both know increases his feelings of persecution. As I move in my chair to accommodate a sore back, I see him tense in the couch. Realizing that this has happened before, I tell him that it has seemed to me that he has tensed up when I shifted in my chair; I then venture that he may have feared I may attack him. He replies that this has often occurred to him, though for some reason he has never managed to mention it, that I should suddenly attack him, especially when at the end of session I walk behind him to the door.

Let us stop the action here. We are not on the terrain of quasi-Newtonian variables but in the basic epistemic field of what Russell (1948) calls 'animal inferences'. Here the analyst intuits and observes feelings or actions and attempts to describe them interpretatively;

here, too, the analysand on his part observes his own feelings, actions, and thoughts and then judges as valid or not the analyst's conjectures, to which, of course, he adds his own. What I pointed out to my analysand is the operation in the here and now of his relationship to me, of an 'animal inference' – call it a drive derivative or the workings of an unconscious relational 'theory' – in this case, something that he recognizes, that he has come already to some acquaintance with, but that he cannot yet 'think out'. He can bear to think it once interpretation provides the requisite 'knowledge by description'. He can then attain a 'correlation in multiple screens', those of his ostensive perception of himself (including his bodily reactions) and of me in the here and now, and of his perceptions on various memory screens of recent occurrences in and out of session and, sometimes, of more remote ones. Such 'thoughts' that cannot be 'thought out' are usually strongly contradictory of the patient's conscious thoughts, as happens in the present case in which the analysand at once feels/perceives that I am going/not going to attack him. This exposes the analysand to the turbulence of paradox. If he can bear the paradox, he gains ostensive knowledge of the operation of his unconscious theories, attaining some tentative reality judgment of my interpretation and, what is more substantial, of the workings of those action-and-emotion instinctual unconscious theories that are the stuff of interpretations.

In due time he may come – or he may not – to mnemic and then cognitive access to more remote antecedents, the 'infantile neurosis'; but, rather than by a search for etiological real-event causes, as Grünbaum would have it, this occurs mainly by way of cumulative correlations, important inasmuch as they throw added light on his current functioning. Thus does cognition about relational affairs emerge from a pragmatic field. To the extent that my interpretive attitude conveys 'neither anxiety nor anger' toward the fact that I believe he feels I'm going to attack him, it provides a more neutral pragmatic context for the content of the interpretation, which allows my analysand a 'double description', an ostensive correlation between what he *feels* is happening on the one hand and what he consciously comes to *perceive* is happening on the other.

Against a requirement for discrete and specific data, the complexities present in the clinical facts or events that are the referent of the Freudian *Deutung* involve at least two logical levels: (a) an ostensive level of *pointing to* facts or events in and out of session (my saying to the analysand that it seemed to me he had tensed up when I moved in my chair), and (b) a metainterpretive level, a wider *conjecture* on the analysand's way of colligating facts or events – that is, on his unconscious theory on what happens in the relationship (my guess that he felt I may attack him). This twofold interpretation, if apt, may lead to a linking of hitherto 'unknown' events or facts (my analysand's grasp that this had often occurred to him on leaving the session). These two levels, the ostensive and the conjectural, stand in a relation analogous to that of object-language and metalanguage: the conjectural level may be thought of as a metainterpretation of the analysand's mostly unconscious ways of interpreting events.

For the analysand to be an epistemic participant in the clinical process, then, it is not at all necessary that he develops those 'formidable cognitive powers' that Grünbaum construes only to reject as impossible: he need not be 'the judge of what was in fact the cause of his neurotic disorder' (1993, p. 16). For Freud's idea of the Tally Argument to stand, it is enough that the clinical process allow the analysand to attain some degree of representability of his unconscious processes and that he thus come to know enough, at the lowest-level observational hypotheses of scientific systems, about the ways in which his 'animal inferences', his pragmatic–affective unconscious theories, function in and out of session and the consequences of that functioning.

Requisites for an epistemology of clinical psychoanalysis

What, it may be asked now, would be the characteristics of an epistemology fit for, to paraphrase Lakatos (1976), the situational logic of psychoanalytic clinical problem-solving? To allow unconscious affective–pragmatic relational events occurring in the session to be regarded not as 'epistemic contaminants', but as empirical events from which ostensive knowledge can be gained, it can be asserted (without any pretense at being exhaustive), that such an epistemology would need take account of several factors: (a) differences in the complexity of both data and causality in the exact and the observational sciences, differences clear to Freud and partly to Mill, this being why it cannot be granted to Grünbaum that Freud shares his idea of what science is; (b) the limits of the experimental approach and of Mill's method of Agreement and Difference, limits of which

Mill was aware, holding that the Method of Difference applies only to cases identical except for a single factor, a situation not to be found, he said, in the case of living beings; (c) the fact that after Darwin 'mind' rests on those relational mental functionings that pertain to our animal inheritance, our 'animal inferences' we are mostly not conscious of, while reason and logic cannot be considered primary mental functionings; (d) the difference, following upon a distinction of diverse levels of mind, between a 'knowledge by acquaintance', which need not be at all conscious, and a conscious 'knowledge by description'; and (e) the need to renounce as absolute the Law of the Excluded Middle and admit that the interacting levels of our mind commonly admit of contradiction and of that nightmare of logicians, the occurrence of paradox. Of this last W. O. Quine (1962) has noted that the discovery of paradox has in fact often in the history of science been the occasion for major reconstructions of the foundations of thought.

This sits well with Bateson's finding that paradoxes are fundamental to epistemic evolutions in the animal kingdom, an idea that I argue is intrinsic to the workings of psychoanalytic insight. Many aspects of Freud's work show the paradoxical nature of psychoanalytic facts: thing- and word-presentations, the phenomena of bisexuality and of sadomasochism, the oft-found coincidence of maximally pleasurable and traumatic events. Indeed, transference enactments will often manifest themselves paradoxically as present traumas whose logical structure is: If yes, then no; if no, then yes. Such paradoxes are alien to Galilean epistemic schemes.

Only in the 'exact' mathematical sciences may refutation arguably assume the ways of rational criticism and experimental testability of discrete, homogeneous, well-behaved variables. In more empirical sciences, by contrast, observation, description, and correlation play a major role. In psychoanalysis in particular, the attainment of 'unprejudiced' observation, description, and correlation by both analysand and analyst opens the road to ostensive refutation of enacted unconscious theories. The approach of the philosopher of science that abandons observational contexts and becomes the judge of observationally based arguments has, in the case of clinical psychoanalysis, no baseline to ground itself but only a personal brand of common-sense psychology (not to mention such outright prejudices as the idea of conscious logic as a primary mental function). Accordingly, the philosopher of science should try to remember what Russell, a more open-minded inductivist, stated in 1948, that 'even the words that we most desire to render scientifically impersonal require for their interpretation personal experiences of the interpreter' (p. 104): it is futile for the philosopher of science to try to hold himself to arguments in observational terrains of which he knows little.

An epistemological equivalent for prediction in our field is inter-science agreement of independent findings. Several highly risky hypotheses issuing from clinical psychoanalysis, such as infantile sexuality, the trauma of weaning, the incest barrier, various features of the Oedipus complex, and that bête noire of philosophers, unconscious ideation, have soundly passed the tests provided by detailed ethological observations of our closest kin, the chimpanzee (cf. Goodall, 1986, pp. 15–42, 444–470, 565–594). Keeping to infantile sexuality and the incest barrier, it must be noted that though the male infant chimp quite early on attempts penetration of estrous adult females enjoying their complacency, which continues while he is a juvenile and an adolescent, this happens infrequently with his mother. Most adult males show no sexual interest in their mothers; incestuous matings between adult males and their mothers are extremely uncommon, and when they do happen, they involve violence amounting to rape. Also, copulations between brother–sister pairs are very infrequent (Goodall, 1986, pp. 466–467).

My aim throughout has been to uphold the psychoanalytic clinical method as inductive, though not, to be sure, in the sense of a Baconian induction that would restrict itself to the cataloguing of similar types (Russell, 1959a). It is in this latter sense that Grünbaum (1993) disqualifies clinical psychoanalysis for attempting to validate its causal claims in what he wrongly considers 'essentially retrospective studies' (p. 29). Rather, the psychoanalyst's work is inductive in the wide, as yet unformalized sense in which Pascal described inductions under the *esprit de finesse* as able to find and describe nodal points out of apparently unrelated and barely perceptible events in complex and seemingly disparate fields (Duhem, 1906, p. 79ff).

As I hope my briefest of clinical examples has shown, it seems fair to say that the psychoanalytic clinical method works in the main *counterinductively* – that is, by allowing analysands to attain at the basic observational level an ostensive reevaluation or refutation of their unconscious theories. It is left to other chapters to detail clinically the ways in which the analysand's insight, and the analyst's as well, relies on the individualizing, refutational component of induction, allowing access to, and ostensive refutation of, unconscious theories as yet unspecified, as contrasted to the generalizing induction of the Galilean approach. The idea of a 'counterinductive policy' (von Wright, 1957) fits my idea of a scientific method appropriate to clinical psychoanalysis far better than the sterile deductivism or experimentalism Grünbaum would foist on it. The vigor of the psychoanalytic scientific method lies in its ability to put into practice, in a systematic way, an observational 'context of discovery' in the domain of mind rather than in any pretense at compliance with verification criteria fit only for well-behaved variables.

A dismissal of the evidential value of psychoanalytic data is, as we have seen, a necessary consequence of the one-sided criteria of Galilean science. But it is groundless to believe that the inferential universe of mind is susceptible to the methods used to study the regularities of the realm of the inanimate. In its necessary reliance on the widely inductive activities of both analyst and analysand, psychoanalysis has no doubt a special place among the sciences and a need for an epistemology, counterinductive in the main, that is yet to be constructed.

If this is valid, it will be the task of our method not to provide general laws in the Galilean–Newtonian sense: rather, we can expect the study of the logic of clinical psychoanalysis to lead into as yet unmapped domains of epistemology. Indeed, it may be that among the motives behind the current contentiousness regarding the scientific claims of clinical psychoanalysis, an intolerance of the paradoxical nature of insight should be taken into account. This would be as it should: paradoxes emerge where conceptual schemes enter into crisis, and from Freud's time on it has been the fate of psychoanalysis to bring existing epistemologies into crisis.

7

DISCLOSURES AND REFUTATIONS

Clinical psychoanalysis as a logic of enquiry

Straddling the natural sciences in its use of observational method and the humanities through its object of study, psychoanalysis is concerned with types of evidence that are beyond the scope of philosophical cogitation. Not surprisingly, most philosophers have not welcomed the newcomer's implicit challenge to cherished methodological and conceptual premises. Freud sketches the impact of his young discipline on philosophy in a short seminal paper, 'A difficulty in the path of psycho-analysis' (1917b), while Bion (1962) traces a complex philosophical history for issues of mental growth. Drawing a distinction between the Aristotelian and the Galilean conceptions of science strikes me as a prerequisite for any understanding of the way in which philosophers and scientists view psychoanalysis.

The two natures of 'natural science'

The roots of two contrasting views on the nature of enquiry and the scientific endeavour can be found in ancient Greece. Aristotle's *empirical–descriptive* tradition traces 'forms' or 'patterns' by observing, describing and comparing 'exemplars': descriptive disciplines, the clinical legacy of medicine included, follow this procedure. A physician's son, Aristotle viewed biology as the principal empirical concern, while he also laid the foundations of logic.

The *empirical–rationalistic* tradition of Pythagoras established measurement, the mathematical treatment of empirical issues and the ontology of number as the basis for reality, and also, with Euclid's *Elements*, the axiomatic method. This was used by Descartes (whose rationalism was often enough blatantly anti-empirical, as Peirce notes with some relish, 1868, p. 40) and by Galileo in his systematic use of experiment, and culminated in Newtonian celestial mechanics, using a new mathematical tool, infinitesimal calculus. This so-called Enlightenment tradition in science turned into an ontology. Newtonian mechanics became paradigmatic for 'theoretical', 'exact', 'hard', 'positive' or 'predictive' sciences that mimicked formal deductive systems, providing a predictive framework within which, if valid, empirical 'elements' would fit. Prediction based on formal deduction became the criterion for 'empirical truth'. The physicist Jean Bricmont voices such yearnings: 'what we understand well, we understand in mechanical and reductionistic terms' (1996, p. 156).

Physics, chemistry and biology at near-molecular levels evolved from descriptive to deductive, Euclidean-like schemes. Reducing their field to discrete, homogeneous, projectible variables, they provide predictions and technologies. This led to a general *infallibilist* conception of science; the Galilean idea of a Universe written in mathematical language, descending from the heavenly spheres, became prescriptive for all valid knowledge: a clarion call for a strict 'inductive ascent' from elementary data along deductive lines. In 'strict inductivism', which Grünbaum advocates, such a strategy, in which 'truth-injection' flows deductively from indisputable elementary data at the base to theory at the top, insists on empirical 'warrants'.

Poincaré (1902), though, found ideas of empirical infallibility fit only for high-school students. To most people, who think about science at textbook levels, the search for empirical certainties remains dominant. This approach fails, though, when we realize that theories are 'forms', and that their predictive efficacies are local, relative and internal to a given deductivist framework. Thus, Newtonian certainties are 'local' phenomena, collapsing, even technologically, in satellite communications, which have to take account of Einsteinian 'forms' of time–gravity interaction. Developments such as biogenetics can introduce 'local' Galilean regularities into the near-molecular levels of the wider Darwinian theoretical framework, but the overall validity of the framework, as well as entire fields such as palaeoanthropology or ethology, is dependent on global 'patterns' or 'forms' that are arrived at through the description and comparison of 'exemplars'. In fact the French theoretical physicist Jean Marc Lévy-Leblond (1996) advises us that presently the notion of truth in science is subordinated to that of validity, in the sense that even the mathematical objects intervening in a theorem such as Pythagoras' happen in a much wider context than the one stated in the initial theorem. Such wider conceptual context is that of 'curved' or non-Euclidean spaces, in which the theorem loses its assumed general validity and is true only in a particular case – that of spaces of null curvature. There is now, he says, a consensus among physicists that every physical theory is apt to describe and understand a segment of reality, and it comes to be properly known only when the limits within which the theory applies are discovered.

Scientific versus philosophical methods

At the core of the controversy on the scientific validity of psychoanalysis is a rift between the philosophy of science and scientific practice (Feyerabend, 1978; Reichenbach, 1927). Following whatever methodological general 'principles' they happened to choose, philosophers undertook to dictate to practitioners what was to be done in quite different empirical fields. Although he is discussing physics, let us quote Feyerabend on the method of scientists and that of philosophers:

> A *scientist* starts with a bulk of material consisting of diverse conflicting ingredients. There are theories formulated in accordance with the highest standards of rigour side by side with unfounded and sloppy approximations, there are 'solid' facts, local laws based on some of these facts, there are heuristic principles, tentative formulations of new points of view which partly agree, partly conflict with the accepted facts, there are vague philosophical ideas, standards of rationality and procedure that conflict with these. Being unable to make such material conform to simple views of order and consistency the scientist usually develops a *practical logic* that permits him to get results amidst chaos and incoherence. Most of the rules and standards of this practical logic are conceived ad hoc; they serve to remove a practical difficulty and it is not possible to turn them into an organon of research. 'The external conditions' – writes Einstein – 'which are set for [the scientist] . . . do not permit him to let himself be too much

> restricted, in the construction of his conceptual world, by the adherence to an epistemological system. He therefore must appear to the systematic epistemologist as a type of unscrupulous opportunist'. The *way of the philosopher* is very different; there could not be a greater contrast. There are some general ideas and standards which are spelled out in detail and there are the principles of the logic chosen. There is hardly anything else.
>
> (1978, pp. 83–84)

Philosophers, then, create 'rational reconstructions' of the process by which scientific knowledge is attained, mainly in 'hard' sciences, and establish these as an organon for any enquiry that aspires to be scientific. Discussing the epistemic strictures that classical (Newtonian) empiricism and the rational reconstructions of the Vienna Circle imposed on physicists in relation to quantum theory, Feyerabend (1980) quotes Einstein to demonstrate that what is at stake there is not 'an 'ontological' issue, whatever *that* means' (p. 91). He argues (p. 91n.) that Einstein was the last of the late-nineteenth-century scientist–philosophers such as Maxwell, Hertz, Mach, Boltzmann and Duhem, who designed philosophies for advancing science, applying and modifying these philosophies in their research. The same is true of Darwin and Freud, though they would not admit to being philosophers in any usual sense of the word.

Two kinds of strictures on enquiry are applied to psychoanalysis. On the one hand there is 'Enlightenment Rational Fundamentalism' (Nanda, 1996, p. 421), with two seemingly opposed branches: 'strict inductivism' (Grünbaum) and 'falsificationism' (Popper); its restrictive definitions of 'empirical' and 'falsifiable' deny empirical status to the psychoanalytic method. Having referred in chapter 6 to the logical constraints implicit in Grünbaum's strictures for the realm of mind, I shall consider these positions only briefly.

On the other side of the epistemic dispute are the idealistic currents of the 'linguistic turn', which take language itself, rather than what it is concerned with, to be the essential issue and which, in today's context of de-medicalization of psychoanalysis, puts forward a polemic that is partly internal to our discipline. There is therefore a risk that the argumentational tradition of philosophy will supplant the observational, clinical one – the 'practical logic', to use Feyerabend's apt term – from which psychoanalysis arose. Deeming psychoanalytic clinical facts to be *irretrievably* 'theory-laden', this current of thinking dismisses efforts to gain ostensive, observational knowledge of the events in the session as naïve realism and empiricism.

On certainty as an epistemic trap

Attacks on the empirical status of clinical psychoanalysis on the part of 'rationalistic fundamentalism' and the idealistic 'linguistic turn' are based on the idea of empirical certainties. This is obvious in the demand made by strict inductivism (Grünbaum, 1984, 1993) that the study of mind conform to physicalist 'guarantees' such as Newtonian guidelines: only data established by an inductive process in which truth flows clearly from the data to the theories is deemed 'empirical' and, as such, properly scientific. Physics, in this view, reigns supreme among the sciences.

Popper's falsificationism grants that we cannot gain access to empirical certainties, and that 'human knowledge is a very special case of animal knowledge' (1982, p. xxxv) – a point, by the way, that Peirce, Russell, and also Searle concede. I agree with Popper's observation (1957a) that social sciences do not follow 'laws'. But his demarcation of scientific empirical knowledge from pseudoscience, with his claim, following Tarski (1931), that *only fully formalized theories can be properly scientific and testable* (Popper, 1982, p. 185) blatantly transfers the demand for certainties to the theoretical apparatus.

The similarity between Popper's and Grünbaum's viewpoints in applying purely physicalistic criteria to all science is clearly apparent in Popper's protest that 'social sciences do not as yet seem to have found their Galileo' (1957a, p. 1); not being 'theoretical', they cannot attain 'large-scale forecasts' (1957a, p. 41). His overall rule for scientific validity is 'falsifiability, or refutability, or testability' (1957b, p. 37); to him every good scientific theory must deductively demonstrate the impossibility of certain events, and its usefulness correlates with the number of possibilities that it rules out. To be acceptable as 'empirical evidence in the scientific scene' (p. 38), the clinical observations of psychoanalysis would have to conform to '*criteria of refutation* . . . laid down beforehand' (p. 38n). This assumes that they should conform to deductivist principles – that is, to reduction to Galilean–Newtonian variables. He further states that 'only by purely deductive reasoning is it possible for us to discover what our theories imply' (p. 51). In this view, only the indirect, rigorously deduced consequences of a theory can indicate its weaknesses. His call for the open-ended use of 'trial and error' is therefore no more than a disguise for a basic adherence to the traditional (hypothetico–deductivist) rules of induction, and on such criteria disciplines based on non-formalized theories, such as Darwin's, or on a taxonomy, or on a description of multi-level processes as with ethology, are unavoidably excluded from the abstract, formal, deductivism-led realm of Popperian science. In fact Darwin can scarcely be deemed a deductivist, if we are to believe what he forwards in his *Autobiography*: 'with the exception of the Coral Reefs, I cannot remember a single first-formed hypothesis which had not after a time to be given up or greatly modified. This has naturally led me to distrust greatly deductive reasoning in the mixed sciences' (1887, p. 141); decades earlier, in his correspondence, he had been even more forceful: 'I look at a strong tendency to generalise as an entire evil' (Barlow, 1958a, p. 160). Not much place, then, in Darwin's mind, for a search for deductive certainties or warrants. In fact, says his granddaughter Nora Barlow (1958b, p. 219), 'his repudiation of those who spin their theories without the constant discipline of factual detail, was the inevitable concomitant of his scientific faith'. Small wonder that Popper finally admits that 'it is far from clear what we should consider a possible refutation of the theory of natural selection' (1994, p. 90) and finds no way to fit Darwin's work in the proper, scientific side of his demarcation between empirical and non-empirical theories.

In response to Popper's view that only conjectures that correspond completely to deductive principles can be considered scientific, Lakatos objects that he turns 'fallible propositions into a "basis" for a hard-line policy' (1970, p. 109). With Duhem and Russell, Lakatos argues that the term 'scientific' cannot apply to a *single* theory considered as an item for testing in crucial experiments, and that to endeavour to do so is, in the logical sense, a category mistake (p. 118ff). For Lakatos the term 'scientific' can apply only to a series of theories, forming a research programme leading to the discovery of new facts. Falsification requires relationships between competing theories, the original 'empirical basis' and the empirical discovery that results from the testing of the alternative theories.

In a seminal paper (1968) Lakatos states that the substantial difference between inductive and deductive logic makes the term logic, used for both, a misleading one. Acutely aware of the heuristic precedence of analysis over synthesis, he maintains that even in a formal discipline such as mathematics we cannot be certain of our proofs. His method of 'proofs and refutations' consists in evolving counter-examples, exploring the structure of one's original assumptions or lemmas by dismantling them into hitherto unnoticed sub-conjectures (1976, p. 9). 'Proof' here then simply means the lack of likely counter-examples – that is, the lack of readily available disproof. He sees this as the route to development of theory and progress in knowledge. However, as this method derives from pure geometry and applies to 'theoretical' sciences rather than observational ones, he retains a Platonic–Popperian view that accords to scientific theories a conceptual universe that is independent of that of the human beings who create it, in which beliefs play a part. His insistence on theoretical anticipation as a key criterion for new facts overlooks the role of ostension in empirical matters.

Continuing the critique of Popperian formalism, and with reference to Duhem's (1906) view that validation of a theory should depend on universal judgements, Feyerabend (1987) reminds us that even in 'mature' sciences: 'scientific theories . . . are never completely formalised or fully interpreted, and the class of basic statements are never fully "given" ' (p. 170). Similarly, Kuhn (1970b, p. 248) warns that the Popperians conflate the clear principles of testability with the shadowy practice of testing, omitting any indication of how the principles are to be applied, which makes Popper's methodology appear to be more of a logic and less of an ideology than it actually is. Scientific activity relies, to a much greater extent than Popperians admit, on shared practices and shared examples that can only be partly expressed in statements and propositions. This dependence on shared examples is a principal meaning of the term paradigm, and being more of an empiricist than his rivals, Kuhn attributes great importance to ostension in the establishment of counter-examples and in the use of counterinduction.

It is characteristic of Popper's constricted views on science and the primacy he accords to the structure of physical science over all scientific endeavours that of the twenty examples of successful refutations 'chosen almost at random' (1982, p. xxvi) in what is perhaps his final major statement on this subject, *each and every one* is from physics. The spell of Euclid, then, falls upon them all, and despite countless disclaimers, Popper's theory-dominated falsationistic formalism follows the route of data-dominated strict inductivism in adopting a reductionistic view of empiricism.

In contrast to simplistic depictions of scientific method as a mechanical process of collecting facts and logical testing of isolable hypotheses, and against calls for a 'unity of science' in a shared methodology, Nobel awardee in chemistry Dudley Hersbach argues that the paths of scientific method are varied:

> Each academic subculture deals with entirely different kinds of questions, develops very different criteria for evaluating answers, and evolves its own languages. That handicaps interdisciplinary communication, but need not be allowed to engender disrespect. Science or any subculture can only treat questions amenable to its methods. (1996, p. 27)

He thus follows Peirce's basic idea that logic learns from empirical enquiry as much as or more than enquiry can learn from logic: 'each chief step in science has been a lesson in logic . . . questions of fact and questions of logic are curiously interlaced' (1877, pp. 6–7). We will encounter this interrelatedness wherever we attempt to make empirical discoveries, and the scientist rises to the challenge by recourse to what Feyerabend calls a practical logic.

On common language and common sense

Geisteswissenschaften – from Dilthey onwards – and linguistic approaches are based on a caricature of a unitary, homogeneous, physicalistic 'natural science' that uses a strategy of working upwards from reliably univocal data, as described above for strict inductivism. With the purported 'empirical certainties' of such 'natural science' are contrasted the uncertainties of human sciences – which often enough slip into a denial of the notion of evidence. Thus, linguistic philosophies (Feyerabend, 1969) tend to be explained only by reference to themselves: they create their own evidence and thus resemble dogmatic systems.

A case in point of the dogmatism pervading 'ordinary language' philosophies, reasonable though it sounds, is Austin's plea:

> Our common stock of words embodies all the distinctions men have found worth drawing, and the connexions they have found worth making, in the lifetime of many generations: these are likely to be

> more numerous, more sound, since they have stood the long test of the survival of the fittest, and more subtle, at least in all reasonable and practical matters, than any you or I are likely to think up in our armchairs of an afternoon – the most favoured alternative method.
> (1956–57, p. 182)

May I add that to hold that ordinary language embodies all distinctions and analogies worth making disregards the fact that *un*knowing is as prevalent a mode as is knowing. Against Austin's plea Feyerabend argues that the linguistic method enshrines unexamined prejudice, and that the success of a 'common' idiom, or of a common-sense view, is hardly ever a test because, even in concrete observational situations, there is no attempt, as there is in the sciences, to break into new fields and test theories (1963, p. 164). In Lakatos' terms (1970), there is no attempt at 'content-increase'. This is true of linguistic contexts that seek no new observations, as in Austin's above (though not in other aspects of his work).

But Moore's point that in our everyday life we find ourselves 'in this strange position that we do *know* many things . . . and yet we do not know *how* we know them, i.e. we do not know what the evidence was' (1925, p. 44) seems a valid one. In fact, he assumes that a 'common-sense view of the world' is in certain fundamental respects wholly true. As an example of conclusive evidence, he introduces his famous 'two-hands' argument: 'Here is one hand and here is another', which actually falls short of *proving* it (1939, p. 149). He concedes to Descartes that he cannot prove that he is awake, but he finds evidence for thinking that this is so, and the same response is valid for nearly all cases; one *knows* many things that one cannot *prove.* This is not surprising, given that the term 'proof' has a variety of meanings. Informally, says Blackburn (1994) it means a procedure that brings conviction; but, more formally, 'proof' means a deductively valid argument starting from correct premises that yields the conclusion. The axiomatic, demonstrative roots of the term are thus evident.

Ostension in everyday life and in scientific discovery

In everyday life gaining knowledge and, even more relevant for us psychoanalysts, emotional growth depend on our ability to test and modify our 'common-sense theories' and the unconscious theories of relationship, which requires ostension of 'exemplars', not deductively demonstrative methods. Pointing to the fundamental importance of insight for emotional growth, Bion describes it in everyday discernment as a *psychoanalytic function of the personality*, as well as describing the painful nature of change towards mental maturity that is central to its operation (1970, p. 53).

The psychoanalytic method can be taken, then, as a special case in which a method of 'disclosures and refutations' gives us as full an observational field as is feasible regarding the ways in which our unconscious theories about relationships operate. To develop my argument that clinical psychoanalysis *is an observational extension of everyday practical logic*, I now turn to Thomas Kuhn's idea of ostension (1964, 1974) in everyday life and in scientific progress.

Kuhn (1974, p. 309ff) imagines a small child walking with his father in a zoo. His father points to a bird, saying, 'Look, Johnny, there's a swan'. Soon Johnny points to another bird, saying 'Daddy, another swan', but his father replies: 'No, Johnny, that's a goose'; and perhaps Johnny's next swan will prove to be a duck, but before long, after appropriate corrections, his ability to identify the water-fowl will be as good as his father's. So to Johnny swans, geese and ducks, mixed together at the start, cluster now in discrete sets, with appreciable distances between them. This simplest mode of ostension requires grouping data in clusters with empty space between them. But the same technique would be viable were Johnny to become a scientist and, if in a less pure form, it is essential to the more abstract sciences as well (Kuhn, 1974, p. 313). He considers the cognitive functions of shared examples prior to any specification of the criteria that they exemplify. The result of this is a simple Venn diagram displaying three non-overlapping classes, and new experiences may well lead to readjustments of class boundaries.

This elementary example of disclosure by ostension of concrete natural events illustrates the resulting redefinition and rearrangement of discrete *classes* of external objects: extension of knowledge modifies both previous theories and the meaning of the descriptive terms used – in our case, those of Johnny's implicit theories on water-fowl. Even the most harmless parts of the idiom used may be based on far-reaching assumptions and must therefore be regarded as highly hypothetical (Feyerabend, 1962, pp. 80–1, p. 86).

Ostension does not apply only to new empirical data: there is also 'thought-experiment', which, Kuhn argues (1964, p. 242), is closer to ordinary experimentation than is usually supposed. Ostension by thought-experiment is based on previous experience; it often confronts the researcher with some implicit paradox in his modes of thinking, and then helps him to modify his conceptual apparatus: its function is to correct previous conceptual mistakes (p. 251ff). From thought-experiments, Kuhn argues, people learn about their concepts and about the world together, and thought-experiments come into play as the difficulties in applying a concept become apparent (p. 258). They illustrate nature's failure to conform to a previous set of expectations and they may suggest ways in which expectation and theory must be revised, often through gestalt switches (1970a, p. 268).

The same applies to ostension of personal relationships and one's notions about oneself, where *un*knowing is most extreme and ostension is hardest to attain. Counterinduction through ostension and thought-experiment with the analysand's unconscious theories about relationship provides a viable epistemic model of the 'practical logic' of psychoanalytic clinical enquiry. But first we need to grasp the profound differences between the logic of discovery and structure of theory-progress in the observational sciences and the deductivist notion that in theory-change explicit new theories must precede refutation of older conceptions. Our example is a major ethological discovery recounted by Jane Goodall.

> 4 November, 1960. . . . He had his back still to me. He turned slightly and, very deliberately, pulled a thick grass stalk toward him and broke off a piece about 45 cm long. Then unfortunately, he turned his back on me again. After a few minutes he climbed over the [termite] hill and moved away on the far side. I identified him as David Greybeard.
>
> 6 November, 1960. By the termite hill there were two chimps, both male. . . . I could see a little better the use of a piece of straw. It was held in the left hand, poked into the mound, and then removed coated with termites. The straw was raised to the mouth and the insects picked off with the lips along the length of the straw, starting in the middle.
>
> (1986, p. 535)

In such modest terms Goodall's diary reports the first observed use of tools by chimpanzees in the wild. Though a narrative, its import derives not from its wording, but from the events described. This crucial observation omits any 'daring conjecture' on Goodall's side and, again *pace* Popper, it does not use any explicit criteria laid down beforehand; here the *less* the theories exclude from the findings, the better. It is not an 'experiment' in any usual sense of the term; though lacking deductive principles, it has the epistemic import of a 'crucial experiment'.

The impact of Goodall's discovery follows in the tradition of the largely unassimilated Darwinian injury to man's narcissism (Freud, 1917b). It refutes the purported empirical generalization that only men are toolmakers, altering a defining characteristic of man. In a way that is reminiscent of Feyerabend's idea that common observational terms contain great theoretical significance, it redefines both terms, 'chimpanzee' and 'man'.

The definition of a fact ranges from a direct observation to a well-grounded conjecture that has no readily available alternative. It is hard to conceive how the kind of conclusive evidence referred to by Moore in the 'two-hands' argument can be refuted by a new theory. Far from testing a deliberate risky hypothesis, Goodall's discovery was a surprise, and contrary to physicalistic epistemological tenets, here the logic of discovery and the logic of verification constitute a single process. It is content-increasing, leading to a progressive 'problem-shift' in Lakatos's sense (1970), but in contrast to his approach (1976), the ability to observe this major counter-example did not require an explicit alternative theory, nor even a 'happy Guess' (Whewell, 1858), just a fortuitous, not entirely random encounter with a theory-bound but not *irretrievably* theory-bound observer. Far from the constraints of formal theory, we encounter a primacy of *knowledge by acquaintance* operating counterinductively upon a range of *implicit, informal* conceptions or theories.

Such a crucial discovery sheds light on the chimpanzee mind and, more generally, on the realm of a non-verbal thought that phylogenetically precedes language, which requires a new research programme, one to be amplified and reinterpreted as new empirical content is gained. This does not take the simplistic form of generalizing induction, 'all swans are white', which provides no new content. New findings will reveal unpredictable diversities, added context and complexity, opening a wealth of possibilities unamenable to a formal tradition. The emergence of relevant findings will, then, not be predictable and will require detailed process observation, which in Goodall's research programme eventually included these findings: that chimpanzees prepare made-to-measure tools for events they anticipate (they will, for example, prepare stones for cracking nuts presumed to be available at distant places and carry such tools to the spot); that they improvise tools in new situations; that mothers teach tool-making to the brood, giving rise to various tool-making cultures in different chimpanzee communities; that such communities can gain knowledge about tool-use from adolescent females with unrestricted migration rights; and that chimpanzees improvise use of hitherto unknown tools to further leadership claims in the group or in internecine warfare (Goodall, 1986; see also Griffin, 1992). Such activities, deeply *meaningful* and involving sophisticated stages of thought and social cooperation, involve emotional and gestural communication, not words. Thought, meaning and social communication, intertwined with emotion, precedes language. At this point the investigations of these two Darwinians, Freud and Goodall, overlap. This basic level of meaning surfaces in Freud's unrepressed unconscious, *Triebe* (drives) and *Dingvorstellungen* (thing-presentations); it obviously does not pertain to *Wortvorstellungen* (word-presentations).

Epistemically, Goodall's discovery comes about ostensively in an *individual* instance, David Greybeard's mound-poking, and it *impacts upon* and *opens up* a range of *implicit and pre-existent, informal* conceptions or theories at several levels. Her research refutes and rearranges, provisionally but irrevocably, concepts ranging from more local knowledge on the chimpanzee's abilities for non-verbal thought (which includes discovery) and for emotive, non-verbal social communication, to general questions about human beings: it gives an insight into the quite distinct levels, both non-verbal and verbal, on which we think and communicate, and it confronts us with our tendency to leave such facts aside and misconstrue our epistemic outlooks. Truth-injection takes place here at all levels; it needs to be both tested and illuminated by new findings.

What does this have to do with the workings of clinical psychoanalysis? A great deal, I suggest. Epistemically, it shows that extending the predictive, deductivist tenets of the sciences of inanimate matter to the domain of mind with the misleading term 'natural science' makes a policy out of ignorance, allowing its partisans to indulge freely in non-observation (Mill's foremost fallacy), usually for purposes of unselective content-dismissal. Such diversely structured communicational levels, a basic emotional non-verbal level of thing-presentations and a superimposed, conscious verbal code of word-presentations, help to explain why paradox plays such an integral part in bringing unconscious material to consciousness.

As I have shown, Kuhn considers that ostension and thought-experiment arise as difficulties with one's schemes come to the fore, and they often confront us with some implicit paradox in our modes of thinking. This has resonances with Freud's 'Remembering, repeating and working-through': 'it is in fact only through his own experience and mishaps that a person learns sense' (1914a, p. 153). Let us now consider a sample of psychoanalytic demonstration of paradox.

A girl consulted me after breaking off a two-year-long, thrice-weekly psychotherapy, in the course of which, eight months before, she had developed a severe phobia. She had to be accompanied at all times, even at home; she also suffered from a variety of somatic symptoms and occasional suicidal impulses. As she told me at length in her first interview, her overt panic attacks started during a traffic jam in the family car. It turned out on my questioning that she had given her family no sign of her acute distress at the time, and then it dawned on me that she was doing just this at the interview. While anxious and expectant about breaking her previous treatment and starting a new one, she talked about her plight in an amiable, smiling mood, close to that of a funny anecdote. I mentioned to her that just as she had been silent about the ordeal felt in the family car, so at the interview she was also being silent about her plight, in the sense that there was a clear-cut discrepancy between what she was saying she had felt during the episode and the smiling, agreeable way in which she talked about it, sparing me as she had spared her family in the car. She recognized this as something that she usually did; interpretive description led to ostension in the here and now and to a thought-experiment about her everyday experiences. Disclosure of the paradox allayed her anxiety about changing therapists and brought considerable relief. It also led fairly directly, during her initial analytic sessions, to long-standing fears of her aggression destroying her loved ones and to the automatic use of her body for appeasement by way of attitude and smiles, and also as a buffer for evidence of felt aggression, which was 'mopped up' into her symptoms.

Later on in her four-sessions-weekly analysis, we were able to map the myriad ways in which this paradox crept into her daily life, in which sometimes she found a way around it, and often did not, in which case she would start having physical symptoms, usually severe ones. In the presence of an object, the paradox encountered at least two breaking points. If the other person responded to her smiling denial, she felt comforted at first but would then start feeling ignored and misunderstood, and she would get anxious and angry, with bodily symptoms such as difficulties in swallowing or shortness of breath. If the other person bypassed her smiling manners and, sensing her anxiety, became solicitous, she felt encroached upon by a benevolent onslaught; a part of the problem was her feeling blamed for draining the other person's emotional resources, which drove her to anger again. This had occurred, to a point of no return, with her previous therapist's attempts to help.

Demonstration of this predicament allowed a way out of the escalating vicious circle and established the basis for viable analytic work. We gained access to major kinds of break-up in which phobia led to fleeting melancholy and suicidal impulses, which happens in the felt absence of a suitable object. (This occurs too when someone present becomes emotionally unavailable, being felt as too involved in his own feelings, or as blaming her implicitly in being felt to be invaded by her needs.) In the transference this happens at weekends: the absence of a containing object is felt as the overwhelming presence of a destroyed, non-existent object, a 'black sun', the outcome of a Hiroshima-like havoc of the mental class of containing objects. Struggling for a non-accusing interpretive way of depicting this most dangerous and exposed area of my patient's mind, I used the story of a man in a toilet in Hiroshima who, in a violent bowel movement coinciding with the Bomb, said to himself, 'God! What did I do?'

Clinically, paradox can arise verbally, but it generally entails an unknown action (in this case my patient's use of amiable manners as a denial of damaging me), on the one hand, and a narrated account closer to consciousness, largely defensive, on the other. The analyst must be alert to the enacted term of the paradox: as my vignette shows, its disclosure opens the way to the analysand's previously unconscious 'theory' (that she might omnipotently destroy me, and those she cares for), and eventually, once enough instances have come ostensively to light, it will lead to its refutation.

Conjectures, proofs, disclosures

The logic of psychoanalytic practice, or, in fact, any research on mind, does not and cannot employ the principles used in physicalistic inductivism. Popper's method of conjectures and refutations is akin to classical strict inductivism, and the term 'conjecture' is part of a set of formal deductivist principles.

In Lakatos' method of proofs and refutations, the term 'proof' means lemma-investigation, enquiry using counter-examples to the unseen assumptions present in formal systems. As a basis for observational sciences this method is the same, except that it holds to no formal principles and gives explicit place to ostension – an essential point drawn from Russell and Kuhn.

Unlike ethology, clinical psychoanalysis is intuitional–observational for both participants. To help attain ostension, the analyst supplies his conjectures to the analysand; but these are not Popperian ones developed as a formal set of principles. They are attempts at purveying a tentative 'knowledge by description' which, in pointing to hitherto unacknowledged aspects, will, if accurate enough, illuminate unknown or obscure aspects of the analysand's psychic realities, bringing about disclosures.

As in our clinical example, the analysand's ostensions are achieved in *individual examples* and then lead to counterinduction on his unconscious 'forms' – that is, on his unconscious *classes* of relationship, and on how he uses them. The analyst's attempts at describing what is the case in the session appeal, at the basic level, to what he grasps from his 'animal inferences' – that is, from his countertransference screening. To Bion (1979, p. 85) the analyst's task is to smell danger, using his primitive, archaic senses. Sometimes interpretations will be akin to Johnny's father's remark 'Look, Johnny, there's a swan', but while the analyst often has better access to evidence as it transpires in the sessions, he does not conclusively *know* the analysand's swans from his ducks or his geese. Tentative discrepancy and analogy based on emotional contact with the analysand's psychic reality are enough for the analyst to work with: and it would be brash for him to view his clinical task as 'getting closer to the truth'. The analyst's conjectural descriptions open the way to disclosure: it is for the analysand to gauge what may or may not be applicable in the analyst's conjectures, and how he uses the disclosures that are prompted. Given that the analyst has not lived through the experiences the analysand *un*knows through repression, splitting, denial and so on, the analysand is the final epistemic arbiter. Here we meet the line that Freud wisely draws between 'psychoanalysis', which is the analyst's proper task and the evolving 'psycho-synthesis' of emergent new meanings, which must be left to the analysand 'without our intervention' (1919, pp. 160–161).

The analyst's task generally falls within a fallibilist epistemology, furthering disclosures based on evolving evidence of discrepancy and analogy. Reliance on evidence of non-concordance is Strachey's chief contribution, contained in the idea that the analysand's insight evolves with the recognition of a divergence between how he realizes he feels or has felt, and how he comes to perceive the analyst consciously. This has two advantages, one technical, the other epistemic. It helps to keep the analyst from a brandishing of 'truth', or, worse, from being a spokesman for reality, which would conspire against his neutrality. It also provides a means of circumventing the overblown philosophical issues of 'truth': a fallibilist policy based on non-concordance, on an awareness of error rather than on truth, presents few targets to the sceptical or idealist rejections of truth defined as *concordance with reality.* And while to Feyerabend (1987, p. 184) the phrase 'getting closer to the truth' makes no epistemic sense, clinically it often enough makes emotional sense: here again, the analysand must be relied upon to *recognize* more than what can be *proved.*

Only in clinical evaluation of the analysand's psychic state or development, which in most cases can be related to more or less clear-cut beacons, must the question of truth as *correspondence with reality* be addressed adroitly by the analyst. In interpretive interventions pointing to enacted and articulated discrepancy at different levels of mind, truth-evaluation can be kept tentative. Here, logic is just an instrument; it opens the way to new observations and thought-experiments in which truth-injections may occur, but it effects no empirical truth-injection.

That our clinical logic of enquiry depends on intuitional–observational extensions of everyday thought is a truism: what the analyst conveys ties in with and extends how the analysand grasps his own ways of thinking, to help him redress them using another perspective. This happened when I helped my patient to see that she had spared her family in her initial panic attack, and then how, in a similar way, she spared me in the interview. It is a truism, too, in that authors agree that finally all science develops as an extension of everyday inductions. Obviously this does not mean that the analyst's practical logic is at the level of common sense: on the contrary, it must focus on that which the analysand *un*knows, which Freud called resistance and Bion called the –K link. Also, my position should not be taken as underestimating the role of our theories, both in facilitating and in obstructing access to facts. However, to embark on the intricate subject of the various levels, from the clinical to the metapsychological, that the term 'theory' embraces in our discipline would go well beyond what I am able to discuss here.

8

COUNTERINDUCTION IN PSYCHOANALYTIC PRACTICE

Epistemic and technical aspects

Basic to our practice is Freud's notion that interpretations must tally with what is real in the analysand's *unconscious* psychic reality. As was previously considered, the analyst's neutrality is the background to an awareness on the analysand's part of the projection upon the analyst of his archaic psychic reality – an idea implicit in Freud's model of the analyst as 'mirror'. Also, only a 'knowledge by acquaintance' on his psychic reality leads the analysand to ostensive insights furthering structural psychic change, the verbal 'knowledge by description' provided by interpretation being in the main preparatory.

Effective insights, then, depend upon ostension, that is, on what can be pointed to with the finger or the eye saying 'this', which happens on both perceptual and mnemic screens. While Freud's term *Deutung* is more ostensive than our term 'interpretation', further precision is needed on how ostension works for the purposes of gaining knowledge on the unconscious mind.

These points are basic to what follows on the role of counter-induction in attaining insight in clinical psychoanalysis.[1] Now I come to the topic of induction, which, being at the core of epistemology, is muddled by its usages in the history of scientific thought. Induction means, generally, inference from the particular to the general, or from the known to the unknown; from Aristotle on, induction depends on observation of individual events, in contrast to deduction, the arguing from general principles or laws to the particular.

Induction, says W. O. Quine (1978), consists, primarily, in the expectation that similar episodes will, to our subjective lights, have similar sequels; it functions according to our innate likes and dislikes, and it guides our acts in common life. Aristotelian science was clearly an extension of everyday inductive methods; it is otherwise for the Galilean method and then Newtonian science, which reduce the complexity of celestial mechanics to the simplicity of discrete homogeneous variables linked by a single formula. This seemingly brought a split between 'common' inductions grounding our everyday actions as well as the organized bodies of knowledge that, following the Latin, are known as *scientiae*, and what to nineteenth-century positivism became the sole kind of properly scientific induction, leading to inductive 'proof' by way of reduction to variables and eliminative induction as typically put to practice in experiment. There soon emerged, however, an awareness that while the process of verification of hypotheses could be assumedly built into a canon, Mill's canon of inductive 'proof', inductive discovery knew no rules.

This seminal period of the theory of science is witness, then, to unacknowledged distinct lines of thought on induction, modelled, respectively, upon Aristotelian science, with its search for pattern and the careful study and comparison of individual specimens, and Galilean science, with its isolation and experimental manipulation of separate, homogeneous variables appropriate for quantification. As stated in chapter 6, both currents are found in Whewell (1858), but what matters for our purposes is that he put forward an ampliative view of induction that seems a good approach to how we employ induction in our everyday life and in clinical work, saying: 'The distinction of Fact and Theory is only relative. Events and phenomena, considered as particulars that may be colligated by Induction, are Facts; considered as Generalities already obtained by colligation of other Facts, they are Theories' (p. 161).

Whewell's broad idea of induction seems valid for our everyday inductions and for observational disciplines, clinical psychoanalysis included. Peirce (1901, p. 150) set apart the 'context of discovery' and the 'context of justification', calling 'abduction' the emergence of hypotheses, 'deduction' the finding of the consequents to the hypotheses, and 'induction' the process of verification – that is, the empirical, usually experimental, testing of the consequents to the hypotheses; but such distinctions lose their edge in observational sciences, where complex, multi-levelled, and context-dependent hypotheses are not fit for point-by-point induction or rigorous prediction. Eliminative induction between alternative hypotheses, the 'context of justification', is tentative here, and the choice between higher-level alternative theories arduous but not impossible (see Hanly, 1992). In any case, methodological fallibilism firmly distinguishes rejection of hypothesis or theories or election between alternatives from disproof, which is to be found, if ever, only in purely formal sciences (Lakatos, 1970, p. 109). Later on Lakatos (1976, pp. 138–139) affirms that the infallibilist tradition is not sustainable even in mathematics, where the 'logic of discovery' and the 'logic of verification' are intrinsically a unit (p. 37).

In fact, Jevons had argued in the nineteenth century that, far from 'warrants', the truth of empirical statements is conjectural, a viewpoint upheld by modern empiricists from Poincaré to Russell. Quine (1980, p. vii) argues, moreover, that scientific statements share empirical meaning in clusters, and it cannot for the most part be sorted out among them, and that even the most experience-near statements may come be denied – witness Cartesian doubt or the idealistic philosophies' denial of the reality of an external world (Quine, 1961). That only propositions linked directly to observation can be definitely refuted or proved does not involve a belief in 'theory-free' pure data: Mill (1852) knew well that the condition for an observation to be reliable is that it be an observation, not an inference, and that observation and inference are intimately blended. This fits with the idea that scientific facts and theories are historical beings, as held by Collingwood (1946), and with the role of surprise in observation on which Russell and Freud agree: a role prominent, as we shall see, in a counterinductive policy.

If induction, in its more general sense, is inference from the known to the unknown on the basis that 'the future will resemble the past', what, then, is to be understood by counterinduction, a policy that takes the way things have been in our experience as a guide to how they will not be (Blackburn, 1994)? Not all logicians accept such a notion: against Salmon, Max Black (1961) holds that the very idea of a counterinductive policy under the motto that 'the future will differ from the past' is self-contradictory and should be dismissed, while for von Wright (1957) a reasoned counterinductive policy is itself an inductive policy; so in his view, which I share, generalizing induction and counterinduction are aspects of the inductive method. Counterinduction as a policy of refutation of earlier inductive generalizations is unlike Popper's (1963, 1983) falsificationism, where only formalized hypotheses can be falsified, and they must be falsified experimentally in crucial experiments. In the case of the analysand, the unknown 'theories' to be elicited and ostensively refuted pertain to the relational unconscious, while the analyst's operational theories range from those working at unconscious and preconscious levels as part of the countertransference, to his more or less explicit theories of psychoanalytic theory and technique.

If to Mill (1852, p. 383) inductive generalization extends to a class of cases something observed to be true in certain individual instances of the class, counterinduction is definable as the observational rejection of such class in individual cases. In this manner, counterinduction goes from an unknowing use of the general to, first, the ostensive differentiation of the particular and then to the grasp of the up to then unknown theory-in-use. In Quine's (1981) terms, this involves making explicit and ostensively refuting unknown observation categoricals.

I shall argue that the psychoanalytic method is a prime example of a reasoned counterinductive policy. Blackburn (1994) comments that it is exceedingly difficult to try to explain what a counterinductive policy consists of, so we can follow Feyerabend to an example from the history of science: a fragment of the dialogue of Salviati, standing in for Galileo, who argues that any perception of movement is relative to an observer, and Simplicio voicing the Aristotelian conception of movement as absolute:

> *Salviati:* . . . Imagine yourself in a boat with your eyes fixed on a point of the sail yard. Do you think that because the boat is moving along briskly, you will have to move your eyes in order to keep your vision always on that point of the sail and follow its motion?
>
> *Simplicio:* I am sure that I should not need to make any change at all; not just as to my vision, but if I had aimed a musket I should never have to move it a hairbreath to keep it aimed, no matter how the boat moved.
>
> *Salviati:* And this comes about because the motion which the ship confers upon the sail yard, it confers also upon you and upon your eyes, so that you need not move them a bit in order to gaze

> at the top of the sail yard, which consequently appears motionless to you. . . .
>
> (quoted by Feyerabend, 1988, p. 67)

Other fragments of the *Dialogue* are just as illustrative. Beyond Galileo's rhetoric, what is relevant is his drawing his partner into a thought-experiment. His new viewpoints for description allow his partner to attain ostensively hitherto unnoticed aspects of his experience, imaginatively pointing with the gaze or the musket on mnemic screens, and achieve through comparisons an experiential 'testing' of his theory of movement: Salviati thus shows Simplicio that his Aristotelian views are not true to his own experiences. Using new viewpoints for describing his partner's experiences, he aims at his 'implicit theories', which now become explicit through a better description. In this case, as in psychoanalysis', this involves a change in the observer's perspective. It must be noted that Galileo's refutation is Aristotelian (rather than hypothetico–deductive) in its method: he draws for the 'thought-experiments' different 'exemplars' from Simplicio's experiences (and from his own!) and has him compare them, ostensively dispelling earlier implicit theories, which allows for new ones.

This shows how fallacious is the idea of a global substitution of Aristotelian by Galilean science, an idea strongly implicit in physicalistic epistemologies such as Popper's and Grünbaum's that upon an Euclidian-like hypothetico–deductive method construe celestial mechanics into a general paradigm of scientificity. They take into account just the qualities of Galilean–Newtonian projectible variables while leaving aside the counterinductive ways new knowledge is built. They leave aside, too, that the applicability of such a formal model is quite restricted: scientific method as used by Darwin to build the theory of evolution is Aristotelian, not Galilean–Newtonian.

An extended use of the admittedly ideal distinctions introduced by von Neumann between tautology and process may help explain how counterinduction works for our purposes. What an ideally pure tautology (such as a logic or a geometrical system) affords is connections between propositions, while a pure description would include all the facts (i.e. all the effective differences) immanent in the phenomena or processes to be described; an explanation being the mapping of description onto tautology[2] (see Bateson, 1979, pp. 86–87).

It would seem that counterinductive use of the psychoanalytic method involves four levels on the part of the analysand: (a) an underlying quasi-tautological level of misconceptual unconscious 'frames' or 'theories' about relationship ruling the analysand's failed inductions; (b) the enacted and verbal derivatives of such misconceptual 'frames', attaining some representability; (c) perceptual and mnemic levels that are partly, but only partly, under the sway of (a); and (d) a capacity to grasp the verbal descriptions and conjectures (i.e. the interpretations) advanced by the analyst about the operation of (a), (b) and (c). I admit, therefore, the operation of two quite different quasi-tautologies in the case of both analysand and analyst, though hopefully used in dissimilar ways: psychic reality, his *unknown* 'deductive' matrix of unconscious 'theories' about relationship, and conscious inferential thought mapped onto language.

I will argue that the psychoanalytical clinical method lets the analysand achieve insight on his psychic reality by giving him the occasion to attain a 'knowledge by acquaintance' of the relational 'classes' that result from his unconscious pragmatic and semantic ways of colligating facts or events; to attain, that is, an experience-near 'reality-testing' in individual concrete instances of the misconceptual 'theories' or 'frames' resulting from early inductive generalizations which, unbeknownst to him, rule his structuring of his relationships and thus provide him with the opportunity to disprove them. The analyst's verbal interpretations are, in my view, subservient to this task: they provide conjectural 'knowledge by description', a temporary 'mapping' by way of an interpretive 'happy Guess', in Whewell's terms, which, if accurate, help the analysand attain a new observational vertex leading to a 'multiple description' on his psychic reality and thereby to a conscious, ostensive refutation or reformulation of his up to now unconscious ways of colligating his relational events. Refutation of his unconscious theories on relationship requires a substantial degree of pragmatic (and semantic) neutrality on the part of the analyst for the necessary ostensiveness to be obtained, this being valid for insights from observations both in and out of session. Let us now sort out clinically the analysand's counterinductive disproof in individual concrete instances of his unconscious ways of colligating events.

Clinical example: part I

As my interest lies in illustrating how the logic of the analytic situation operates, mainly in the analysand's counterinductive, ostensive disproval of his unconscious 'frames' or 'theories' on relationship, I will be very brief as to the history and psychopathology.

Aged 20 at the time, he was brought to analysis at age 15 by his parents who, hitherto convinced of his intellectual poverty in spite of his deftness in dealing with quite complex mechanical objects, were taken aback by the finding of an IQ of 131 at a test made at his paediatrician's prompting. Except for a sole and quite disturbed friend he would contact occasionally, he had no links outside his family, and he lived mainly in what to the parents was a state of distraction, truly of mindlessness. So he had no chance for useful attention at school and read only a few lines at a time; in fact, it was usual for him to fall asleep in class as soon as the teacher would start speaking. In spite of a number of psychopedagogic treatments in childhood, he was fully two years behind his age level at school, and this only because his mother would read volumes to him as exams approached, which, when he did manage to pay attention, he would remember phonographically. Underlying unconscious terror was, at the time he came in, obvious toward a grandparent, and it had led, more generally, to an inhibition of play and aggression that lifted only in a peculiar context: he was an excellent marksman and an enthusiastic hunter. It took him years in treatment to contact with, and then acknowledge feelings of anger or rivalry.

His progression in a classical analytic setting, four times a week, was at first maddeningly slow, but firm nevertheless. We came gradually to understand a basic split in his universe: on one side the world of the Adults, the annihilating Big Ones he avoided or submitted to, the place of all excitement that he cannot 'think'; on the other side his own place, the no-place of the submitting-child-subject-to-annihilation, a place allowing no pleasure, nor any success (this became strikingly clear: whenever he did get a very good grade at school, he would panic, and the following day he would manage to get the lowest grades, which calmed him down immediately). The world of the Adults was felt concretely as a combined-parental-couple locus he was not able to discriminate into separate individuals, so it was a major relief, which he brought up himself, when he managed to feel mother and dad as persons distinct from each other, which allowed him thereafter to handle his contacts to each of them in distinct ways. This happened after years in analysis, when he had gained some social life outside his family and was to a goodly extent out of his protracted postautistic state. He had also gained private spaces for himself, places he did not feel intruded upon by adults. This started on his sailing alone in a small boat for hours on end in a relaxed, vital mood; it continued by his taking his small brother or his cousins for a sail as passengers, enjoying it as long as he and no one else was the captain on board. An enlightening incident threw light on the quite covert rivalry and violence underlying the basic split in his universe: out hunting, targeting his telescopic sights on a big buck deer, he was suddenly struck in a very emotional way by the thought that the buck was unaware of what was happening. When he brought this to his session I mentioned (but this had become clear to him on narrating the event) that what had struck him so was coming in touch with the fact that this was the way he usually felt, both in life and in the session: as the one being targeted on the wrong side of the gun.

This was certainly so when he neared a contact with pleasure or sexuality. By that time he had a sweetheart but seldom mentioned her in the session, and then weeks or months after the relevant event, such as his having his first sexual relations. As happens with post-autistic patients as distinct from neurotic ones, he brought no daydreams. For example, he never spoke about his masturbatory fantasies, but despite this reticence it had been often possible to show him concretely how, as far as pleasure and sexuality are concerned, he experiences me unconsciously as an annihilating rival. It was a momentous time when he did bring in a daydream, the only one that ever came into treatment, but one, he said, he had entertained in many variants: he was the sole man in the universe, he was the only partner to the sole girl, and the only possessor of every gun, car, boat, or plane in the world in which his girl and he unendingly go on and on at his whim. By way of a highly ideal contrast, this daydream provided him with some intellectual grasp on his intolerance to rivals, but no changes came out of it.

Let us now explore in detail the operation of the method as it leads to the analysand's attainment of effective insights by counter-induction on his up to then unconscious processes. At a Monday session he spoke both vividly and at length, which was not the usual custom. He had been quite angry, and to some measure he still was: on Saturday he had gone out sailing with his small brother and two close friends, but instead of handling the sails, his friends just loafed on deck. He became so angry that he threatened never again to invite them; in his fury he lost the mainsail sheet into the mast and had to jury-rig a new one, but in spite of his anger his friends kept on handling the radio transmitter. At some point I asked about his fiancée, S., who usually goes sailing and whom he had not mentioned at all. He responded that she had stayed ashore because of a sore throat. I then remarked amusedly that keeping track of S., and generally, of whatever has to do with sexuality, was a task that he very much throws upon his analyst.

To this he agreed and, amid mild stuttering, said that he realized that when something sexual comes up, he goes mute and has trouble speaking for the rest of the session. Something of that sort had happened to him over the weekend with his grandfather, the one he had been terrified of at the time of starting his analysis and of whom he was now quite fond. Though he was aware that on other sailboats people were fooling around with the radio, he kept asking his friends to stop fooling with the transmitter (it must be said that as such talk went on over authorized channels, not those reserved for emergency use, it did not have the transgressive character he felt it to have). He could not get beyond the idea that the Coast Guard was going to come over the radio at any time with a stark command to stop talking nonsense and clear the radio channel. His friends paid no attention to his protests, and then some girls came on over the radio ('we never knew who they were, they were phantom girls') and they started joking (he, too, though he does not make this explicit), finally swapping phone numbers. Quite attentive to what was going on, his small brother told the story to the grandfather; he would have never dared do so, though by this time he knew full well that the grandfather enjoyed such stories.

I then interpreted to him at some length, in a somewhat humorous vein, that whenever pleasant or exciting events come up, the Coast Guard, the grandfather, and the analyst in the session come to be felt by him like Geneva's morals police in Calvin's time, whose function was to enquire into and obliterate the inhabitants' pleasures. The police had free access to everyone's privacy and the authority to send anyone to the stake for his pleasures, especially for sexual ones. He replied this is just the way he experiences the Coast Guard – watching closely whatever 'exciting' (i.e. sexual) events happen at sea. After a silence he added that on realizing how he experiences the Coast Guard, he can now feel what has been interpreted to him so many times, that when something sexual comes up the analyst turns into a Big One watching him in critical, threatening ways. On saying that he now *feels* what was interpreted, he acknowledges passing from merely intellectual 'knowledge by description' to 'knowledge by acquaintance'.

Some preliminary comments

The weekend scene displays, both directly and in indirect, projected modes, coexisting aspects of his psychic reality: foremost his angry identification with the Big One concerning his stepping upon the pleasurable sexual 'nonsense' of his friends. This identification both is and is not a presence of the analyst, and it is a part of the acting out. But also, the roles of his 'nonsense-talking' friends, putting into play their adolescent sexual excitement, and his small brother's curiosity stand for split-off projected enactments of his own feelings. Splitting is no longer rigid, as it was in the early stages of analysis; at present it is fairly porous, and we may assume that in unacknowledged ways these latter role-enactments are 'known' to the analysand, which may help explain why his anger had no impact. However, to the extent that his psychic reality shifted partly from an identification with the persecutory Big One to a covert sharing in the ongoing sexual excitement enacted by his friends, the role of the persecutory, unconscious, annihilating father–penis passed on to the Coast Guard, and then to the grandfather he cannot share his story with, and later on, in the session, to the analyst, enacting all three to various degrees, the persecutory father–penis claiming for itself, as did Freud's (1912–13) mythic father of the primal horde, a monopoly on women and pleasure. But then, after the second intervention, the analyst rather easily moved on to be felt in the role of a benevolent grandfather – that is, as a more benign paternal imago allowing and sharing in some level of sexual play. This is in neat contrast to the obliteration of action, pleasure, and play amounting to a dematerialization in Ferenczi's (1932b) sense, which had signalled the early years of analysis.

A verbal narrative description in the form of a clinical example telescopes a long, involved multi-levelled process into a given sequence. That said, may we comment that, from a classical Kleinian standpoint, our material illustrates an acting-out of the transference, in the sense of the deflection of a part of what the analysand feels towards the analyst to others in his present life, with whom he enacts his conflicts (Klein, 1952). The said acting-out is 'benign' (Rosenfeld, 1964), part and parcel of an evolving analysis in severe patients. This concept of acting-out rests on a conscious standard, the relationship to the analyst as an actual individual. How the analyst may be said to be, immaterially, so to speak, present or absent in the said acting-out forces us to a logical distinction between the analyst as individual and as transference object within an unconscious relational 'frame'. In this last sense, I shall presently argue, the analyst is very much present in the acting-out.

The first preparatory intervention enquiring about the absence of his girlfriend from his narrative can be taken as a statement on a 'fact', his suppression of his sweetheart and his leaning on me to rescue his sexuality. Posed in deliberately conjectural terms, it brings to his attention an aspect of the underlying relational pattern he enacts, while I do my best to evade enacting the persecutory role he assumedly attributes to me. This persecutory transference role is the one the analysand overtly enacts in his narrative, that of the annihilating monopolizing paternal penis which threatens to throw him out of the 'channel' of his adumbrating and attaining a link with enjoyable sexual female objects, internally and in real-life situations. From this viewpoint the analyst is very much present in his weekend by way of an identification of the analysand with the role the analyst is unconsciously felt to incarnate.

The second intervention, worded as a 'story' in terms of a historical analogy to the Geneva morals police, is more directly interpretative. It is a complex description encompassing the assumed analogy in the analysand's unconscious link to three dissimilar 'individuals', in Susanne Langer's sense, pertaining to distinct ostensive screens, perceptual and mnemic: the Coast Guard, the grandfather, inasmuch as he is feared, and the analyst, three admittedly quite different individuals who, being recruited by a given unconscious theory or 'frame' into an unconscious relational 'class', play an analogous role to the analysand's psychic reality. This intervention attempts to be true to the evolving covert violence in the situation, while keeping as distinct as possible that which is being interpreted from the interpreting analyst as an individual – that is, the message from the messenger. It can be contrasted with a more direct form, such as 'You are telling me that during the weekend you felt me as interfering, like a jealous father, in your wishes to enjoy yourself (or in your sexual enjoyment)', which would tie relational events singly to the analyst as an individual and is less closely descriptive of the evolving dynamics.

In ways he contrasts with mere intellectual verbal 'knowledge by description' such interventions allowed him, towards the end of the session, to attain an *experiential* correlation between the descriptive 'mapping' that interpretation purveys and his unconscious ways of colligating events. Construal of an interpretive mapping of the unconscious 'form' or 'frame' the analysand puts into play as it evolved through several individuals, recruiting them into an unconscious relational 'class', has brought forward a reality testing, advancing an ostensive distinction between the individuals involved (the Coast Guard, the grandfather, and the analyst) and the unconscious 'form' or 'frame' that had up to then encompassed them. To the extent that he attains such reality testing – that is, that he recognizes and consciously refutes the unconscious 'frame' through 'knowledge by acquaintance' of the projective component – the analyst as individual stops being felt as incarnating what he is interpreting. In other words, a conscious 'multiple comparison', verbally from interpretation, ostensively on perceptual and mnemic screens, of his way of perceiving the analyst as part of the unconscious 'frame' of an archaic object opened the road to a new felt perception of his analyst's functioning as a real object. He thus attains in the link to his analyst a genuine distinction of his up to then projected psychic reality and factual reality.

Clinical example: part II

That structural psychic change has come forth is apparent in the next day's session, which started on his recalling – in itself a most unusual feat – the previous one, saying that our talk about the Geneva morals police had been quite useful. Then he turned pleasantly to further weekend material. On Sunday they had gone sailing again. They had twice overtaken a larger boat that luffed successfully, taking their wind off. But on a third attempt he had charged on, claiming his right-of-way loudly, thus forcing the larger sailboat to give in to avoid a collision that, according to the rules of the sea, it would have been responsible for.

This omitted fragment of the weekend narrative shows, perhaps for the first time, an overt reference to a use of, and a pleasure in, aggression at the service of demarcating personal spaces in front of rivals: a significant change as concerns his invariant submission to the Big One with an introversion of aggression on his mental apparatus, leading to dematerialization. The same is true of his demeanour in the session, exposing quite straightforwardly his joy in holding his right-of-way in a context of plain rivalry. Impulses to collide with the analyst are not as yet directly accessible; when this is mentioned, he does not dismiss them, however: he knows now that important feeling-states are often unavailable to him. We are both aware that direct experience of aggression towards the analyst must be left to future evolutions.

The paradoxical context of interpretation

My approach to the concrete stuff of unconscious relational 'theories' or 'frames' starts from Matte-Blanco's (1975) idea that the unconscious does not know individuals, only propositional functions defining the class. Given that the term *propositional function* belongs to logic, I'll first define it. 'Socrates is mortal' is a proposition affirming something of some 'individual' (be it a person or an event). '*X* is mortal' does not affirm something of someone: it is a propositional function that can give way to a myriad propositions when the variable '*X*' is replaced by values that satisfy it. A propositional function (or *propositional form*) defines a class – that is, the set of those values that satisfy it: in this well-worn example, the class of mortals.

That the unconscious patterns or *forms* analysts deal with are not bound to individuals as such is, of course, present in the idea of *Triebe* and in the old term 'imago'. Going into this subject fully would merit a chapter by itself, so I will just take as my example how some four decades ago an intellectual father of Latin American psychoanalysis, Enrique Pichon Rivière, used to express the analogy backing transference interpretation: 'here, now, toward me as it was elsewhere, in the past, with others' – which is to say that the analysand's unconscious equates his relationships to dissimilar individuals and dissimilar moments, and to say also that interpretation seeks to attain a conscious awareness of such unconscious ways or forms of colligating relational events. The idea that relational inductive generalizations resulting from early inductions are built on propositional forms that do not discriminate between individuals as such and also, to varying degrees, do not discriminate between oneself and others, explains that they operate 'deductively', recruiting into their preformed patterns dissimilar individuals, events, or happenings, and that it is patently difficult to attain their conscious refutation as a result of experience in individual instances.

On attending to the patient's verbal and non-verbal utterances, the analyst tries 'to catch the drift of the patient's unconscious with his own unconscious' (Freud, 1923b, p. 239), which allows him by way of 'countertransference working-through' (Urtubey, 1994) to weave his hypotheses on the interplay of multiple and conflicting action-and-emotion relational events: on how these are enacted towards significant people on the outside as apparent in the analysand's narrative and on how these, in turn, relate to the evolving link to the analyst in the session where, says Freud (1912), the fights take place between intellect and instinctual life, between understanding and a tendency to act that, he points out, express a hostile or an unduly intense transference (1914a).

This leads to the core role of analytic neutrality in ostensiveness; after Freud, Strachey (1934) holds that the patient is on the brink of experiencing the analyst as his archaic object, which means he experiences the analyst simultaneously with the qualities of the archaic object and as a factual individual. That *the analyst is/is not* the archaic object bestows the formal qualities of paradox[3] to the interplay of analogic archaic unconscious propositional forms or patterns (psychic reality) and an evolving conscious thought which grasps discrete facts (factual reality) and codifies them in digital verbal language. How the paradox is exacerbated on being interpreted will now guide my re-view of interpretative strategy.

Listening to an interpretation in a persecutory or sexualized context actualizes for the analysand's psychic reality the archaic object to which the interpretation refers: as everybody knows, one should not speak of the devil because the devil cometh. This is a main motive for Bion's (1975) warning that a probing of the unconscious is inseparable from emotional turbulence and it first exacerbates the emotional problems that it attempts to solve. Attempts at interpretive verbalization foster to some degree a coincidence of the messenger with the message he conveys, of the individual who interprets and the class of unconscious action–emotion propositions that are the referent of the interpretation. This must, I believe, hold some priority for interpretative strategy. (In the literature this comes up as the issue of 'tact', the full weight of which to Freud's and Ferenczi is known nowadays owing to Grubrich-Simitis' [1985] studies.) Whenever the analyst is experienced too much as an archaic object, interpretations will not be able to purvey descriptive 'mapping', and they will not then assist the analysand in distinguishing psychic from factual reality.

The clinical material shows how a carefully worded preparatory intervention calling attention to how his fiancée, standing also for his own sexuality, had been obviated in his narrative, brought about some degree of paralysis of free association and a mild stuttering on his part: an analysand prone to find himself on the wrong side of the rifle's sights comes to feel unconsciously at risk on any 'Big One' analyst's intervention on his sexuality. It is crucial, then, that ways of interpreting the transference strive to effectively keep apart what the analyst as transference 'frame' is felt to be enacting and the analyst as an interpreting individual, assumedly 'neutral' as to action. So, though active at purveying appropriate new descriptive viewpoints, he must remain as neutral as is humanly possible at an enactment level.

As it is close to the spell of unmitigated terror, this material is more stark than most on how the basic paradoxical situation is exacerbated when interpretation is (unconsciously) felt as a threat of enactment of the archaic object. This is clearer in postautistic patients than in aggressive narcissistic ones, but in these too an evolving renunciation of narcissistic defences as treatment progresses exposes the child-in-the-adult (Ferenczi, 1932b) – that is, the infantile self – and brings us close to issues of vulnerability.

Ostensions on transferences as enacted meaning 'frames'

Enacted meaning 'frames', Money-Kyrle's 'unconscious theories', proceed 'deductively', leading to missed inductive generalizations in the here and now of the session: they recruit, to use Caper's (1995) apt term, the analysand's perception of his analyst into given, preformed ways of colligating and attributing unconscious meaning to events. Transference as a higher level, metacommunicational, unconscious, enacted meaning 'frame' is the 'context' of a conscious verbal interchange that at best alludes to it by way of the analysand's occurrences. Reference is a conscious affair but, as Etchegoyen

(1986) warns, verbal interchanges in a –K link luring the analyst away from grasping unconscious psychic reality are a main part of each and every analysis.

To return to ostension: being complex, immaterial, and multi-levelled enacted meaning schemes, there can be no direct ostension of transference relational 'frames': they cannot be pointed to saying 'this' in any simple way. Awareness of transference will depend on our grasp of complex, mainly unconscious 'inferences', the diverse 'derivatives' of which must be grasped again and again by the analyst from enactments and allusions in the session and the narrative of what has transpired out of session on the basis of analogies, of 'happy Guesses'.

Here, as Smith (1995) quotes from Russell (1959b, p. 39), 'surprise is a criterion of error' – that is, it is an opportunity for attention to, and for counterinduction on, one's implicit theories. Gribinski (1994) quotes Freud's letter to Ferenczi of August 1915: 'I consider that one should not make theories. They should arrive unexpectedly in your house, like a stranger one hasn't invited'. Likewise, 'counter-transference occurrences' (Racker, 1968) coming by surprise upon the analyst point to clinical 'facts' when our multi-levelled conscious and unconscious ways of colligating events in the session meet incongruously the analysand's unconscious ways of 'deductively' structuring the relationship at a process level and his ways of alluding to it. That clinical 'facts' meet the analyst, counterinductively, whenever his expectations and assumptions are disproved by the events in the session fits in with Feyerabend's (1962) pragmatic theory of observation. Our ways of observing contrast at least two acknowledged or unacknowledged 'theories': one (our consciously available expectations) ties in closer to the analysand's conscious verbalizations; the other (not conscious and even less formalized) erupts, often unexpectedly, from preconscious or unconscious thought and countertransference screening.

As said, the analyst's interpretation, schematically, addresses the analysand on two logical levels: (a) an ostensive one of pointing to, of calling attention to and describing, events or 'facts' based on countertransferential hunches on how the analysand's psychic reality operates, and (b) a metainterpretive level, a wider explicit conjectural mapping on the unconscious 'theory' or 'frame' colligating relational events. Only amid resistances, as part of an advance in a process of insight, does ostensiveness come to be gained – be it on our royal road, dreams, or by way of enactments or verbal occurrences.

According to Etchegoyen (1986), extra-transferential interpretation of present conflict on the 'outside' is preparatory, tactical rather than strategic. Its risk, he says, resides in the fact that the patient may receive it from a transference outlook as threat, blame, complicity, or seduction. It must be added, though, that transference interpretations just as well tend to be heard as emerging from the archaic object the analyst incarnates: as our clinical material shows, too much transference concreteness of the annihilating 'Big One' led to a mild stuttering and to some paralysis of thought upon a simple exploratory question. At any rate, direct interpretations that refer simultaneously both to the analyst and to the archaic object he incarnates often can be only a final stage of an interpretative cycle as a result of which full conscious contact with 'personification' of the archaic object in the analyst has become tolerable.

Transference interpretations, when not grasped due to the hostility or the intensity of the underlying transference, can lead to a repetition in the session of the original traumatic situation. Though unavoidable to a point, this must be kept in mind, as it was by Ferenczi (1932a, 1932b), to whom traumatogenesis in the session was a main concern. A neutral stance demands moment-to-moment attuning to what goes on: countertransference monitoring is the key here. Neutral benevolence towards the feeble contacts with his aggression on the part of a postautistic patient will differ from that required for handling the demeaning onslaught of a phallic–narcissistic analysand or a psychopathic one: countertransference scrutiny provides here, if not ready answers, some useful beacons, should we go astray.

The role of language in enactment

My emphasis has been on the analysand's unconscious pragmatic enactments in the session as metacommunicational 'frames' to the relationship, but the analysand's words are not alien to the process. Language is, in von Neumann's terms, our fundamental tautology allowing description or 'mapping' of the process level of psychic reality and its enactments. Distinction of tautology and process in our domain, though, while valid and important, is only relative: the analysand's use of language in the session is also part of the process.

To the post-Saussurian linguists' idea of language as a system of signs emerging within a community of speakers as a 'pure' tautology with no referents external to itself, and to the logicians' idea of language, after Frege, as a tautology having both meaning and referents, psychoanalysis adds new dimensions. The analysand's use of language is under the impact of the evolving unconscious, and it is put to use to impinge on other people's minds: in Poland's (personal communication, 1995) terms, 'words are awesomely powerful carriers of action'. The analysand's speech, then, maps the external objects that are its referents, but it is modified and acts as a 'carrier' of unconscious emotion. Speech refracts the unconscious in highly personal and changing ways: here language differs from pure deductive tautologies such as Euclidian geometry, subject to no changes in its mapping of, say, a terrain. André Green (1984) rightly insists that language as used in the analytic setting allows us to listen behind the most banal statements to an otherwise imperceptible richness of meanings.

J.-M. Quinodoz (1994) presents a singular example on the use of language as part and parcel of defence. His patient Jacques referred to his parents by their first names in the session, erasing the differences between generations; led by unconscious psychic reality, use of language was put at the service of erasing his dependency link to the parents. This verbal enactment illustrates how, as held by Matte-Blanco (1975, 1988) consciousness thinks in terms of individuals but the unconscious recognizes only 'classes': consciously Jacques acknowledged his parents as such, but unconsciously he did not, as far as he was personally concerned, recognize the 'class' of parents or a relationship to the analyst-as-parent. By his use of their first names, he wiped out emotional contact with the parents' and the analyst's generativeness, as well as his own situation as its offshoot and receiver.

Attempts at verbal description or mapping of the evolving unconscious, be it by the analysand's free associations or by the analyst's interpretations, introduce a selection and a distortion: the map is not the territory, and a description is not reality, whatever reality may be. Any particular interpretative vertex is just a vertex for description of a complex multi-layered process, and often it is the joint use of descriptions under multiple vertices that brings forth the requisite ostension. Choice of terms introduces a bias, be it in the session or in the attempts to conceptualize what happens in the session: so, the term 'unconscious theories' is too intellectual for a 'process' operating as unknown tautologies, this being why I also use alternative terms such as 'unconscious relationships', 'unconscious frames', or 'unconscious propositional forms'.

Unconscious tautologies and internal objects: the 'Class-Object'

What is important beyond the terms chosen is to grasp these 'unconscious theories' as emotional in the sense of conveying unconscious affects, pragmatic in the sense of covert enactments, and relational in the sense of addressing someone present (in the session the analyst) inasmuch as he incarnates an atemporal archaic object.

As I understand it, and here the Darwinian standpoint plays a role, these unknown tautologies assemble in so-called 'internal objects', sets of unconscious propositional forms configuring the analysand's primordial links, and thus his pragmatic and verbal enactments as well as his conscious cognitive ways of structuring his 'reality'. Such an outlook puts right seemingly contradictory features of the Freudian *Triebe*: the power and rigidity of its fixations and that the object is the most variable part of the *Triebe*: as promiscuity makes especially clear, the fixation of the *Trieb* is to a partly representational 'form', while variability of its objects refers to a variability as to *individuals.*

What muddles comprehension here is the issue of 'one-member classes': the main initial biologically determined links are to 'one-member classes' such as 'Mum' or 'Dad', not to individuals as such, and the early '*Class-Objects*' where class and individual coincide are to be at least partly 'negativized' (Green, 1993) in the course of essential mental evolutions. In his Leonardo paper Freud (1910) hints at this when he conjoins acknowledgment of the mother as individual and early grief at the loss of fusional bliss with the breast. Acknowledgment of the other individuals emotional 'otherness' would then involve an ostensive 'negativation' in concrete instances of the said propositional forms. Which means that gaining some distinction between what is projected and the 'individual' is part of everyday life, and psychoanalytic method is just a way of furthering ostensive distinctions not yet attained. Where 'negativation' of primitive affect at the level of the *Class-Object* has not been attained, emotional closeness will evoke unbearable dependency at the level of the symbiotic link, and so it will be felt unconsciously as being *at the mercy of the primary Object,* be it of its 'coldness', its recriminations, or its attacks. Close, intense affectionate links will come then to be felt as a 'softening' of the self vis-à-vis the primary Object, and they are apt thereby to become terrifying, giving rise to switches into crises of fury, or to claustrophobia and flight from the partner. One example may be given by a patient who, on the occasion of emotion and crying of his girl during coitus, asking him never to leave her, feels an unbearable impulse to abandon her, the ensuing internal recriminations pushing him, and often leading him to reverse the situation by becoming 'hard' and sharply recriminatory towards her. In his session he grasped that what had impacted him was an implicit recrimination in her request not to be left; this had been felt – in his terms, when he was able to consciously 'think' the incident – as a 'stab', in quasi-hallucinatory fashion: having 'softened up' in the affectionate contact entails a risk that contacts at the level of the '*Class-Object*' take such stabbing quality to him, which well explains, I believe, the ensuing entrapment in her. His ability to recognize such a state of affairs had been preceded in the previous session, much to his surprise, by his realizing that when he managed to regard her from an 'outside', more objective viewpoint, he'd feel her as a stranger, and affect for her would vanish, he did not feel love for her anymore. This first insight assumes, I believe, somewhat greater tolerance to a distinction between the 'Class-Object' and the girl herself as an individual, and was, I gather, a requisite to his quasi-hallucinatory insight. Another example of an impossibility to establish a distinction of 'Class-Object' and individual is that of a female analysand who came to recognize patently in the session, also to her surprise, that she had, up to then, put forward explicitly her emotional demands to her partners only after she had explosively put an end to the relationship: she realized then that up to such break-up time she had felt her own requirements – and her implicit recriminations – as destructive of the affectionate link – so much so that she had not even managed to 'think' them.

This is far from being a question of purely sensory events. We deal here with primary emotional processes at the level of the symbiotic part of the personality: uncontainable, explosive *hyperaffects* that are, to be sure, full of sensoriality. These hyperaffective processes must be contained and described in detail as they evolve outside and inside the session. In cases such as those just mentioned, more and more commonly nowadays, promiscuity often becomes a main defence: not only does each serially 'new', fleeting relationship allow a contact with the primary Object in a link controlled by fleetingness itself, it also reassures that one has come out alive and whole from earlier bonds.

When the operation of the unconscious comes to be understood in terms of relational propositional forms rather than in terms of individuals, the connection between the two senses of the term 'transference' in Freud's work, the wider one of transference as a component present in any relationship, and the more restricted technical sense referring to the analyst must probably be rethought. 'Transference' and 'extratransference' interpretations vary as to the individuals they make overt reference to rather than in the propositional forms involved. 'Implicit' transference interpretations do describe the ongoing transference link without referring manifestly to the analyst as individual.

Final remarks

As contrasted to Lacan's beguiling but in my view thoroughly misguided idea that 'the unconscious is structured like a language', this chapter upholds the idea that 'the unconscious is structured as affective–pragmatic relational tautologies'. Helping the analysand through adequate interpretative descriptions to an ostensiveness on such affective–pragmatic quasi-tautologies is a main part of the analytic work that in 'Lines of Advance of Psychoanalytic Therapy' (1919) Freud compares to chemical analysis: getting the analysand to grasp his heavily composite unconscious mental formations: breaking them into their component elements, that is, into *individually* ostensive constituents, allowing counterinduction on his unconscious 'theories'.

Study in logical terms on how the analysand attains a knowledge of his unconscious 'theories' about relationship offers a strongly complementary perspective to Etchegoyen's contributions on the validation of interpretation in the clinical setting. A firm allegiance to method, and attention to the manner in which clinical psychoanalysis proceeds *per via di levare,* are not the least of the gains the author has profited from in his 30-year-long association as supervisee, co-worker, and friend of Horacio Etchegoyen.

9

Logical and communicational levels of transference

My purpose in this chapter is to study in terms of logical levels the theory of transference, which, says Money-Kyrle (1978a) in his final paper, being perhaps the most mysterious aspect of psychoanalysis, is what makes analysis possible.

Betty Joseph on transference

Let me illustrate my ideas on the clinical material in Betty Joseph's 'Transference, the Total Situation' (1985). Stressing transference as a *framework*, she quotes Klein (1952) to the effect that it should be thought of in terms of *total situations* transferred from the past into the present, as well as emotions, defences, and object relationships. These total situations must include everything that the patient brings into the relationship, specially 'how he is using the analyst, alongside and beyond what he is saying' (p. 447), grasped mostly through the feelings aroused in us – that is, through the countertransference in a broad sense. Interpretations bring the patient's basic assumptions in the analytic situation into the open, so that these can be experienced as his psychic reality; only later, and slowly, should they be tied to history. If interpretations and understanding, says Joseph, 'remain on the level of individual associations, as contrasted with the total situation and the way that the analyst and his words are *used*, we shall find that we are being drawn into a pseudo-mature or more neurotic organization and missing the more psychotic anxieties and defenses, which manifest themselves once we take into account the total situation – which is being acted out in the transference' (p. 453, emphasis added).

Her clinical material is as follows:

> The dream was: there was a kind of war going on. My patient was attending a meeting in a room at the seaside. People were sitting round a table when they hear a helicopter outside and knew from the sound that there was something wrong with it. My patient and a major left the table where the meeting was going on and went to the window to look out. The helicopter was in trouble and the pilot had bailed out in a parachute. There were two planes, as if watching over the helicopter, but so high up that they looked extremely small and unable to do anything to help. The pilot fell into the water, my patient was wondering whether he would have time to inflate his suit, was he already dead, and so on.
>
> I am not giving the material on which I based my interpretations, but broadly I showed him how we could see the war that is constantly raging between the patient and myself, which is shown in the way in which he tends to turn his back, in the dream, on the meeting going on at the table, on the work going on from session to session here. When he does look out knowing that something is wrong (as with the helicopter) he sees that there is an analyst, myself, the two planes, the two arms, the breasts, watching over to try to help him, but he is absorbed watching the other aspect, that is the part of himself, the pilot, that is in trouble, is falling out, dying – which is the fascinating world of masochism. Here I mean that he shows his preference for getting absorbed into situations of painful collapse rather than turning to and enjoying help and progress.
>
> At the time he seemed, as the session went on, to get well into touch with these interpretations, and to feel the importance of this fascination with his masochism.
>
> (Joseph, 1985, pp. 449–450)

On the following day the patient related that after working on the dream he had felt concerned about his rejecting and fighting and his excitement when he gets so involved; while to some point this was insight, he spoke in a flat, almost boring way. This, Joseph showed him, was a silent war, to which he gloomily replied: 'There seems to be no part of me that really wants to work, to cooperate'. As she was starting to show him that this could not be quite the case, since he actually comes to analysis, she had realized that she would be acting as an active, positive part of him projected into her. In this way, she was trapped into either living this positive part, which he would not feel his, or agreeing that there was no part of him willing to cooperate. This the patient said he understood, but he was able to do nothing with or about it: now the silent war in the dream was lived out in the transference. Some emergent memories gave the clue that the problem was in the acknowledgement and the recognition of his improvement, which would mean giving in to his elders and giving up some of the pleasure of defeating her. While the patient no longer felt stuck, he felt it was the analyst's initiative, as 'a kind of Pied Piper', that had pulled him out, just as, as a child, he had felt seduced by his mother. Then he quickly, very quickly, added, says Joseph, that there was also the other fear of getting caught up into excited warm feelings, like the feeling he used to call 'puppyish'.

On representation in dreams and action

The unconscious mind shows to Matte-Blanco (1975) the qualities of a space of more than three dimensions, and *hyper*spaces of more than three dimensions cannot be visually imagined. We can visualize a two-dimensional square having lines for its sides as well as a three-dimensional cube having two-dimensional squares for faces, but we cannot visualize a four-dimensional hypercube with three-dimensional cubes as its 'faces'. In analytic geometry a space of a higher number of dimensions can only be represented in a space of a lower number of dimension through repetition of its elements: a bi-dimensional triangle is represented one-dimensionally by three elements, its sides. The same tendency to a repetition of elements is true, says Matte-Blanco, of dreams. To depict the ways in which the unconscious experiential psychic 'hyperspace' of more than three dimensions attains representability in dream-space through the repetition of its elements, Jiménez (1990) has taken up Joseph's material as follows:

1 The patient's self is represented at least twice in the dream: once as the 'observing' ego which turns its back on 'the table

> where the meeting was going on' to look out of the window at the helicopter and the pilot and which is fascinated by this vision of danger; and once as the pilot himself falling into the water. We therefore have here a split in the self, in which the observing ego is pervaded with masochistic fascination and excitement, as will become clear in the subsequent elaboration of the dream.
>
> 2 The analyst–object also appears split, firstly as the enemy which is not represented directly but is present through the war atmosphere, and secondly as the two planes flying so high that they are unable to help. This is then the typical split between a 'bad', persecuting analyst and an idealized analyst. The major who accompanies the patient to the window is probably also a representation of the analyst, who is caught up in the masochistic manipulation. . . . We could proceed further and suppose that the allusion to 'people sitting around the table' is a representation of the analytical situation, in which the analyst assumes different transference roles which the patient projects on to him. Hence the analyst is represented at least twice and perhaps three or more times.
>
> (p. 462)

Both Joseph and Jiménez work on the basis of a series of to-and-fro analogies between the representational contents of the dream on the one hand, and action and emotion as they evolve in the link to the analyst on the other. What they call a 'split' is the coexistence of contradictory relationships in both dream and action, addressed to the person of the analyst. Joseph's main emphasis is on how these 'splits' appearing in the dream are made explicit by their being lived out through action in the session. These contradictory relationships can, in Matte-Blanco's terms, be seen as unconscious propositional forms unfolding in the link to the analyst. Further on I consider this material in terms of Bateson's views on the 'logics' of relationship, but first I must introduce his concepts.

Bateson on the logical levels of 'relationship'

Bateson states (1955, p. 150) that beyond the seemingly simple denotative level ('the cat is on the mat') two quite different sets of hierarchical levels must be taken into account: the *metalinguistic*, in which the object referred to is the language itself, and the *metacommunicative*, which refers to the relationship setting the 'contexts' and 'metacontexts', that is, the different levels of hierarchical '*frames*' *for the action and emotion relationship* of the interlocutors. These 'frames' are usually implicit: tonal, gestural, and situational rather than verbal; they pertain to the analogic action and emotion codes of our mammalian *Anlage* rather than to the digitalized verbal codes of language.

All along mammalian evolution, attempts to discriminate between categories pertaining to different logical levels tend to assume the qualities of paradox, which to Bateson (1973) are intrinsic to an evolving communication. It was argued in chapter 1 that ostensive insight comes through out of the evolution of a pragmatic paradox which, in terms of a cognitive use of language, can, in its simplest form, be stated thus: the analyst '*is/is not*' the archaic object. In Freudian terms, the paradox can be said to involve the 'psychic' reality of the unconscious thing-presentation, on the one hand, and the 'factual' reality of conscious thought linked to word-presentations on the other.

Language, says Bateson, following Russell, is an attempt at 'explanation' – that is, at 'mapping' a process level that, in the case of the psychic reality that analysis purports to 'map', is relational, hyperdimensional, and primarily unconscious. It is well known to logicians that everyday language fails to discriminate between the different levels of language (object-language and metalanguage), as evidenced by the paradox of the liar. It must be added that it fails to take into account the multi-levelled structure of relational frames.

From the standpoint of the theory of logical levels of language, the language in which we speak is one level higher than the language being spoken about (Reichenbach, 1947, p. 223); so from a conscious cognitive standpoint verbal statements about a 'factic' reality would by definition be considered a metalevel to relational psychic reality. But while this may be correct from the cognitive standpoint, we must be aware that, by proposing his hierarchy of metacommunicative frames, Bateson is positing what can be called *a theory of pragmatic relational levels* modelled upon, but dealing with elements with qualities quite distinct from, those of the theory of logical levels in language. A conceptual leap is here present: as both Sharpe (1940) and Matte-Blanco stressed, verbal language was built up for describing physical objects, and its sole approach to a description of psychic reality is through 'physical' metaphor. So, only events happening in three-dimensional 'physical' space can be ostensively denoted and described in language, and, as we shall presently see, the functioning of the pragmatic relational levels of psychic reality and that of logical levels in language would seem to run, in a crucial way, contrarily to each other.

Freud and Bateson agree, from their own perspectives, on the primacy of unconscious relational reality as contrasted with conscious linguistic reality. From the standpoint of technique we must take into account this (unconscious) pragmatic priority of psychic reality: in Batesonian terms, that 'the relationship comes first, it *precedes*' (1979, p. 143), this primacy being valid too for its action and emotion context and metacontext 'frames'. Bateson goes as far as to say that *an important relationship is the most general 'context of context of context'*, and *within* it 'contexts' (events) and 'contexts of contexts' (classes of events) are set (1973, p. 246–249; 1979, p. 130). Important relationships are of two main kinds: that to the nurturing mother, and that to the head of the pack or group.

While not easy to grasp, this Batesonian line of thought is hardly surprising. As analysts – but this is definitely not the case for logicians and philosophers – we have learnt from Freud that *the world of verbal statements and logic is but a conscious subset to a wider world of unconscious relationship*. The denotative level, the *object-language* (Reichenbach, 1947) which refers to physical individuals and facts or events, seems simple and 'primary' because it is – as Freud made clear of word-presentations – readily available to consciousness. It is the analyst's task to find ways to bring to light the fundamentally analogic metacommunicative 'contexts' and 'metacontexts' of relationship.

The analyst's neutrality

Bateson (1973, p. 250) argued that by ignoring the theory of logical types, behavioural scientists can claim to some six decades of obsolescence. Whether or not this so, a concept of transference encompassing varying levels of relational propositional forms can, in my opinion, be shown in Betty Joseph's definition of transference as a 'total situation' in which, to use her own terms, how the patient 'is using the analyst, alongside and beyond what he is saying' (p. 447) – that is, the 'action-relationship' – sets the *frame* or 'context' to what the patient puts into words. The 'frame', then, is unconscious and relational and is disclosed as enacted transference, and we consider as 'events' or 'facts' that which, coming to be denotable in the three-dimensional spaces of the dream or of action, can be ostensively described.

'Psychic' reality must become in some way 'factic' to be ascertained consciously: it can be unconsciously and then consciously grasped only as it unfolds in that peculiar royal road to the unconscious, the 'physical-like' tridimensional space of fantasies or dreams, or in perceived or remembered tridimensional physical space; that in such ways it becomes verbally describable is an assumption underlying Sharpe's (1940) and Matte-Blanco's idea that psychic reality cannot be described except metaphorically through physical analogy.

It was pointed out before that in an important way, levels of language and pragmatic relational frames appear to function in contrary ways. What can more readily become conscious and be enunciated in language as 'facts' seems to pertain to an emotionally and relationally *lower* dimensional type; from experiences of a higher – and less verbalizable – dimensional type would seem to derive, in the final instance, all meaning. The 'action' and 'emotion' relational 'frames' to the interchange pertain to a level of a higher number of dimensions than tridimensional 'factic' space, this being the level of *transference as 'context' and 'context of context'* to the verbal messages addressed to the analyst. Benevolent neutrality, Freud's prescription for the analyst's attitude, helps set the higher receptive 'frame' to the patient's evolving transferences – that is, to the unconscious relational 'contexts' and 'contexts of contexts' he posits in the session. In the analytic situation the unconscious relational 'class' object of psychic reality (the internal object) is incarnated in the analyst as physical, tridimensional 'factic' object and can then be subject to a first unconscious and then conscious ostensive 'reality testing'.

The elusive relational 'context of context of context': the analyst as 'base'

The higher dimensional 'context of context of context' can perhaps be adumbrated by each analyst on the basis of his experiences in the session but not directly shown or described: this higher dimensional context is, it seems to me, what Money-Kyrle called the 'base', the primal link to a breast–mother 'to which the body-ego orients itself as its "home" ' (1968, p. 424), from which the other kinds of links branch off, and on which sanity depends. Classic terms such as 'regression' no doubt relate to it, as is the distinction of an 'early transference' coming into analysis through repetition (Ferenczi, 1932b; Etchegoyen, 1982) – that is, through the ways the patient uses the analyst. Matte-Blanco's 'symmetrization of classes' approaches it in terms of symbolic logic, but use of the theory of types adds in my view further precisions.

In looking, in Betty Joseph's material, for clues having to do with the patient's contact with this elusive and all-embracing level corresponding to the breast–mother transference and the analyst-as-base, I consider the following clues:

1 In the dream, the patient 'was attending a meeting in a room *at the seaside*'.
2 Also in the dream, 'the pilot fell *into the water*, and the patient was wondering whether he'd have time to inflate his suit, was he already *dead*, and so on'.
3 As the sessions evolved, the patient no longer felt stuck, but he [said he] felt it had been the analyst's initiative, '*as a kind of Pied Piper*', that had pulled him out, just like, as a child, he had felt seduced by his mother.
4 The patient's quick acknowledgement of a fear of getting caught into excited warm feelings he used to call 'puppyish'.

Joseph's material describes the many-sided vicissitudes of a process of insight, but I will restrict myself to what can be shown by these clues. There can be few doubts that the meeting in a room at the seaside and the pilot falling into the sea, dead if he did not manage to 'inflate', refer to a contact with the wider relational 'frame' to the material. While the patient can be said to be *personified*, in a split-off way, by the pilot, his higher-order unconscious relationship to a primal object – irresistibly attractive and deadly – 'framing' the material is not: it appears on the one hand as an *atmosphere*, the war atmosphere, and on the other as a boundless expanse, the sea. It can be argued, and this is indeed the case with other patients, that the boundless expanse takes on by itself this double dimension, both beautiful and deadly. In literature this is strikingly pictured in Baudelaire's *Hymne à la Beauté* [Hymn to Beauty]: '*Viens-tu du ciel profond ou sorts-tu de l'abîme, O Beauté'* [Did you fall from heaven or surge from the abyss, O Beauty?]. In the guise of the far-off aeroplanes that are unable to help the wider context is indeed hinted at, but in terms of its negative, the non-helping analyst. The person of the analyst appears in various ways in the dream, but mostly as she pertains to relational 'contexts' split-off from the wider unconscious 'frame'.

Later on, at the time when the patient no longer feels stuck, this more general frame evolves from the unconscious psychic hyperspace 'atmosphere' or 'boundless expanse' to tridimensional personification in the analyst in the session as 'a kind of Pied Piper', an irresistibly beguiling and sinister character attracting child unconscious aspects to their death by drowning. So at this point in the session a wide-ranging unconscious 'symmetrization of classes' operant in the transference has come to be ostensive and then put into words: Pied Piper analyst equals (or 'realizes') seductive–sinister mother.

It would seem that only then, when this sinister aspect of the higher-dimensional 'context of context of context' has evolved 'carnally' by personification in the three-dimensional-space link to the analyst, can 'reality-testing' come into play. The multilevelled structure of unconscious relationship and the dynamics of ostensive insight can be tied in at this point: as pointed out in chapter 1, the analysand's reality testing is perforce ostensive, and it comes about in the measure that the analyst's neutrality withholds the validation of archaic relational reality. In Joseph's material, only after she is *ostensively* perceived as a Pied Piper can this relational link be refuted and she be acknowledged as 'non-Pied Piper'; the childlike unconscious aspects can then evolve, allowing the patient to get in touch with warm feelings to breast–analyst – though perhaps the patient still 'inflates' himself somewhat on calling these feeling 'puppyish'.

It is my impression, and probably on calling attention to the transference as 'frame' it was Betty Joseph's assumption too, that crucial changes in analysis take place at the level of these higher-order unconscious 'frames'. This would explain the discrepancy, after successful analyses, between the broadness of psychic change and the analysand's relative paucity of conscious memories of his analytic process and of pertinent interpretations.

10

The double work on the clinical evidences, and the nature and limits of symbolization

In memoriam Agostino Racalbuto

From Freud on, in psychoanalysis the terms mind or psyche cover different levels, from the consciously graspable and verbally enunciable to the enacted level that Freud somewhat mysteriously calls the unconscious 'thing-presentations'; these, coupled with the drives in the realm of the unconscious and the repetition compulsion, might be better named 'presentations of relationship'. On speaking of the realm of the unconscious, I refer not only to the repressed, but also to what the later Freud calls the unrepressed unconscious, which gives the background for Matte-Blanco's (1975, 1988) fundamental assertion that while the conscious mind thinks in terms of individuals and their qualities, *the unconscious does not recognize individuals, only classes.*

Before going into the clinical material, let me say that my approach to objectivity centres less on testing my interpretations or theories than on how the analysand explores *his/her* 'unconscious theories': that is, on how she/he gains viable 'evidence-realism'. As I see it, our clinical work involves, for *both* analysand and analyst, an evolving logic of disclosures and refutations, with no way to separate neatly the contexts of discovery and verification.

'Theory-realisms', be they Platonist like Popper's or 'strict inductivist' like Grünbaum's, take as premise the feasibility of reduction of the phenomena in all sciences to homogeneous 'well-behaved' variables such as those in classical Newtonian mechanics: such mechanistic/formal stances conflate objectivity with strict predictability – which, to put it mildly, does not fit either the nature of psychic processes or that of the clinical interchanges. My stance on objectivity leans on a '*pattern-realism*' mapping the unfoldings of the repetition compulsion at the crossroads of an unconscious logic of classes and a conscious logic of individuals. The multiplicities of such 'pattern-realism', where advances in *evidential mapping* are conjecturally brought about by the analyst's interpretations, allow the analysand, by way of 'multiple correlations' in his perceptual and mnemic screens, to access and modify his/her up to then unknown 'unconscious theories'.

A caveat at this point: the clinical material shows the analysand traversing a variety of paradoxes, which complicates description a great deal and may be seen as putting an unfair load upon the reader; however, such a load mirrors the burden on the analyst in the clinical process. The evolving clinical sequence shows the ups-and-downs in the process of a woman approaching 50 who, contrary to what two patients of mine suggested, namely her overbearingness and transgressiveness, came in as a run-down emergency, as she put it in her first telephone call.

On opening the office door for the first interview, I met no one there: then I saw her, collapsed as a hunched form in the corner to my right; a moment passed before she responded. After coming in, she stated off the cuff that she feared an imminent breakdown, that she would stop functioning: thought deserted her when most needed, and she chose wrongly where it most mattered. Two earlier analyses brought support in difficult times but little grasp of what had gone wrong. She had kept off treatments for years after interrupting a five-year-long Lacanian analysis by running from the couch after an interpretation felt as unbearably traumatic: as she wryly remarked, 'I'm a veritable example of subjective destitution'. Thinking that I was her only hope, she came after years of considering how the two patients of mine to whom she was close had evolved.

When I mentioned her collapse at the door, she was rather surprised and said she had not noticed it, but that it fitted what she knew about her collapses. Collapse at the analyst's office door may rightly be considered as a first *clinical fact*, to be unfolded and enquired upon along the process. However, it is the analysand's contact with such evidence and then its recognition in terms of her acknowledged history that instances an operative mapping of her psychic processes, a viable if initial insight. While arguably having a kernel of predictability on the rigidities of the unconscious processes propelling them, the requisite unfoldings occur via in principle *un*predictable 'transformational cycles' (Bion, 1965).

On her close link to my two patients, I told her I was unsure about the requisite space for treatment, and asked her to evaluate this. She was late for a second interview, saying that she had felt my doubt as a cataclysmic rejection; coming again was a huge effort. Though reassured by my decision to treat her, she made it clear that she felt entitled to a grudge. She came back, she said, because for the first time in her analyses she had felt she associated freely. Based on what had already unfolded, namely her collapse in front of the closed office door and her traumatic therapeutic history on the couch, as well as her cataclysmic feelings of rejection, I asked her whether she would rather work face to face for the time being. Much relieved, she confirmed that on the couch she often fell into insurmountable silences.

From infancy on, blighted expectations had led to psychic paralysis: in her words, to 'falling into a hole'. Her first marriage, when she was quite young, was to an older divorced man anxious to have children: as she put it, 'To him I was a womb, to breed the children he yearned for'. But her transgressive wishes to break away from a highly dysfunctional family can also not be ignored. Her last marriage, to a quite immature man, had left her with all sorts of debts: while relieved at the rupture because their life together had been chaotic, the lack of human presence again threw her into her psychic hole.

After collapsing, she went blank, finding relief in the bathtub, where she stayed for hours, and then it took her days in bed to get back into shape, only to collapse again because of new mishaps. On journeys abroad she was vital and resilient, but she had no idea why. Back in town, her vitality and enthusiasm faded after a fortnight; thereafter she collapsed, which she attributed to feeling drained by tasks at work and at home. We learnt in due course that kind gestures felt as motherly, such as a warm email from a friend, often helped her out of her collapse.

On the fragility of her emotional 'base' (Money-Kyrle, 1968) – or, as Tustin (1986) puts it, of her place in the 'womb in the mother's mind' – the first analytic weekends were proof to her of my aloofness and lack of interest. Incidents in the session turned devastating; when after a Tuesday's session I said 'till Thursday' instead of 'till tomorrow', her universe collapsed: though consciously she saw this as a minor error, it renewed her impression of my not being dependable, as well as her felt destiny of being arbitrarily rejected.

As the months went by, she gradually came to better observe and register how her world collapsed. But this, in turn, posed a paradox: insights were poorly distinguishable from falling anew into trauma, and they ushered in self-reproaches on her inability to think, so she dismissed insights as worthless. We came to grasp that she had no awareness of her anger and then would explode on minor issues, such as happened when a friend against whom she had an undetected gripe dropped a piece of cake on her rug: she went into a fit of boundless fury, saying things she had not thought before and had not intended to say. Work on such incidents allowed her some contact with her split-off furies as distinct from her all-too-available hopeless collapses. Nonetheless, since she felt that her hates were insoluble, contacting them was again felt as useless.

Exploring her frozen hates led to a frozen infancy and a frozen mother, who often said that children were but a bother: she dressed her daughters primly and did not allow them to play so that they would not get dirty, and she allowed no choices: dolls were the only toys for her sisters and for her. My patient's main game was to be mother to her younger siblings; she did not rebel, as did a younger sister, whom the mother would then harshly punish. She sees herself as having been a withdrawn and sad child, saying this is what photographs show. The only happy memories from her childhood she could recall at the start took place not at home but at her grandparents' house nearby, and later on at school, which was felt as a blessing as it allowed an alternative to the emotional wasteland at home. About her mother she says that she lived in houses full of mirrors, fascinated by her own image; her only tender contacts with her involved a reversal of roles, as they took place on lengthily combing her mother's hair, which the mother much enjoyed. My patient, who was dark-skinned while her sisters were fair, received black dolls as presents; later on, in adolescence, her mother used to tell her that no man would love her, because her skin was dark and no one would cherish her dark nipples. She saw her mother, even now in old age, as undaunted and immortal, with neither wrinkles nor feelings ('I never saw her cry'); she envies mother's invulnerability while seeing herself as run down by affects and by mother's critique: only once in her life has she stood up to her, but cannot remember in what context. Similarly, she often feared in the session that I might eject her arbitrarily, or that she might feel expelled through some error of mine.

To her surprise, work on these issues brought up memories of loving people, one of them caring for her in infancy, the other in later childhood; with this last she spoke fluent French, and she realized in the session that on trying now to speak French, she loses her voice. She also better grasped her usual behaviour with her adolescent son and the son's father who, after promising to come, would not show up: this inevitably took her by surprise, and she went to pieces on finding that she was unable to provide the boy with a worthy father. At other times father and son, in complicity, invaded her flat, eating and drinking everything in sight and romping around like kids. Unable to stop their invasion, she felt despoiled and collapsed soon afterward. Such incidents were understood in terms of the splitting-off of her own aggression jointly with her self-positing as an irreparably orphaned girl: much to her relief, by working on this she gradually came to set some limits.

This brought a memory from age 5, at which time mother's adored brother had died in an accident close to Christmas-time. After his death, Christmas was never again celebrated at home. Work on this memory allowed her to view mother as not only devastating but also as devastated, which lessened mother's felt invulnerability and her fear of her. She thus eventually came to see her family of origin not only as unjust and cruel but as being themselves disturbed in themselves and in their monetary mishandlings (amounting to despoiling and self-despoiling family-wide delusional enactments): thereafter, for the first time she came to be able to bear and sort out some entangled inheritance issues.

Though consciously she appreciates my unobtrusiveness and puts this appreciation into words, her negative transference shines through in her often coming late, in her persistent feelings that analysis and the need for thinking things through are part and parcel of the injustices of life, in her hugely resenting my fees, and in a depressed mood in the session due to her rancour at my not alleviating her pain as fully as she felt I should. Her unremitting unconscious demand for a mother who would alleviate all malaise was put into action out of session in a role reversal whereby she enacted the role of an enthusiastic mother to her adolescent son, and to her grandchildren.[1] Here also, though, she fell into the 'hole' whenever her loved ones did not respond as she expected, or when they happened to leave. Gradually she grasped that her costly maternal crusades provided for others what unconsciously she desperately demanded for herself: she often went to pieces in the attempt, as the following incident illustrates. She was at home in the morning, her son was close to waking, and it came upon her to offer him a special treat for breakfast. At a nearby bakery she found wonderful croissants, but then the idea crossed her mind that her son would not grasp how much they witnessed her love for him, and she collapsed on this idea, bodily sensations included. On taking heed of the dynamics of her emotional collapses, she became better able to receive affect, first from a small favourite granddaughter, then from her friends. But the more tender the affect, the worse were the ensuing separations: on departing, her loved ones 'fell off' her inner world, she again entered an emotional wasteland and fell into her psychic 'hole'. The vicissitudes of a long weekend in the countryside abroad illustrate the ongoing paradoxes. She had felt quite attentively cared for at a small inn and felt very well there, but on coming back to the city she spent a day in a state of stupor and the next one in a fury at herself for thus being, as well as being furious at me for not helping her be otherwise.

Shortly afterwards, on coming to her session, she became furious with a man walking by stiffly in a manner she felt characteristic of locals while foreigners she found to be more natural, free and relaxed; this helped us grasp why she felt so bad in the city and that she could imagine herself doing and feeling well only when away from it. The infuriating starchy stiffness was traced to mother's artifice and coldness in relating, and she sarcastically added it was good that I am not short in height, as her mother is. Here we find what Matte-Blanco calls a *symmetrization of classes*, as it turned out that the city itself was equated to a frozen/freezing unconscious mother embodied in its starchy inhabitants, the analyst included. As we shall see later on, such equation, which after Klein and Segal is known as a symbolic equation, might be better called an *iconic equation*, where iconicism is linked to a massive failure in symbol-formation.

Her inability to become openly angry at me, flagrant at the start, then connected in her mind with what, being a teacher, she had read about deprived children who, when angry, bite and lacerate themselves instead of getting angry at their parents. Starting to show anger, she recalled a dream at age 5 in which she was furiously sticking knitting needles into a breast. This remembered oneiric image she linked to her asking her parents for money to buy knitting needles, which her father had refused, saying it made no sense to spend money on such things; this she took to mean they had no place for her – nor for children generally. On recounting the dream, she had felt vivid wishes to stick needles into me. I then managed to tell her that as I saw it, the dream might be alternatively thought of in two ways, the most obvious one in terms of her now frequent wishes to attack me, or alternatively, reversing the roles, as illustrating her dilemma that the more she feels me as a breast, the more she herself feels exposed to lacerations and pain.

Contact with her Furies again flared up into an all-or-nothing dilemma: thus, though she no longer smokes, she lights up a cigarette in the session, saying, 'better to smoke than to kill you'. And it is true that on coming to the fore, her Furies can hit: at about that time, angry at the boy's father for not sending money, she took a taxi and went to his office, armed with a can of paint, which she duly splattered over documents and furniture.

Clues came up on why after the wreckage of another marriage she did not fall into her empty depression and had been able, instead, to keep active and to successfully work and study. This marital rupture had involved overt, at times physical violence, and afterwards she was able to keep up her studies and a defiant political militancy against the then ruling military regime, at which period she dressed up in a sort of Maoist uniform despite not being a Maoist. She felt happy and sure of herself in her rebel uniform, which she used at all times, night outings included, until it came apart.

In a dream, she was with her granddaughter and a 3-month-old baby; her grand-daughter was telling her that the baby was dirty, and on checking the nappy, the baby talked, saying he/she was dirty: she had felt afraid in the dream at realizing that she herself was the baby, this being why her own efforts felt so strenuous. The next day, while on errands around the city, she had to stop along the way at several cafés that sustain her just as travels do, and had ended up exhausted. During the day she had several soft bowel movements, which had never happened before and which she linked to the baby's in the dream (analysis had relieved her, shortly before, of a constipation that had required her to take strong laxatives from infancy on). Later in the day she had an amiable telephone call from her gym teacher, whose group she had missed for days: she had gone there but would not enter, as she felt that she would not be recognized. She noticed the discrepancy between the warm telephone call and her own inability to keep receptive attitudes alive, realizing that this happened all the time in connection with her absent children and grandchildren. Also, she commented that the call had got her out of the 'hole', and she came to reflect calmly on the damage brought by her not being able to retain a viable memory of her affects. These insights made her feel better, but they also heightened her conflict with me, as 'nothing should get better, because whatever is treasured turns unpredictable and then collapses'. Inasmuch as progress in analysis brings her to a state of trauma, the process is designated by paradoxes and it often approaches a negative therapeutic reaction. The fact that analytic insights and progress again and again evoked the traumas of swindle, she linked to how she had felt cheated from infancy on, such as the innumerable times she had had to leave the pleasurable enclave of her grandparents' house in order to go back to the encapsulated coldness of her home and her mother.

A triumphant–revengeful association in face of the trauma of encapsulation by her trapping–voiding–swindling objects (her analyst, of course, included) shows up in her recalling the final images in a Swedish film that she had happened to see two full decades earlier, where the protagonist felt her sanity go to pieces falling into schizophrenic annihilation. As she went into psychosis, she wilfully contemplated how her children, her husband, and also her analyst – whom she had invited for dinner – ate the poisoned grapes that she had served at the table.

The clinical unfolding of the evidence

Let me begin by recalling that not long ago, at a presentation at the British Society, I was greeted with a roar of friendly laughter when, asked about the nature of evidences, I responded that the trouble with evidences is that they are not evident. Then, in order to regain my footing and stitch things together, I managed to add that evidences not being evident is the reason why we psychoanalysts need to stick to the method.

The *unfolding process* – that is, the process whereby evidences unfold – is a favourite term that Matte-Blanco employed to highlight a central issue of clinical processes. Coming back to what in the clinical material I characterized as a first *clinical fact*, my analysand's collapse in front of the closed office door, here my surprise delimited and highlighted what I took to be a relevant, indeed a striking piece of evidence involving twin, allied dimensions of ego collapse and relational collapse. But even such a glaring piece of clinical evidence does not readily surrender its various layers of meanings: oncoming evidences do not charitably relieve us of the work of enquiry: on the contrary, they bolster it and are steps into it. Even when, as happened here, they are thrown in one's face, clinical evidences are anything but transparent.

Clinical evidences cannot be thought of as 'theory-dependent' in any strong, deductive sense of the highly composite term 'theory'. As shown, conversely to deduction taking premises as a start, clinical evidences often come into being by themselves, bouncing by surprise into the rather loose nets of our 'background knowledges', to use Hacking's (1983) felicitous terms. What is at stake is an *inference to the best available explanation*: in our field the many-layered, changing and often paradoxical complexities, both relational and cognitive, compound and expand the meaning of the very term explanation.

What the analyst voices as interpretation leads to *descriptive insights* with scant potential for psychic change. To acquire a potential for psychic change, they must usher in *ostensive insights,* taking their support from a knowledge by acquaintance ingrained in the analysand's own experiences, past and present. The fact that interpretation can of itself lead only to descriptive insights separates the *via di levare* of enquiry from the *via di porre* of suggestion and propaganda. Thus genuine insights on her/his psychic realities require as an added step that the analysand ostensively grasp and then evaluate, directly in actual instances, the content of what is going on – the analyst's interpretation included.

Our clinical task involves thus a *dual work on evidences*, an operant logic of disclosures and refutations working on different levels for *both* patient and analyst. My clinical presentation emphasizes how access to the evidences of her unconscious functioning – to her 'unconscious theories' – was obtained by my analysand. Such access to evidences on her unconscious functioning has required her traversing highly contradictory anxieties and wishes, a paradoxicality resulting from the unfolding of her various ego-splits and relational splits.

Iconic equations and symbolization

As mentioned, my patient's collapse at the office door was relevant to me but not at first to her, she not having noticed it: when told, she recognized it as fitting a life-long pattern of experience. Thus a punctual event instanced an ostensively recognizable dynamic whose manifold unpredictable further unfoldings, enacted and verbal, will allow its different aspects and dimensions to be clinically accessed and made available for working through. In what follows, I shall illustrate how insights occur at the crossroads of an *unconscious* logic of classes and a conscious logic of individuals, where representability is attained in concrete particular instances. We thus clinically access unconscious equivalences (*symmetrizations* in Matte-Blanco's terms) where the unfolding of the analysand's 'unconscious theories' operating in terms of unconscious 'classes' turns graspable, often, as illustrated, by way of surprise, leading to the counterinductive[2] assessment and refashioning of such unconscious 'theories'.

Given that counterinduction must be shown rather than explained, I shall take as my example of ostensive, counterinductive enquiry on psychic evidences my analysand's evolving grasp and tolerance of her unconscious psychic reality, mainly in the unfoldings of what in Hanna Segal's terms is a symbolic equation as it evolves in two different transformational cycles (Bion, 1965). As might be surmised, the first transformational cycle involves what was singled out as a first clinical fact, my analysand's collapse in front of the closed office door which, even before meeting me personally, set the issue of her ego-collapses as a result of blighted expectations squarely in the frame of the transference link.

The second transformational cycle chosen for illustration pertains to the incident where walking to my office she became furious at the unbearable starchy stiffness of the locals compared with the fluency attributed to foreigners, which led associatively to a vivid recognizance of the personal impact of her own mother's bodily stiffness as part and parcel of her emotional coldness. By way of the psychic evolutions taking place in such transformational cycles, we both came to realise, through a series of representational devices in the form of traceable individual images, how the link to an internal unconscious stiff 'frozen mother' equated in her psychic reality such seemingly dissimilar individuals as are the closed office door, the prospect of laying on the couch, the 'starchy' locals, the unbearably inhospitable city, and her analyst's absences and errors – all of which were felt as extended embodiments of her mother's felt coldness.

Such disclosing of a main equation of hers fitted no previous consciously held theory, either hers or mine. The equation involved core affective as well as enacted components, so it should not be thought of solely, or even predominantly, as an unconscious *cognizance* mishap. Being in nature emotional and iconic rather than properly symbolic, the ongoing paradoxes can hardly be resolved at once: therefore the process must sustain the paradoxes, as Winnicott (1971) stressed. But my point is that, furthermore, it must be able eventually to resolve them through insight – that is, by way of access through the relevant evidences to one's conflict-laden 'unconscious theories'. And it must also be stressed that only inasmuch as psychoanalytic holding keeps the unconscious anxieties within certain limits will access to the relevant evidences unfold.

Symbolization in the psychoanalytic process and in other fields of endeavour

What Hanna Segal, in her classical papers, called 'symbolic equation' involves a massive failure in symbol formation and thus must be fully recognized as an *iconic equation*: this requires a delineation of the differences between the type of symbol-formation attainable by psychoanalytic insight and what disciplines in the philosophical and the social fields understand by symbolization. To put it in a nutshell, the philosophical and social fields adopt as premise the notion that the issues of meaning fit the frame of a *linguistic determinism*, whereas signification resides in the linguistic code itself, a prime case being linguistic structuralism with its passion for formalization and its conflation of the formal and the objective: there the linguistic code as a socially shared code is elevated to being the place meaning resides in, taking up a ruling role as *symbolic order.* Such a stance, which marked the 'structural moment' of Continental philosophy in the 1960s, retains full weight in Lacanianism, despite its arguably not reflecting the final thinking of Lacan. On the other hand, from its inception on the mark of psychoanalysis as a clinical discipline was its attention to a *psychic determinism* where meanings – which include drives, affects, and anxieties – reside primarily in psychic events located outside language. These psychic facts need to be accessed in the clinical process of analysis as they unfold in particular instances and events: in its search for such psychic facts located mainly in actions and affects – that is, outside language proper – clinical psychoanalysis finds its potency and its specificity. As Freud puts it, after Goethe, in *Totem and Taboo* (1912–13): in the beginning there was action.

A sharp redressing of the sense and function of symbolism characterized the Marburg school of neo-Kantianism, where under the guidance of Ernest Cassirer symbolization turns into the main function of human consciousness, making man, in his words, into a 'symbolic animal': but in such a momentous shift, maintains the Russian linguist Natalia Avtonomova (1991, p. 73), symbolic forms turn into a sort of 'organ of reality' thanks to which the real becomes comprehensible, visible to us: we are thus said to access an objective perception as a condition for objectivity in a field of knowledge extended to prelogical forms and modes of conceptualization, including fantasies and dreams. According to Avtonomova (1991, p. 74), the doctrine of Marburg neo-Kantianism with its formal interpretation of the symbol paves the way for Lévi-Strauss' interpretation, marking the next step in an objectivation of the unobjectivable, whereby symbolic forms give way to *symbolic systems*: language, marital rules, arts, science, religion. These symbolic systems express aspects of physical and social reality as well as the interrelations of these two types of reality, their hidden interplay being to Lévi-Strauss the unconscious. Language as symbolic system is accorded epistemological priority based on its undeniable structurality, and to Lévi-Strauss it is only through its analogy with language that the cognition of any other symbolic system is made possible: a linguistic interpretation of symbolism turns into the condition for the possibility of knowledge.

There is only a step here to the Lacanian primacy of the Symbolic Order, its rule over the other orders (the real and the imaginary) being fixed in language. Putting together the ideas of a Symbolic Order and the primacy of the linguistic signifier, Lacan attributes to the preverbal infant his/her living in a purely *imaginary* illusionary unity with his mother: attainment of the linguistic stage allows access to the Symbolic Order, which requires the acknowledgment of the father's symbolic role in the family and renunciation of any authoritarian vindication towards the mother. In accessing the symbolic order, the subject's becoming starts to be determined by the rules of the relations between the signifiers – that is to say, between linguistic forms freed from even the loosest links to the signifieds (the objects of the world or the objects of thought). As Avtonomova reminds us (1991, p. 76), according to Lacan the subject is what a signifier represents for another signifier. But then the concept of the symbolic is impoverished by a triple reduction of the symbol – to the language, to the sign, and to the signifier – which in her opinion is particularly problematic as concerns the unconscious: despite the hypertrophy of the linguistic method, here language as a chain of signifiers is deprived of any real content because being closed upon itself, it has nowhere to apply its force and spends itself in its own closure (1991, p. 78). We encounter here the two *a priori* that André Green (2002, p. 368) discloses in Lévi-Strauss' work: the anti-naturalist obsession, and the obsession to build a system (unconscious) outside meaning and thus deprived of content. The result, in the words of the Lacanian historian of psychoanalysis Elisabeth Roudinesco (1991, p. 234), is that in the context of the theory of the signifier the unconscious is assimilated to a *machine à penser*, to a language-driven thinking machine from which the primordial and the instinctual are evacuated.

The notion of symbol as the living category of the cognitive process and of cultural reality embodies – Avtonomova crucially argues – an intrinsic tension. Insofar as a symbol always accomplishes the function of a sign, it can be connected to a signified, but it never reduces itself to such a connection, and reaching beyond it penetrates a domain that cannot be defined univocally: the destruction of this mysterious side – that is, the destruction of how the known reflects the unknown, of its 'aura of openness' – degrades the symbol into a sign. From Kant on, she recalls, a symbol comes into being inasmuch as it is impossible to objectify univocally a given content, and this being the case, we can only allude to it (Avtonomova, 1991, p. 70). Pursuing a classic Kantian distinction, she considers that symbols exist to grasp ideas with no need to objectify them: under the form of symbols we access the cogitable, not the knowable. Given that psychic phenomena do not take place in the space of representation, as happens for other 'external' objects, then it will be impossible to develop a psychology as a 'theoretical' science fulfilling the criteria of universality and necessity that demarcate for Kant the knowable from the cogitable (p. 72). But it must be highlighted that the Kantian gap between the knowable and the cogitable was built on making Galilean–Newtonian mechanics paradigmatic for certain knowledge: in such a stance, brandished again and again by physicalistic epistemologists such as Popper and Grünbaum and adhered to by much if not most of the philosophical–literary establishment, only reduction to 'well-behaved' variables allowing point-by-point prediction gains the title of knowledge and is admissible as science. However, the pretence at empirical certainties on which Kant built up his gap between the cogitable and the knowable fell by the board during the twentieth century: to give a prominent example, Einstein pointedly maintained in 1924 that 'insofar as the propositions of geometry apply to reality, they are not certain; insofar as they are certain, they do not apply to reality' (Landsberg, 2000, p. 706). Charles Peirce's comment, several decades before, that the notion of empirical certainty is 'irresistibly comical' (1897, p. 3) applies well to the Kantian distinction between the cogitable and the knowable. On such distinction the currents feeding structuralism uphold the primacy for the human sciences of formal, arbitrary systems of representations derived from linguistics and ultimately from phonology (Lévi-Strauss, 1974). While such attempts at universally valid formalism did dominate an epoch, they go right against the tide in that today scientific concepts in every field are acknowledged as both open and context-dependent. Perhaps even more relevantly to our issues, Tustin (1981a, p. 130) observes in the case of the psychotic child that in order for language to be able to help him make something out of his utter devastation, he needs to be held by a therapist who is alive to the child's capacity to devastate the skills he has acquired instead of using them in a progressive way. These children can use language as autistic objects that block communication instead of facilitating it; thus, she says, language can deteriorate and become 'dead', words being used like rocks to throw at people: what must be attended there is the *use* of words rather than their content.

What precedes on the nature of the symbol highlights *openness* as its core quality. In this sense the term 'symbolic equation' seems inappropriate: as illustrated in the clinical material, symbolic equation amounts to a massive failure of symbolization characterized by closure; it acts 'deductively' by equating and assimilating such obviously dissimilar aspects of reality as the closed door of my office, the collapses into silence on lying on the couch, the city and its inhabitants, the departure of her loved ones, and in many respects the analyst. Pointedly, such phenomena of iconicism surge on under the pressure of an emotion, in the case presented under the pressure of a powerful unmet expectation of primitive maternal receptiveness and containment. This 'deductive' assimilation of dissimilar constituents bearing the brunt of an unconscious emotion and the corresponding anxieties marks the quasi-tautological ways of cognitive *mis*understanding, which functions as a misconstrued and misconstruing *machine à penser.* As shown, the analysand's unconscious theories can only be accessed and mapped as they evolve through a series of particular concrete instances; ostensive insights on how she conjoined facts and events in concrete instances allowed my analysand to traverse the ongoing psychic paradoxes: our method thus amounts to an empirical science of the individual event.

This can help us draw the differences in nature and function of the processes of symbolization attainable in the clinical setting and those in the social setting as exemplified by one of the few psychoanalytically well-informed philosophers, Cornelius Castoriadis, who described himself as Freudian and had by the time of his writing been treating patients for twenty years. Given the vastness of his published work, I can only provide a bare sketch. To Castoriadis (1996) language shows the work of the social imaginary as instituting imaginary, because in and through language, the social imaginary significations operate that keep a society together: totem, taboo, God, *polis*, nation, money, party, citizenship, virtue, or eternal life. Such social imaginary shows the creative capacity of the anonymous collective that emerges whenever human beings come together and results each time in an instituted, singular social form. To Castoriadis human knowledge and human action are, then, simultaneously psychic and historical–social: to find in the individual something that is not social would, he holds, need to reach the ultimate nucleus of the psyche where the most primordial desires, the most chaotic modes of representation, the most brutal and most savage affects are at work. And, he maintains, we can only reconstruct such a nucleus.

In such a socially focused approach, symbolization is both linguistic and imaginary, an anonymous social creation that, including, among others, totem, taboo, God, *polis*, nation, money, party, and citizenship, has no discernible relation to insight, only to social practice and cohesion. In psychoanalysis, however, symbol-formation is personal and results from traversing an emotional experience: it requires, as Meltzer (1986, p. 23) puts it after Bion, that emotional experiences be accepted, observed, and thought about. Another issue would be whether it is valid that we can only *reconstruct* the level of the psyche where, as he puts it, the most primordial desires, the most chaotic modes of representation, the most brutal and most savage affects are at work. For better or worse, such a level is not as difficult to access clinically as Castoriadis supposes: often it crashes upon us, as in the case presented above it fell across in front of the office door even before the patient had met me as analyst. Of course, enquiry on this nucleus needs to evolve in manifold events allowing analysand and analyst to gain, from what goes on in psychic reality, an ostensive 'knowledge by acquaintance'.

A closer look at the clinical material shows that the manifold symmetrizations of the early maternal link form a *multipolar paradox,* each pole sporting affects and anxieties. At the primordial levels that concern us its components range and oscillate clinically between (a) the frozen mother, on to (b) a devouring Moloch–mother (Racker, 1952), and (c) the fusional oral–orgasmic mother (Rado, 1926). My analysand's confronting the ensuing psychic dilemmas included her putting into action the maternal functions in 'delusional goodness' on the one hand, and on the other hand her cataclysmic falls into the oblivions of the 'black hole' when her intense but utterly fragile unconscious expectation of a readily available motherly object went bust.

That action is mostly on the part of the analysand allows better conditions for observation: what probably calmed my patient after the first interview, despite her rancour at my doubt on my availability, was not just associating more freely but also grasping what went on, which was central vis-à-vis her terrors of massive collapse of thinking. Also, receptiveness and unobtrusiveness – what Tustin (1981b, p. 171) called 'fit' – are crucial for free association and for grasping what goes on. My analysand's noticing her being able to free associate, a finding that prompted her to start treatment, happened with no interpretations on my part: it related to a 'fit' brought by the analytic attitude, where neutrality and receptiveness must be understood as regulative ideas rather than as premises that can be fully satisfied.

The above is relevant to the theme of *the new* in the psychoanalytic process, which to my mind happens in ways far removed from what is fashionably put forward – namely attributing the birth of the new to the analyst's poetic wordings, which woos the analyst's voluntarianism and protagonism. Directly in keeping with Freud's (1919) careful distinction between psycho*analysis* and psycho-*synthesis*, the idea here is that the genuinely new comes into being upon the unfolding of the evidences in the clinical process, it being mostly the analysand who unwittingly brings them in. Dominance of paradox in the clinical unfoldings requires that many interpretations be two-sided, covering both sides of the ongoing unconscious dilemma. As noted, interpretations work on two levels: as ostension markers and as 'meta-theoretical' conjectures about the analysand's unconscious 'theories'.

That, as held by constructivism, truth is *made* rather than discovered seems truer for advertising, politics, and rhetoric than for clinical enquiry. While much that is genuinely new comes forth in the course of the psychoanalytic process, the analyst does not *make* truth. He builds a setup and a holding to frame complex unfoldings, which the analysand then accesses, helped on by whatever worthy interpretive conjectures the analyst comes to muster. Thus seen, epistemic weight falls less on the interpretations as such than on the distinctions brought by the analysand's evolving ability to grasp and process incoming disclosures. Our method proceeds *per via di levare*, and in discerning psycho*analysis* and psycho-*synthesis* Freud accords the analysand, at each point of the clinical process, the role of epistemic arbiter. Our voicing interpretations does not elevate them to being truth-injections: however, their pertinence and their precision – their fit with the ongoing psychic realities – is indeed crucial.

Such a stance is accurately Freudian: as he puts it, the analysand's 'conflicts will only be successfully solved and his resistances overcome if the anticipatory ideas [i.e. the interpretations] tally with what is real in him. Whatever in the doctor's conjectures is inaccurate drops out in the course of the analysis; it has to be withdrawn and replaced by something more correct' (Freud, 1916–17, p. 452). It is accurately Freudian also in distinguishing between psychoanalysis, the analyst's conjectural task, and psycho-synthesis, the analysand's work on his emerging evidences and meanings: a work that takes place, urges Freud (1919, p. 160ff), without our intervention.

The analysand is the epistemic arbiter at each step of the process: that what we enquire on has happened and happens to her/him stands firm despite the fact that traumatic experiences have had an impact, by way of alterations of his ego, on how she/he filters emotions and deals with evidences. As Etchegoyen (1986) points out, the analysand often systematically disregards or twists the evidences. However, openness to further incoming evidences and sustained enquiry and interpretation of how the analysand filters and handles them – that is, on how her/his epistemic prisms operate in the various splits of the ego – are our best bet for getting things into track. Evidences impinge as counter-factual on existing unconscious conceptual frames, which opens the road to new findings and allows the analysand's and the analyst's mind to operate, in Hanly's (1995) terms, as *critical realism.*

There being no God's eye epistemic view available, the above does not require that the analyst renounces what his psychoanalytic experiences have taught him, nor does it involve any epistemic relativism on his part. It just precludes ascribing to what he voices the role of truth-injections.

11

THE ANALYTIC MIND AT WORK

Counterinductive knowledge and the blunders of so-called 'theory of science'

Jorge Canestri's kind invitation to revisit my 'Counterinduction in psychoanalytic practice: epistemic and technical aspects' (chapter 8) prompts me to reassess how the psychoanalytic mind works, the debate on its epistemic place, and wider issues of 'theory of science'. What follows builds on Freud's conviction on the link between everyday thought and scientific thinking, clinical analytic work being part and parcel of scientific work; indeed, as he puts in the *New Introductory Lectures,* 'Scientific thinking does not differ in its nature from the normal activity of thought' (Freud, 1933a, p. 170), and, furthermore, 'Progress in scientific work is just as it is in an analysis' (p. 174). Based on a coincidence of therapy and enquiry, my approach focuses on the clinical situation as a double work on the evidences, analyst and analysand being involved in a logic of disclosures and refutations where both gain knowledge from the experience.

In the process of accessing the evidences of his unconscious life-stream, the analysand traverses contradictory anxieties and wishes resulting from his varying levels of mind and his ego-splits and relational splits. This contradictoriness adopts the form of paradox, the analysand's conscious 'theories' about himself often being at the core of his *un*knowing. The interaction, then, involves an enacted, mainly unconscious pragmatics (Freud's thing-presentations), and what is verbalized, having a neat if often skewed and tendentious link to reality. Winnicott's (1951) assertion that the clinical process must sustain the paradox points to an indispensable technical first step, it being a main goal to eventually resolve paradoxes through insight.

The clinical exposition presents a two-pronged unconscious dilemma, pre-oedipal and oedipal, posed to the patient's observing ego, which being itself part of the conflict is centrally involved in *un*knowing. Evolution comes from gaining knowledge by acquaintance from various sources: memories, dreams, instances in and out of session; these evidences impinge counterinductively on the patient's pre-existent 'theories', unconscious and conscious. Much – though by no means all – evidential mapping is mediated by the analyst's interpretations; however, it falls on the analysand to finally sort out what is pertinent and what is not.

This approach is true to Freud along several dimensions:

1 that thought is primarily unconscious, as held from the *Studies on Hysteria* (Breuer & Freud, 1895) on;
2 Freud's statement in a letter to Ferenczi of August 1915: 'I consider that one should not make theories. They should arrive unexpectedly in your house, like a stranger one hasn't invited' (Gribinski, 1994, p. 1019); thus evidences, which are always multiple, impact on thinking, allowing us to revise our 'theories, and this counterinductive epistemic posture is at the opposite pole from deductivism, which derives knowledge deductively from premises.
3 the limit between psycho*analysis* as the analyst's task, and the analysand's evolving psycho-*synthesis*, refurbishing his personal meanings 'without our intervention' (Freud, 1919, pp. 160–1);
4 that 'it is in fact only through *his own* experience and mishaps that a person learns sense' (Freud, 1914a, p. 153, emphasis added): my epistemic focus rests mainly on a careful mapping of dysanalogies and errors, not on overblown notions of truth;
5 that the analysand's 'conflicts will only be successfully solved and his resistances overcome if the anticipatory ideas [i.e. the interpretations] tally with what is real in him. Whatever in the doctor's conjectures is inaccurate drops out in the course of the analysis; it has to be withdrawn and replaced by something more correct' (Freud, 1916–17, p. 452); therefore, analytic interpretations are *conjectures in search of evidential disclosures*, rather than being truth-injections.

Counterinduction must be shown rather than explained or defined. My example is of a boy just over one year in age as he carries on a 'dialogue' with the building's lift in front of its door, shouting: *col, miní* (his baby-talk Spanish for 'lift, come'). Calmly at first, then imperiously, he was finally shocked and angry that the lift did not respond to his call. Summoning the lift just as he does his caretakers discloses an *iconic equation* whereby he assimilates it in the felt *class* of his caretakers and deals with it as he does with them, by voicing his wishes. Given that the lift does *not* respond to his enacted wish-driven requests, the boy will – counterinductively – modify his personalistic 'theory' about lifts.

As Freud knew well, children's thinking proceeds from the animate to the inanimate: the child puts apart from himself a world of wish-driven animate objects and only later comes to acknowledge the attributes pertaining to those objects. Psyche evolves from an action-intentional universe of *self-attributed* ways of relating and meanings, to a later delineation of conscious understandings of attributes as pertaining to the objects themselves.

In the case of our baby boy, we depend on context and observation to grasp what went on, including what his enunciation means. His ongoing experience with a lift felt as animate will eventually lead him to differentiate animate objects (as he evidently feels the lift to be) from inanimate ones. As his mounting imperiousness shows, revision of error must from early on traverse emotional barriers of active *un*knowing. Similarly, the analysand's unconscious 'theories' will 'deductively' assimilate a world of emotional and relational attributes addressed mostly to personal objects, himself included.

I will now proceed to the clinical exposition.

Clinical illustration

Let me expand on the course of a patient, now in his 40s, accessing the interplay of oral and genital anxieties.

The patient had consulted in his early twenties due to apathy, being stuck in his studies, dire social difficulties, indecisiveness, and an inability to approach women; he didn't even masturbate. Lack of enthusiasm and of personal agency was the unifying theme: he felt that what he did was forced, with no assurance of doing it properly, and in any case it brought him no pleasure. His apathy, and his apathy towards women, he attributed to some inborn lack, but we recognized along his drawn-out treatment that it responded to deep-seated terrors: here his conscious 'theories' about himself were part of the *un*knowing.

Shortly it emerged that the motive for seeking consultation had arisen months before when he had stopped at a red light, and a transvestite had opened the car's door, jumped inside, and kissed him on the mouth. The ensuing fright gave him no relief. A strong attraction to transvestites intertwined with his terrors, prompting fears of being homosexual. In the analysis of what I then considered a severe obsessional stage and I now, at two decades' distance, consider an obsessional restitution of an autistic state, progress was slow due to the obstructions to insight, but nonetheless consistent.

A childhood memory that emerged in the first year of analysis illustrates the phallic anxieties that formed one prong of the unconscious pincers deadening his psychic space. At elementary school he was poor at sports but a fast runner; he was ahead in a race up to the time close to the finishing line, when he realized he would win: at this he panicked, slowed his pace, and came second. (Needless to say, confronting rivals has never been his forte.) He also recalled fears about his parents: when they went out together, he was terrified that they would die.

In this initial stage of analysis sexuality evolved in encounters with transvestite prostitutes who masturbated or fellated him, then in a short liaison with a girl, and from then on in long affairs. His first amorous 'crush' in the analysis and his first sexual relation ever was with a work companion he felt fascinated by and who seduced him – a beautiful, fleeting, nomadic girl he then chased after for over a year, until she left the country. Being on the chase spared him from fully confronting his anxieties of entrapment. His next relationship, with a troubled if lively divorcée a decade older, lasted for a couple of years: there he took the initiative, as the age difference mitigated his fears of engulfment while allowing him to gain some clues about them.

As to the pre-oedipal prong of his dilemma, fusional impulses ruled his links to women upon amorous or physical contact, leading to entrapment and to excruciating feelings when threatened by loss of their approval, not to say their anger or actual demise. Thus he was up in the air, externally and internally. At times he verged on mimetic robotization in his attempts to anticipate and fulfil the woman's wishes, which turned all-powerful; their expectations that he deliver on his 'commitment' had missile-like impact, and self-recrimination on those grounds was a constant.

Phantasies of being masturbated by feminized, cross-dressing inmates while being in prison emerged as soon as he started to masturbate, early in treatment. Images of transvestites helped him to attain erection approaching and during vaginal penetration: thereby he often thought of himself as homosexual, and at times homosexuality seemed to offer a way out of his lack of zest and apathy to women. He lost his erection and excitement when the woman was much excited; his terror when the woman fellated him shows the oral impetus of these genitally expressed anxieties.[1] A surprise erection when talking on the telephone with a girl came as a counter-induction to his conscious theory about his 'apathy': this event, mentioned in passing, allowed me to show him that what he saw as sexual apathy appeared, conversely, as an overexcitability he cannot contain.

After five years in analysis he decided to interrupt, having graduated, gained some degree of professional efficacy, and an ongoing if not really satisfactory amorous relationship; that his father paid my fees also played a role. He came back more than a decade later, at first consulting sporadically over practical decisions such as an offer of full-time appointment as technical adviser that was incompatible with his free-lance work. He had declined it because of the responsibilities involved and his having to renounce his independence, but thereafter he was disturbed at the thought of having committed a grave error. In those consultations he mentioned in passing a terrifying phantasy on nearing orgasm in an intensely felt relation: the door opened and a man came in to attack him; at the time he resumed analysis he vaguely remembered this fantasy, but it sounded alien.

All in all, he claimed that he had been satisfied with his progress: now, though, his work and his love life stagnated. He was more aware of losing his independence in amorous relations where he played the fiancé like it or not, and he felt stuck in a years-long relationship that he experienced as an emotional and sexual wasteland. In fact, what brought him back to treatment was that his fiancée, on a work stint out of the country, asked him to join her for a week. He was torn between feeling that such a fake solution would hinder his shelving a dead-end engagement and an urge to join in to avoid losing her. Besides, he feared damaging a new affair meant in good measure to flee his present stuck relationship; but he was again afraid that this new affair would entrap him. After thinking about re-starting analysis for years, this dilemma brought him back to the analytic couch.

This decisional stalemate was an example of his never being confident of acting correctly and on his own wishes, as distinct from doing what he felt obliged to do. The longstanding fiancée he was separating from was an amiable, rather distant girl a few years older; at the start he had felt relieved and proud of her autonomy and lack of emotional demands. Their sexual relationship was pale; she ideologized her frigidity, holding that clitorideal stimulation is a must for women. While internally resentful at her lack of response, consciously he colluded with her ideology and mostly blamed his own lack of passion. Years before they had considered having a child, which she urged and he postponed. Then an early menopause took away her chances for childbearing; he dearly blamed himself for this, which increased his difficulties in separating. That he felt women as unflinchingly right in their requests, expectations, complaints and gripes, and in their personal ideologies, built up an unconditional realm amounting in Ferenczi's (1909) terms to maternal hypnosis. Though initially he felt no anger, and he thought my enquiries about his anger were beside the point and it was still difficult for him to access anger, submissiveness was most notable as concerns women. Being possessed by what we called the 'Kryptonite effect' (after the meteorites coming from his home planet that deprived Superman of all his might) was the greater the more emotionally involved he was, which emptied him of personal agency.

On the other hand, increased pleasure in coitus exacerbated his homosexual fantasies and anxieties, as happened during an enjoyable coitus where he found himself, in a kind of psychic somersault, taking the position of an attractive woman in coitus – passing, under the brunt of his anxieties, in Ferenczi's term (1914), to subject-homoerotism. This in turn prompted a nightmare. He was at his childhood sandbox playing with a small girl, and a car ran over the girl; he spent the rest of the dream desperately searching for her in desolate and dirty places and sewers, where he finally found her all damaged, and he woke up terrified. (On enquiry the dream car turned to be the same make as his father's at that time!) Relevantly, while working on the dream he recalled having the night before an intense coitus while half-asleep, and then, much to his surprise, manifested explosively a wish to be 'a sexual working stallion'. However, on the next session he had forgotten his virile manifesto, and I was able to point to this forgetting.

His link to his parents was appreciative but emotionally deadened, and he saw them rather as a unit; though they are in good shape, he is apprehensive about their health. Regarding his mother, he has no overt conflicts, but he was now better aware of being exceedingly careful to keep his distance. His father is a reliable, stable, successful professional man who knows how to keep out of conflicts; notably, my patient has never clashed with him. The father's car dream likely depicts a major unconscious clash with his father leading to damage and feminization of a part of himself. How this issue was to come alive in the transference in order to be worked through was, of course, another matter.

At the time of the session to be described, some five years into the second course of analysis, progress was considerable in his ability to work, and for the first time he felt he was living a life of his own, which happened initially, and still mainly, when he was out playing golf. He had attempted to learn this sport in childhood, taught by his father, to no avail. In fact, in adolescence he strongly equated his inability to play golf with his incapacity to contact girls and his conviction that he would never have a viable erection. As already described, during this second stage of his analysis he had a couple of rather long relationships with women: he now knows he is rather attractive but feels women choose him instead of his choosing them (he does not approach until given obvious signals). He lost all feeling of initiative as the relationship settled and was more and more trapped in the women's demands for affective long-term commitment. This set up a vicious circle of parasitic possessiveness whereby closeness and enthusiasm led to entrapment.

As the relationship turned into a prison, he finally got the lady frustrated enough to break away. This brought on strong feelings of loss as well as relief at getting out of the bind; however, with each break in his successive relationships feelings of loss were less cataclysmic, while relief at freeing himself turned acceptable, and he came to grasp that the intensity – at times the persecutory character – of the loss resulted from an unbearable guilt at killing both the amorous relationship and the woman involved. On that basis he was much concerned about how his partners fared after the break-up and was relieved when they found new engagements. His last relationship, lasting a couple of years, was fairly satisfactory for over a year, and at that time he had his best sexual encounters ever, as he grudgingly admitted. This, though, heightened the sense of entrapment, and he gradually lost zest; the mounting and often ill-humoured demands of his fiancée for him to marry her led to a break-up that she decided on, but that in the final stages he consciously fed.

He came into the session, took to the couch, and said he had got up with no zest – as routinely happened on Monday mornings. I mentioned that he seemed to leave aside, as he usually does, his feelings of anger at getting up and starting the work-week, and perhaps in coming to the session. Smiling, he said this might be so, and that in fact it was an unusually lively weekend. (Such a comment was itself unusual, given his huge difficulty in admitting enthusiasm – partly due to a feeling that this elicits my rivalry.) Also, after the weekend he had a series of dreams he does not recall, except his being enticed by cross-dressers in prison – with the difference, he noted, that now it was the prison wardens who were the transvestites.

Over the weekend he had gone to the cinema with an ex-fiancée of many years whom he hadn't seen for some time; he was thrilled at the idea of something sexual. Knowing she would resist the emotional impact of a sexual revival allowed him, he came to realize, to feel the thrill as his own and not as a response to a demand of hers.

This theme was much present the following night, when he went out with a woman, M, whom he had met shortly before, with whom he had had some lukewarm sexual bouts.

He had doubted whether he wanted further outings with her, but somehow this came to be. After a week with no contact, she called in undemandingly, and he found himself inviting her for dinner. So they went, and on taking her back, he felt tired and pressured to again go to bed with her. To his relief she said that her sister had come and was sleeping there; he then felt obliged to invite her to his apartment, but found the idea that she would be likely to stay for the night unbearable. Rejecting the idea made him feel much better. Then he told her he would come the next evening after his golf game, which she took well, and he was glad at having administered the affair based on his wishes, not on her felt demands.

The following evening he had a good erection and ejaculated inside her – which he usually is anxious about and has trouble with. They stayed in bed relaxed, and an hour later, rather to his surprise, he tried coitus again; this time he did not manage to ejaculate inside and had masturbated with her help, but nevertheless felt well after. Then they went for dinner, and he took her home with no plans for new outings. While glad about the weekend, this contentment soon soured, both as regards the girl and his link to me. He said he felt that based on his enjoyable weekend I would start pushing him for a deeper 'commitment' with the woman – which we both knew telescoped into marrying her and having children.

I told him his language condensed a double system of meanings: the term 'commitment', while seemingly coming up in terms of a *felt* link to the woman, turns into a command; though first saying he enjoyed his weekend because he had felt he was acting on his own, this gave place to a feeling of slavish 'commitment': enjoyment thus reverted into an obligation, and I was felt as railroading him into the 'commitment'. His agreement reinstated the problem. He said that if he were to go out with some other girl, he would feel – and feel that I felt – that he was not doing so because he wished it and liked this other girl more but, conversely, because he was evading emotional 'commitment' with M.

Thus interpretations turned into mandates of mine on what he was supposed to do – not to fail in his 'duties' to the woman, or alternatively not to let his own pleasure pass by. Thereby his place for decisions or wishes felt as being his own simply vanished. What may seem a semantic issue, an idiolect condensing a double system of meanings for the term 'commitment', amounts – internally and transferentially – to an enacted iconic equation akin in its dynamics to the dream of father's car: interpretations were felt as enactments that hit upon and sidelined his agency.

Concerning the dream mentioned in passing, I told him some changes might be happening. While he felt me as a sort of analytic prison warden to whom he submitted by transcoding interpretations into mandates, the dream hinted of pushing the prison wardens into the feminine role – which probably meant his wish to display a masculine one.

Perhaps as a result of these interpretations, over the weekend at the golf course he played on par three times in a row, something that had never happened before. Characteristically, he dismissed his enthusiasm over this; however, this coexisted with an underlying, overblown thrust to play from now every hole on par, as shown by his disappointment at a bogey in the following one. That he played the next hole very badly brought – predictably enough – myriad self-recriminations. However, the next session brought the first definite virile phantasy impersonation in his long treatment: a daydream of being Robert Capa, the famous war cameraman who lived fully in action, fearlessly at the brink, and who – he mentioned – enjoyed lots of affairs with beautiful women, Ingrid Bergman among them, and had resisted her push to marry him.

I shall now consider a Monday session a few weeks later. It had been a rather unusual weekend, and he had a dream just before waking. He was with L (his last long-time fiancée) at an ice cream parlour where a famous academic man attended. He asked for a long drink that had ice cream and a blend of liquors; but he felt that this famous academic was not attending him as he should. He wanted to go on the road with the girl, and though worried about driving after drinking alcohol, he decided to go on. He had had two other short dreams: in one of them he tenderly embraced his last fiancée, amid sexual excitement. The other dream made him ashamed, and he said he had never had one like it: it was an erotic dream with his mother: it was just an image, she was younger than she is now, and he caressed her leg.

This weekend was also unusual. On Sunday it rained, and his golf tournament was cancelled. On Friday night he went with his old fiancée, S, to see a classic film he liked very much. Though tired, he enjoyed himself; at the cinema they had embraced tenderly and pleasurably, rather as friends; he noticed having an erection but it was very relaxed and pleasurable, and he was happy on coming home. However, he found it symptomatic that the next morning, over a message from S asking him to call her back, he panicked and fantasized all kinds of reproaches and claims of hers, foremost that he marry her. So it was quite a relief when, on the telephone, having run out of cash, she just requested a small loan. I told him then that his enjoyment is manifest only while free enough in a personal space undisturbed by possessive claims, and these claims are felt explosively as a result of minor incidents.

What he brought up next throws further light on his troubles with his maleness. Before going to the cinema with S, he found on the Internet a cross-dressers' phone number. On calling, he was told of a meeting within the week, and that despite not being a cross-dresser, he was welcome as a man. This he found exciting, being the only man amid feminized submissive crossdressers; this he felt as becoming much more of a man than he managed to regarding women. As far as can be gathered, he felt the submissiveness of feminized men as a reassurance against his not easily recognizable fears that his masculine sexual pleasure and activity was a sort of hubris exposing him to annihilating warfare on the side of his unconscious oedipal rival.

After the weekend he said that at the Saturday tournament he had missed many putts but winning the long drive made him glad. Then he organized the day under no pressures, playing golf and then going to an experimental cinema festival. At night he had an erotic dream, which was unusual and puzzled him. It was a dream with Aurora, the middle-aged Indian maid who cleans his apartment – to his eye as unerotic a woman as they come. She undressed and he had a big, hard erection, while her body became that of an attractive girl, quite different from her own; when he was expecting her to grab his penis, he woke up. He linked the dream with winning the long drive, especially since two people made sexual jokes: an older player said that after his big drive all the girls would come after him, and somebody's wife wryly said that winning the long drive sounded very masculine.

I commented that Aurora's presence in the dream might depend on her likely submissive attitude; that following on what came up about the cross-dressers' meeting, sexually unenticing as they went on like girls, fooling with each other rather than submitting to him, might mean that winning the long drive as a form of masculinity and the woman's submissiveness built the context for his big erection in the erotic dream, as he felt his relations with women as the more strongly asymmetrical, the more attractive he found them. When asymmetry is eclipsed by Aurora's submissiveness and lack of attraction, he can feel masculine and excited.

My analysand's inhibitions on pleasure can be grasped, in terms of Matte-Blanco's conceptions of the unconscious functioning in terms of classes, as an infinitization of both phallic and oral dynamics. Chapter 8 reported a huge infinitization in a post-autistic adolescent whose sole waking fantasy was being the only boy in the universe, partner to the only girl with whom he was the sole possessor of every car, plane, boat, and gun in this world. As Franca Ferraro (2001) stresses, phallic logic tends to absolutize, which led my analysand to an either/or psychic dilemma with no possible place for both his oedipal rival and himself. That he got no kick out of the transvestites' meeting, where the girlie display was to one another instead of submitting to his masculinity, supports this idea.

Here we find the dynamic primacy of a traumatic background: contacts with cross-dressers and closely delimited erotic intimacy with his long-time fiancée, S, are bearable and thus enjoyable because they involve what Hardin and Hardin (2000, p. 1249) call a 'leaveable' object: in the case of the cross-dressers, because they are only mimetic womanly forms, and in the case of contacts with S because they both respect a contract of non-possession, having renounced each other. In such fashion the traumatic conflation and infinitization of the genital and the oral is controlled.

On theory-realism and pattern-realism

The conceptual aspects of my enterprise highlight the mishaps brought by what in unified terms is known as the 'theory of science': I shall build my argument in Freud's wake, showing how our clinical work makes good use of what to Popper's theory-realism is the worst of all possible epistemic scenarios: namely, 'the method of having no theory at all' (1979, p. 365). Freud's method of free associations, and of free-floating attention on the analyst's part, puts to work in the realm of the psyche our best attempt at using the 'method of having no theory at all'.

Now, the term 'theory' covers a gamut ranging from 'a system of ideas or statements explaining something, esp. one based on general principles independent of the things to be explained; a hypothesis that has been confirmed or established by observation or experiment and is accepted as accounting for known facts', on to 'the formulation of abstract knowledge or speculative thought; systematic conception of some thing. Freq. opp. to *practice*' and, loosely, 'an unsubstantiated hypothesis' (*The New Shorter Oxford English Dictionary,* 1995, p. 3274). To Popper, 'theory' means *formal* theory, positing as mandatory the use of formal theories in realms where no formal theories are extant. The same goes for his use of the term logic. Aristotle knew that a *formal* logic demands that its component elements be identical – which is not the case in many realms of empiry, least of all the psychic. This makes it necessary to distinguish between *informal* 'background knowledge' or informal 'theories', on the one hand, and *formal* theory operating as a 'logic'.

Informal logic, which examines the complexities and contrarinesses of arguments in natural languages and traces the main ingredients in our patterns of inference, lacks, says Tully (1995), the precision and elegance of a formal theory. Moreover, as the logician Hans Reichenbach (1947) noted, formal logic studies purely cognitive statements, while those given to someone in the flesh are instrumental and pertain to pragmatics, not to logic; in addition, in the actual process of knowledge abstract statements must be verified in terms of directly observable states of affairs. As Ayer (1956, p. 17) put it, what verifies the statement that I have a headache is my feeling a headache, not my having a feeling of confidence that the statement that I have a headache is true. The process of knowledge as it happens in clinical psychoanalysis deals not just with statements addressed to someone but also, and centrally, with the ongoing emotional difficulties that distort actions and statements or preclude them and, importantly, with how statements come to arise.

Theory-realisms subordinate the idea of objectivity to reduction to variables and predictability. The seemingly opposed kinds of theory-realism Karl Popper spearheads as falsificationism and Adolf Grünbaum as strict inductivism are mirror images of each other: via different roads they put up as requisite the formalization of the conceptual apparatus, they forward reductionistic definitions of what is deemed empirical, crucially defining scientific objectivity as reduction to well-behaved variables and predictability.

Concerning psychic processes, Popper's top-down theory-realism and Grünbaum's 'bottom-up' one share the assumption of the mechanical nature of mind. They do not make it explicit, but it underlies, to give a prime example, Grünbaum's demand that the causal groundings of theories of mind comply with the sort of baseline that the law of inertia provides in the realm of physics. The premise that to be deemed scientific the study of mind must proceed in mechanical terms is voiced openly by Wittgenstein – who was first engineer, then logician, and later philosopher of language – in his *Lectures and Conversations on Aesthetics, Psychology and Religious Belief*: 'Paradigm of the sciences is mechanics. If people imagine a psychology, their ideal is a mechanics of the soul' (1938, pp. 28–29). Thus, out of what Charles Peirce (1883, p. 215) saw as the two and only two kinds of thought, mechanical (formal) and anthropological, Popper and Grünbaum admit as science only what is framed in formal–mechanical ways. Popper states in his book *Objective Knowledge* as revised in 1979 that his *objectivism* purports to skip the psychological problems of induction, and it operates on *strictly logical grounds* (p. 26). But it happens that logic is a highly composite field providing no clues on *which sort* of logic is to be used: this is valid for all fields of empirical enquiry and for the formal sciences, mathematics included.

The unitary label 'theory of science' deriving from Comte and the Vienna Circle, which marks Popper's unremitting logicism, utterly disregards the dissimilar nature of scientific endeavours. It was clear to Aristotle more than two thousand years ago that misguided attempts to force the precision of a given research beyond what the phenomena explored allow backfire and introduce distortion.

Popper follows Aristotle in that (a) all science, and all philosophy, are enlightened common sense (1979, p. 34); (b) in that the growth of all knowledge consists in the modification of previous knowledge – either its alteration or its large scale rejection – and (c) that knowledge always comes from some background knowledge (p. 71). Freud would no doubt agree.

But Popper parts ways with Aristotle, Darwin, and Freud when, after acknowledging that science is enlightened common sense, he decries as particularly misleading for the theory of knowledge the primacy accorded to observation (1979, p. 34): his scientific mind is a theoreticist mind operating within the classical physics from which he draws his examples on how all science supposedly works. Newtonian celestial mechanics models Popperian science, built on the belief that, as Hacking crucially quotes him, 'science has a pretty tight *deductive structure*' and that 'all sciences should employ the same methods, so that the human sciences have the same methodology as physics' (Hacking, 1983, p. 5, Popper's italics). However, says Hacking, such deductivist postulation gets scant support from the history of the sciences: even in the history of physics many are the instances in which surprising observations preceded and provided the impetus for the formulation of theory. Later on Hacking (1992) distinguishes our background knowledge and expectations – unsystematic and mostly taken for granted – framing any possible observation from the high-level theories that most often play no direct role in experiment.

Popper's deductivist–formalist premises amount to what Quine (1957, pp. 118–119) calls a *legislative postulation* instituting truth by convention, unencumbered by attempts at justification of its viability for the realm of mind. In so doing, he overlooks that postulates, 'though they are postulates always by fiat, are not *therefore* true by fiat' (Quine, 1957, p. 131). Much of what goes by the name of 'theory' is but postulation; however, as Quine pertinently quotes from Bertrand Russell, 'the method of 'postulating' what we want has many advantages; they are the same as the advantages of theft over honest toil' (1964, p. 133).

In the empirical disciplines the term 'theory' encompasses a gamut going from '*formula-theories*' embodied in mathematical formulae, the prime example being Newton's formulae for universal gravitation (so-called 'Newtonian mechanics'), on to '*frame-theories*' exemplified in Darwin's theory of the evolution of species. Frame-theories are not formalized, do not sustain strict deduction, and serve as general background settings for thought, to be amplified, detailed, and accommodated by further observations. Gooding (1992) underlines that philosophers of science streamline scientists' activities into logically transparent structures, into *normative reconstructions*, highlighting non-situational and theoretical goals at the expense of contextual and practical ones. What I call frame theories correspond to the explicit parts of our background knowledge. For our clinical purposes, we must deal, additionally, with an ever-present background of *un*knowing, the analysand's 'unconscious theories' (Money-Kyrle, 1965), simultaneously enacted and emotional, which organize his experience in unknown 'deductive' ways.

The priority Popper grants tightly formalized deduction as the unitary method for all sciences disregards the huge differences between the inanimate and the animate. That all science is universalistic and non-contextual is a solid Pythagorean–Platonic–Cartesian notion: Plato, in the *Republic*, argued from the geometrical theorem that only Forms, abstract entities outside space and time, are fully real, while our commonplace realities are not: the theorem becomes paradigmatic while infallibility as *necessary* truth demarcates knowledge from mere opinion, entailing that knowledge demands a world of changeless objects (M. Williams, 2000).

In face of Popper's and Grünbaum's *theory-realisms,* a quite different stance must be considered: a *pattern-realism,* which harks back to Aristotle and Darwin, encompassing the huge and varied field of the observational sciences – the human sciences included. The view that all sciences employ the same methodology effaces what distinguishes, for example, ethology from physics. As was mentioned in chapter 6, Bateson's dog helps to approach the issue of causes and motives. Kicking the dog would not be deemed 'causal' in a physicalistic sense, because it does not entail 'an invariable connection' (Bouveresse,

1991, p. 73). The motive (or cause, or reason) is that a dog is not mechanical. Being animate, his response to the kick will be strongly context-dependent: results will depend on whether he is or is not your own dog, and even if he is your dog, on what type of dog he is. There is nothing teleological about this, it just shows that work on these domains requires a *logica situs*, a situational logic making room for Complexity of Causes, in John Stuart Mill's (1852) hallowed terms. So this is *not* a nomological domain fitting Popper-Hempel mechanical-like 'covering laws': even this simplest of examples, Bateson kicking the dog, shows that historical factors (being or not being the dog's master, among others) must be assessed in each case.

For Popper, as for Wittgenstein, only a *formalized* theory is truly a *theory*: hence Copernicus and Darwin did not discover true theories, only a fertile point of view (Wittgenstein, 1980, p. 18e). In such formalist vein Bouveresse argues, following Wittgenstein, that 'Freud's theory – like Darwin's – is related more to what we can call the "morphological" approach than to causal explanation properly speaking' (1991, p. 131), namely causal in mechanical terms.

What is decried as a 'morphological' approach is the sort of *logica situs* befitting observational sciences: thus, the demand that the study of the evolution of species be reducible to physics is preposterous, and it is just as preposterous to assume that a science of psyche should do so. A *logica situs*, a situational logic, must rely on ostensiveness. Moreover, the tension between passivity and agency intrinsic to many psychic happenstances does not permit dichotomies between 'causes' and 'reasons'.

In the case of the observational sciences Mill hit the nail on the head better than Popper's 'theory-realism', avowing in *On Liberty* that 'the truth depends on a balance to be struck between two sets of conflicting reasons . . . and it has to be shown why that other theory cannot be the true one" (1859, p. 98). But it is Mill's inspirer and arch-adversary William Whewell who provides an elastic-enough inductivist frame fit for the sort of scientific thought that, far from formal logic and formalized theory, makes due place for Darwin's and Freud's ways of enquiry and concept building:

> Induction *is* inconclusive *as reasoning*. It is not reasoning: it is another way of getting at truth. . . . It is known from observation, but it is not *demonstrated*. . . . Induction is, as Aristotle says, opposed to syllogistic reasoning, and yet it is a means of discovering truth: not only so, but a means of discovery of primary truths, immedi-

> ately derived from observation. . . . I have elsewhere taught that all induction involved a *Conception* of the mind applied to facts.
> (1850, p. 317)

In induction, then, 'there is always a *new conception*, a principle of connection and unity, supplied by the mind, and superimposed upon the particulars' (1858, p. 163). That scientific induction involves the joint evolution of Conceptions and Facts means that 'Conception must be formed before it can be defined' (1849, p. 284). Man, he holds, 'is the Interpreter of nature; not the Spectator merely, but the Interpreter' (1849, p. 281), and he expounds 'the difficulty of getting hold of the right conception, as a proof that induction is not a mere juxtaposition of facts' (1849, p. 282). He does not mince his words on the obstacles involved in arriving at a conception suitable for binding together the observed facts: 'the process of obtaining new conceptions is, to most minds, far more unwelcome than any labor in exploring old ideas. The effort is indeed painful and oppressive; *it is feeling in the dark for an object that we cannot find*' (1858, pp. 181–182, emphasis added). We cannot aspire to exclude ideas from our facts, but we aspire to improve the ideas we put into play: 'We are not able, nor need we endeavour, to exclude Ideas from our Facts; but we may be able to discern, with perfect distinctness, the Ideas which we include' (1858, p. 125).

What Whewell calls *consilience of inductions*, which happens when findings collected from one class of facts provide *an unexpected explanation for a new class of facts*, is a main criterion of their validity. Freud, from quite early on, explicitly relied on this ampliative side of inductions, their opening into unexpected directions joining previously unlinked events: 'anyone who is engaged in the construction of hypotheses will only begin to take his theories seriously if they can be fitted into our knowledge from more than one direction' (1895, p. 302). Though Whewell explicitly purports to leave out of his enquiry the 'emotions, thoughts and mental conditions' (1858, p. 159), nonetheless his describing the scientist's struggle at finding the right conception might as well be describing every analyst's and every analysand's struggle to attain the right conceptions, allowing insight and psychic growth.

Darwin and Freud found counterfactuals essential in building up their scientific concepts (Ernest Jones, 1957, p. 304, relevantly called Freud the 'Darwin of the mind'.) While Wittgenstein's associate and editor, the Finnish logician Georg-Henryk von Wright, pursued in 1957 a logical concept of counterinduction, it might be likely argued that counterinduction functions in the main outside and against ratiocinations, and as such it cannot be defined in properly logical terms. Speaking from logic, Rescher (2009) admits that no purely formal logical resources will resolve the issue of discrepant counterfactuals, and, accordingly, some logical–external, 'material', or substantive mechanisms must be introduced; counterfactual reasoning, like inductive reasoning, is ultimately a primarily functional project whose management requires pragmatic resources. His recalling that 'Logic as such does not tell us what propositions are true but only which inferences are valid' (p. 36) pulls the rug from under the entire Popperian logicistic enterprise. In fact, had he taken heed of his own statement, against Marx's attempts at sociohistorical prediction, in *The Open Society and its Enemies,* to the effect that 'science can predict the future only if the future is predetermined' (1945, p. 93), he could have spared himself a lot of spilt ink.

Against the Popperian demarcation argument, Blackburn highlights, after Lakatos, that a nineteenth-century Newtonian would have been quite unable to conceive of circumstances that would lead him to declare the general principles of mechanics false. This being so, he asks: Why demand higher standards from psychoanalysts or social scientists than from physicists? (1984, p. 256). As explained above, the case of Bateson's dog requires a *logica situs*, a situational logic making room for Complexity of Causes, accountable to local and historical factors. When historical factors are involved, says von Wright (1971) causal events create new situations requiring practical inferences that could not have been made before; Bateson's kicking the dog a second time would be influenced by what came out of his first kick, both participants having been modified by its outcome. This involves an *inferential* method where, as specified by Whewell for all empirical enquiries, induction means *inference to the best available explanation*, as distinct from formal deduction.

On background knowledge, unconscious theories, pattern-realism, and counterinduction

Psychic concepts attempt to grasp a relational realm. Relational concepts in the domain of the psyche are 'open' concepts: they are intended to cover 'vague' objects, which must be enquired into and discerned in depth in each case. Are not what we call love, or anger, or, in the case of my analysand, apathy 'vague' objects in the sense of being complex, changing and unfolding over time, and of having no predeterminable limits? As they approach vague objects, our psychic notions are perforce open concepts, which come to life as unfolded and redefined anew on being put to use in each singular instance.

Pattern-realism entails that analysand and analyst undertake a mapping of the various unfoldings of the repetition compulsion (the analysand's unconscious theories), at the crossroads of an unconscious logic operating in the main in terms of classes, and a conscious logic drawn in terms of individuals. Such multiple unfoldings need to traverse a variety of ongoing paradoxes on the road to psychic evolution and growth. Centrally, as against the mechanical objects ruling the Popperian conception for all scientific endeavours, *the 'object' that clinical psychoanalysis deals with is, at the same time, both subject and object* (both dimensions are present in the Freudian understanding of *Selbst*): a *historical, evidence-seeking subject/object,* and, what is more, she/he is both an *unknowing* and a *knowing subject.*

This peculiar scientific endeavour, clinical psychoanalysis, amounts to a huge observational, counterinductive extension of everyday practical logic. Thus my approach to objectivity centres less on testing my own interpretations or theories than on how the analysand gathers and tests (and modifies or refutes) *his/her* 'unconscious theories': in other words, my focus is on helping the analysand to gain reliable 'evidences-realism', mainly by way of his current experiences.

Going back to my argument in chapter 8, it must be recalled that my idea about the counterinductive use of the psychoanalytic method distinguishes four psychic levels on the part of the analysand: (a) an underlying quasi-tautological level of *mis*-conceptual unconscious 'frames' or 'theories' about relationships, both misconceived and misconceiving, which rule the analysand's failed inductions; (b) those enacted and verbal derivatives of such mis-conceptual 'frames' that attain some representability; (c) perceptual and mnemic levels that are partly – but hopefully only partly – under the sway of his mis-conceptual unconscious meaning 'frames'; and (d) a capacity to grasp the verbal descriptions and conjectures (i.e. the interpretations) advanced by the analyst, as well as their relevance for the evidential interchanges that take place in and out of session.

Thus we find two quite distinct sets of quasi-tautologies going, the analysand's and the analyst's, though hopefully in dissimilar ways: psychic reality, the *unknown* 'deductive' matrix of unconscious 'theories' about relationships, and conscious inferential thought, itself under the partial sway of the unconscious. Interpretations operate on two levels: as markers for the ostensible and as 'meta-theoretical' conjectures posed by the analyst about the analysand's 'unconscious theories' that happen to be modelling the session. Here receptivity to the *un*expected in incoming events permits that it operates counter-factually, impinging on and modifying our unconscious and conscious conceptual frames, which opens the way to *new* findings and allows the analyst's – and the analysand's – realism to operate, in Charles Hanly's (1992) terms, as *critical realism*.

Last but not least, only psychoanalysis takes into account the daunting topic of the never fully accomplished psychic differentiations and the confusions between self and object. In order not to further complicate exposition, this topic has been alluded to in the material only in passing, but differentiations between self and object are a concomitant of every step in psychic evolutions, and here the working out of the relevant evidences in attaining evolved conceptions is difficult indeed. In present-day patients individuation – that is, a sorting out of self and object – is increasingly problematic: as was pointed out three decades ago by André Green (1980), non-neurotic patients are in the majority. This leads to an intolerance of the psychoanalytic setting and, more generally, to an intolerance of insight and learning by experience, given that the properly habitable psychic space, in everyday life as well as in the session, is restricted and delimited by two equally unsustainable poles: on the one hand a mimetic–fusional pole leading to ecstasies and then to a terror in which much too often entrapment in the other plays a role, and, on the other hand, a pole of separateness leading, often abruptly, to the anguish of primordial depression and thereby also to terror. A third pole often contributing to the ongoing paradoxicalities is that of heroic or risky enactments, a counter-phobic pole put at the service of ego-hardening. In such a psychic context, as presciently stated decades ago by Joan Riviere (1937), approaches to the depressive position are experienced as a catastrophe.

POSTSCRIPT

'What hath God wrought?' A plea for insight in media society

So far so good. It is my hope that the clinical and conceptual march throughout this book, investigating the argument that, epistemically, clinical psychoanalysis is a huge observational extension of every day practical logic, being mainly counterinductive and then ampliative – that is, it opening towards and connecting hitherto unknown or unconnected facts – has been fruitful. All along I have tried to show how doing science in psychoanalysis is alien from the rational reconstructions of hypothetico–deductivist visions of science. My closing remarks will be limited to the daunting topic of the fate of insight in media society.[1] My 'The crisis of culture and the crisis of psychoanalysis' (Ahumada, 1997d), which was published in English as the Introduction to *The Logics of the Mind: A Clinical View*, held the view that the so-called 'crisis of psychoanalysis' derives from a crisis of reflective thought in society, as it passes from family-rearing and a culture of writing towards acculturation in 'virtual' realities, whereby the media redefine normality as ever more multifarious. Passage to 'virtual realities' leads to an ideal of unfettered self-realization and ambiguity, wherein banalization abolishes contact with unbearable feelings of lack and loss.

The initial passage to the virtual realities of media society might be traced to the invention of the telegraph; thereafter came radio, cinema, TV, and then the multifarious Web-based devices. '*What hath God wrought*?': in these prescient words did Samuel Morse's pioneer message from Baltimore to Washington inaugurate long-distance telegraphic transmission (Postman, 1982, p. 68), opening the way to a new era. The very next day a Baltimore newspaper hailed 'the annihilation of space'. The telegraph, says Postman, eliminated in one stroke both time and space: disembodied information took us into a world of simultaneity and instantaneity, moving local history into the background while amplifying the instant and simultaneous. The end result, he says (1982, p. 98–99), is the adult–child, a grown-up whose intellectual and emotional capacities resemble those of children, in a cultural context that deems it desirable that a mother should look no older than her daughter.

Relevantly enough, in homage to the historian of ideas Isaiah Berlin, the literary critic Robert Darnston (1997) listed among the lost arts, along with the Latin pronunciation of the ancient Romans, the *vitraux* of Chartres, the tiles of Delft, and the intonation of the *Minnesinger*, those assumedly extant arts, motherhood, and conversation. That the primordial art of motherhood, and the evolved art of conversation, be thought to be on the wane highlights a crisis of emotional insight in media society, bearing directly on the oft-mentioned crisis of psychoanalysis. Those temples of amusement – sports, gyms, TV sets, video games, and media chat – take over centre scene in lieu of in-depth personal conversation; whereby protagonism displaces reflection, the personal trainer replaces the psychoanalyst, and we come upon a momentous shift in the psychopathologies.

Freud's *Civilization and Its Discontents* (1930) dwells on man's malaise upon his renouncements, amid the civilizing process of the enlightenment and a culture of neuroses; he foresaw, however, that in his mimesis with techno-artefacts man became a prosthetic god. Soon afterward, in *Brave New World*, Aldous Huxley (1932) ushered in a new age. A few years later, in 1937, the philosopher of history and art Roger Collingwood raised the alarm about the heightened social role of amusement and the watertight bulkhead between its world and the world of common affairs. The 'make-believe' of amusement differs radically from that of childish games, which is very serious work. Amusement, he said, bifurcates experience into a 'real' part and a 'make believe' part. Practical life becomes emotionally bankrupt, amid an inability to take an interest in ordinary affairs. The kind of work on which civilization depends turns into an intolerable drudgery, whereas boredom, or lack of interest in life, becomes a constantly recurring state of mind; the feverish attempts to deaden the nerves dispelling this boredom by means of drugs or criminal activities soon lose their bite, and the dose must be increased.

A quarter of a century later, David Riesman signalled, in *The Lonely Crowd* (1961), the ever-expanding role of peer groups, introducing the terms 'inner-directed' and 'outer-directed', and four decades after Collingwood another historian, Christopher Lasch, drawing on psychoanalytic sources from Freud to Melanie Klein and Kernberg, argued in *The Culture of Narcissism* (1979) that historical forces had made the concept of selfhood increasingly problematic. The new narcissist is superficially relaxed and tolerant but fiercely competitive in his demand for approval and acclaim; he demands immediate gratification and lives in a state of restless, perpetually unsatisfied desire. Amid a waning of the sense of historical time, for him the world is a mirror: despite illusions of omnipotence he cannot live without an admiring audience. This happens, he says, in the context of the mechanical reproduction of culture where, on the proliferation of the visual and auditory in a 'society of the spectacle', we inhabit a swirl of images and echoes, giving much of modern life the character of an enormous echo chamber. What is there taken as mental health is the overthrow of inhibitions and the immediate gratification of every impulse: the voyage to the interior, Lasch maintained, discloses nothing but a blank, while the world, even in its emptiness, is but a mirror of himself.

Society, he holds, impinges on private life, making deep and lasting friendships, love affairs, and marriages increasingly difficult to achieve. Erosion of lasting intimacy results from a *flight from feeling*: personal relations turn risky as they no longer carry any assurance of permanence, and under such conditions more and more people seek emotional detachment, pursuing sex only where they can define and limit their involvement in the relationship. As a patient cited by Warren Poland (personal communication, 1995) bluntly put it: 'I fuck, I do not love'. In the prevailing conditions of the proliferation of visual and auditory images in a 'society of the spectacle', narcissistic traits come up, to varying degrees, in almost anyone: a protective shallowness, an avoidance of dependence, an inability to mourn, a dread and loathing of aging and death, an inability to feel oneself part of a historical stream, a fear of binding commitments, a desire to keep one's options open, and an incapacity for loyalty or gratitude. The ever-present media images and the overexposure to manufactured illusions lead to an indifference to reality, if not to the collapse of the very idea of reality – confirming Collingwood's concerns. He further argues that a 'new illiteracy' rages at all educational levels and not only in mass education: such decline in literacy reflects a retreat from intellectual discipline of any kind. Later, in *The Minimal Self: Psychic Survival in Troubled Times* (1984), Lasch noted that while the older definition of identity retained connotations of sameness, definiteness, and continuity, from the 1950s on it came to refer to a fluid, protean, and problematical self, socially bestowed and sustained, defined by the social roles performed, by the groups to which one belongs, or by the deliberate management of impressions or 'presentation of the self', which blurs the limits between self and others while weakening or eliminating the link between identity and continuity of the personality. As held by Eugenio Gaddini in 1984, along the twentieth century the neuroses gradually gave way to character disorders, and then to narcissistic and borderline states. We now witness an upsurge in autistic–mimetic psychopathologies and an ensuing seriality of unthought events, which fit under the term 'autistoid' coined by Bernd Nissen (2008). Here I join Symington (1991) in putting autistic disturbances at the root of narcissistic ones.

What can one say about visual media effects? This huge theme can only be touched upon. At its extreme we find Juan, a boy who believed that he was an animal that had been bred mainly by the TV program *Animal Planet* between six months and two years of age. After several years in treatment, lonely and angrily embracing himself in the session, he cried: 'I want to be with the TV, who is my Mum. Carmen [his mother] is Lisa's Mum': Lisa being his younger sister. However, a TV set cannot be a mother, let alone a 'good-enough' one: as Justin Call (1980) pointed out, it is the infant who, in the first hours after birth and thereafter, initiates visual reciprocity with the mother. The baby is 'the initiator and primary architect of the game, while the mother is the follower' (p. 276); the mother follows the clues in the infant-initiated reciprocity, which can be called 'holding' or 'emotional containment'. A 'dumb box' cannot be a Mum; it is a tireless provider of what Tustin (1986) called 'autistic shapes', but this is not an adequate substitute for the art of motherhood.

To illustrate the mindlessnesses displayed by the *un*thinking serialities shaping up the neo-normalcies of media culture, let me take two examples. The first is a narrative of a mother whose 15-year-old son had, weeks earlier, confided to her that he had just had his first sexual relationship. Encouraged by his frankness, she asked him how it had come to be: he responded, as if stating the obvious, that it happened in the dancing place where they meet. There were big sofas, and at a some point or other, instead of dancing, a girl and a boy had a sexual relationship while the others looked as if nothing had happened. He explained that this was the way to have relationships, adding that nobody talks as they were now doing – not his friends with one another, nor with their parents.

Just as this upsurge of the ephemeral and impersonal was leading me to classify what precedes as just an adolescent, wayward local use in a provincial town, I was called to my senses by an analysand coming from a top-notch international university, commenting on his troubles in adapting to how sexual relationships happened there. Everyone – people in their early thirties – drank beer to oblivion; then twosomes went off together, and only on waking the following morning did they gather who they had had mindless sex with. Each then departed on his own, and life at the university went on as if nothing had occurred: after anonymous antics that it would be idle to call amorous, a 'reset' command reinstated full anonymity. Can such antics be deemed 'experience'? As the other side of the coin to what was described in the second clinical material of chapter 3, where a single individual and the 'class' of females coincided in a Class-Object, here we find ourselves amid the hyperbole of seriality in a 'make believe' sexuality: in the protagonistic flight from emotional dependencies that characterize media culture, sexuality is disengaged from individualities.

We are in a different realm from Freudian *psycho*sexuality. Not much trace there of Bion's *psychoanalytic function of the personality*, a function correlative to the German word *Arbeit*, work in the plainest sense, which has a weighty place in Freud's contributions. We find there, as part of *Aufklärungsarbeit*, the work of enlightenment, both a *Deutungsarbeit*, the work of interpreting what is going on, and a *Durcharbeitung*, the working through on what has been gathered. As quoted, for Freud it is only on becoming aware of their mishaps that people learn sense, and in the same vein Peirce (1905, p. 89) stated that in order to be such, experience requires breaking through resistance to change, and there needs be an element of effort in this.

In order to further grasp what is happening, one might consult best-selling advocates in their different varieties, from the techno-guru to the postmodernist. Among these last, the MIT Lacanian sociologist Sherry Turkle, maintaining in *Life on the Screen: Identity in the Age of the Internet* (1995) that, when she lived in the late 1960s and early 1970s in the hothouse of Paris intellectual culture having, as its gurus, Jacques Lacan, Michel Foucault, and Gilles Deleuze, she was taught that the self is constituted by and through language, that sex is an exchange of signifiers, and that each of us is a multiplicity of parts, fragments, and desiring connections. These Gallic abstractions she met concretely two decades later in the world of chat rooms, where the self is multiple, fluid, made and transformed by language, sex is an exchange of signifiers, and understanding follows from navigation and tinkering rather than analysis. She takes as given that everyday technologies change the way we see the world, that life on the screen is without origin and foundation, and that the postmodern is a world without depth, a world of surfaces where the self is decentred and multiple and alienation leaves place to an anxiety of identity. That the fake becomes more compelling than the real is to Turkle a step towards reaching a deeper truth; it seems more sensible to take it as a flight from feeling and a demise of insight amid a celebration of *un*knowing. In so saying, let us recall something said in a 1967 lecture by Winnicott (p. 582): that 'our patients, more and more, turn out to be needing to feel real, and if they don't then understanding is of extremely secondary importance'.

Mindless states, worldwide rather than local, usher in what Lasch called a 'new illiteracy': based on studies of the Swiss Federal Office of Statistics, under the title 'On Course for the Poorhouse' the editorial of an official Swiss magazine (Eckert, 2005) highlighted an alarming rise in modern analphabetism. Despite having completed their education, over a fifth of the students cannot master tasks requiring minimal reading skills, which leads to social marginalization and virtually no chance to be employed. That this happens in one of the best educational frameworks available worldwide shows the potency of this 'new illiteracy' affecting those who, having had the chance of an education, cannot profit from it. As these lines are written, a survey in Buenos Aires on youths contemplating university studies found out that only 15 per cent of them had a clear notion of what career they will engage in; the rest were divided roughly equally between those having no idea of what they planned to study and those undecided about committing to further study (Parmat, 2010). The issue, as there stated, is uncertainty about life in general. So we might well ask ourselves: are we on course for an autistoid society?

Currently the expanding impact of autistic spectrum states is taken into account mostly in relation to children. Thus, while Leo

Kanner assumed the incidence of early infantile autism at 1/10,000, Christakis, Zimmerman, DiGuiseppe, and McCarthy (2004) estimate, based on the current literature, that ADHD affects between 4 and 12 per cent of children, having become the most common disturbance in infancy, more so than child neuroses.

Learning from experience, and emotional maturation, require thoughtful effort in concrete life-events, as Freud was quite well aware. This contrasts with the ideology on the basis of which, as described in the Introduction, Kandel spoke in favour of the neurosciences, urging that psychoanalysis abandon the subjectivities of insight and introspection and adopt the Pavlovian language of stimulus–response. Such a notion of what objectivity consists of furthers a Cartesian ideology of man-as-machine. He is not the only one to do so: four decades before Kandel, coming from a quite different background but similarly attributing to itself – in its passion for formalization – the rigour of a scientific program, structuralism, a similar idea on what knowledge consists of had been brandished by Claude Lévi-Strauss in his inaugural lecture at the Collège de France in 1960: 'The emergence of culture will remain a mystery as long as we do not arrive to determine, at the biological level, the changes in structure and functioning of the brain' (quoted by Dosse, 1992, p. 222).

It is true that psychoanalysis cannot provide *episteme*, definite and immutable knowledge: it simply furthers by other means the sort of work on which sanity depends. The issue is that under the spell of the mirage of man-as-machine and of proper knowledge as *episteme*, the pangs of learning from experience evaporate. That the hardships on the road to emotional 'experience' are shorn out of the sort of objectivity heralded by the neurosciences is at the core of their appeal: the implicit promise is that the need for traversing the pangs of 'experience' and emotional growth can and will be bypassed through the use of technologies, chemical or otherwise – including those geared to amusement, where the fake is more compelling than the real. Which, propelling the 'common sense' of the age, is grist to the mills of the current media-driven autistoid mindlessness.

According to an African saying, to educate a child, you need the whole village. The big question is: how does this work out in the Global Village?

So I end with a plea for insight.

Glossary

Abduction: According to Peirce, a kind of inference by which new notions emerge; comparing it with the chick's ability to choose the right pickings as soon as it breaks out of the eggshell, he likens this 'instinct for conjecture' to what Russell will call 'animal inferences' and we would regard as 'unconscious thinking'.

Consilience of inductions is, for Whewell, a main way of verifying hypotheses, and it happens inasmuch as these are able to bind together – in what he calls a mysterious step – theretofore unrelated and unlinked kinds of facts. As he puts it, 'if we can predict new [kinds of] facts which we have not seen, as well as explain those which we have seen, it must be because our explanation is not a mere formula of observed facts, but the truth of a deeper kind' (1849, p. 294). That such was Darwin's, and also Freud's, main verification tool comes as no surprise in Darwin's case, as he had read Whewell in depth and corresponded with him; Freud, in turn, knew his Darwin well.

Context of discovery/context of justification: Peirce drew a distinction between the 'context of discovery' and the 'context of justification' of hypotheses. He called 'abduction' their emergence, 'deduction' the finding of their consequents, and 'induction' their empirical testing. However, in the observational sciences where complex, multi-levelled, context-dependent hypotheses do not allow rigorous deduction or prediction, such distinction loses force.

Counterinduction is a term introduced by the Finnish logician Georg-Henryk von Wright; the term, reversing the usual logic of induction, means taking the way things have been as a guide to how they shall *not* be. Blackburn (1994) finds it surprisingly difficult to formulate a consistent counterinductive strategy. In my own approach, counterinduction advances from an unknowing use of the general to, first, the ostensive differentiation of the particular, and thereafter to a grasp of the up-to-then unknown theory-in-use; this involves first making explicit and then ostensively refuting unknown ideational categoricals.

Deduction: A type of reasoning that allows the construction of complex ideational systems starting from simple elements (its 'premises' and 'axioms'). It had its start in geometry with Pythagoras' theorem and is the kind of inference that characterizes the formal or ideal disciplines, such as mathematics, geometry, and symbolic logic. Euclid's axiomatization of geometry provided the ideal for the 'exact' sciences: first cosmology, and then, more generally, physics (see **physicalism**). That such axiomatic systems aspiring to certainty through lack of internal contradiction are purely ideational and in themselves involve no direct reference to empiry came to be generally accepted only recently, in the nineteenth and early twentieth centuries. Informally, the term deduction is often used to refer to any sort of inference, as famously happened in the case of Sherlock Holmes.

Empiry is a term that includes that which the world (foremost, in our case, the *affective–relational* world) is kind enough to make available to our knowing. It has not been easy along the history of science to distinguish what belongs to empiry from what does not: as was shown in the Introduction, in the early days of Western science and up to the nineteenth and twentieth centuries, Euclidean geometry was thought (for example by Kant) to be a necessary, a priori background to our knowledge of empiry. For whatever it is worth, the classical philosophical description takes empiry to be whatever knowing happens to come to us through our five senses.

Empiricism: In its widest sense includes each and every way of learning from experience, from the basic level of knowing that Bertrand Russell calls 'knowledge by acquaintance' onwards. Its roots can be traced in Western science to Aristotle, and it is the dominant stance in the observational sciences – that is, in those sciences not susceptible to **reduction to 'variables'**. It is to be contrasted with **rationalism**, insofar as it accords no epistemic primacy to theory. However, in the 'exact' sciences modelled on some axiomatic, the meaning of the term 'empirical' shifts radically, being restricted to those data susceptible to reduction, as happens in the case of Grünbaum's 'strict inductivism'.

Epistemology: From the Greek *episteme*, knowledge; it tends to apply mainly to the study of scientific knowledge. For Blackburn (1994) epistemology can be seen as being dominated by two rival metaphors: the first that of a pyramid, with the philosopher trying to describe secure foundations and modes of construction, the second that of a boat or fuselage with no foundations and owing its strength to the interlocking of its parts. The metaphor of the pyramid applies well to so-called 'strict **inductivism**'; the metaphor of the boat or fuselage seems suitable for observational sciences. The notion of a unitary epistemology has usually taken the way of **physicalism**, taking classical physics as its ideal science; the alternative stance – that, as Feyerabend (1995) puts it, 'science is not one thing, it is many' – leaves aside the idea of a unitary epistemology.

Fallibilism: See **Infallibilism/fallibilism**.

Hypothetico–deductivism is the epistemic stance according full primacy to formal axiomatic 'theoretical' systems as applied to the study of empiry in all fields. It can be illustrated by the primacy of Euclidean geometry throughout the history of cosmology, from Ptolemy through Copernicus, Galileo, Newton, and Laplace: only hypotheses framed in mathematical formulae (**variables**) were deemed 'empirical'. A rigidly mechanical version of determinism was part and parcel of so formulaic an outlook, as exemplified by Laplace's assertion that given full knowledge of the universe's state and its laws, one would be able to predict in detail any of its future states. Modern variants of hypothetico–deductivism include 'top-down' strategies such as Popper's falsificationism, where emerging theoretical, formalized 'bold' conjectures are then put to the test of an empiry that can refute them but never prove them, and 'bottom-up' strategies such as Grünbaum's 'strict empiricism', where truth is supposed to flow upwards from a foundation on basic empirical theories such as the law of inertia.

Induction involves a variety of notions, which are caught in the perpetual tensions between **rationalism** (see **deduction**) and **empiricism**. In the widest sense it includes all the ways in which knowledge on matters of fact is gained, in passing from the unknown to the known, or from the unobserved to the observed, both in everyday knowledge and in scientific knowledge. It is contrasted with deductive knowledge (such as Geometry, Algebra, or Arithmetic), which deals with purely ideal or formal issues: in Hume's terms, with 'relations of ideas' rather than 'matters of fact and existence'. The 'problem of induction' (Hume's problem) he famously raised, arguing that 'In vain . . . we should pretend to determine any single event, or infer any cause or effect, without the assistance of observation and experience' (1717, p. 30); 'all inferences from experience suppose, as their foundation, that the future will resemble the past . . . if there be any suspicion that the course of nature may change, and that the past may be no rule for the future, all experience becomes useless, and can give rise to no inference or conclusion' (p. 34). That the course of nature may change does not invalidate knowledge build-up based on observed regularities (flame and heat have always been conjoined together, as is obvious, he says, even to a mere infant), but it precludes attributing to empirical knowledge a strong rationalistic basis. This is acceptable to **empiricism** but not to **hypothetico–deductivism** (such as **physicalism**), where scientific induction is redefined as ancillary to findings fitting into formal deductive frames: induction in such stances means the empirical testing (i.e. the verification or refutation) of previously evolved deductive formulae. While induction as it is understood in classical hypothetico–deductivism assumes that 'theories' and 'facts' are logically independent of each other, later approaches, such as Whewell's, acknowledge that it is not possible to fully distinguish our 'facts' from our 'theories': exploring his facts and revising his theories are two sides of the same coin in every scientist's practical research tasks. In Whewell's view, induction (which he calls 'discoverer's induction') requires that a *new* conception colligates the facts: it is thereby ampliative, inasmuch as new conceptual knowledge is tentatively generated (see also **consilience of inductions**).

Infallibilism/fallibilism: In its Greek origin and thereafter, on to Descartes' 'clear, distinct, indisputable' concepts, simplicity and certainty ruled the idea of science. The idea that empirical concepts are always fallible and can never be definitive is widely accepted today; however, while currently few if any would openly admit infallibilist goals, such aspirations covertly define the idea of science both in formalistic stances such as Popper's and in 'strict inductivism' as maintained by Grünbaum. The idea of fallibilism we owe mainly to Peirce, who thought of 'truth' as an ideal limit.

Knowledge by acquaintance/knowledge by description: A century ago, in a presentation made to the Aristotelian Society, Bertrand Russell stated that knowledge depends in the final instance on direct, unmediated acquaintance with its object, that description itself depends upon acquaintance, and that no amount of description can replace direct acquaintance, so that even the words that we understand ultimately depend on ostensive definitions, i.e. on a knowledge by acquaintance.

Ostension, ostensive definition: Something is defined ostensively when the thing defined is actually addressed by pointing, in person. For Russell, who introduced the term, ostensive definitions are only possible in relation to events that have occurred to oneself, while for Thomas Kuhn ostensive definitions are central to both everyday learning and to scientific advances, linguistic philosophers discount their value.

Physicalism is the epistemic stance maintaining that physics is the overarching science, whose concepts and methods are taken to be ultimately valid and sufficient for all fields of enquiry, psychic processes not excluded. So-called Cartesian dualism is largely a physicalistic stance on mind inasmuch as only conscious will and deliberate cogitation, which man shares with God, are removed from the otherwise purely mechanical realm of mind.

Propositional functions/propositional forms: The notion of propositional function was introduced into logic by Frege. 'Socrates is mortal' is a proposition affirming something of someone; '*x* is mortal' is a propositional function that as such does not affirm nor negate; it defines a 'class' of those values that can satisfy *x*, the class of mortals. According to Matte-Blanco, the unconscious psyche does not recognize individuals as such; it operates in terms of propositional functions. Given that in symbolic logic propositional functions work at the level of written statements and that they do not affirm or negate, while unconscious instinctual drives do not primarily occur at the level of statements and they can only be enacted, it seems preferable to use the term 'propositional forms'.

Rational reconstructions are the end result of the philosopher's activity in streamlining and giving additional logical (or perhaps just didactic) form to the scientists' findings and results. The issue is the point up to which such logical streamlining does or does not respect the scientist's findings and results: it is good to recall at this point Peirce's caveat that logic learns from science at least as much as science can learn from logic.

Rationalism in science, deriving from the successes of Greek geometry, is built upon the systematic use of deduction and the axiomatic method, pursuing as its goals necessity and simplicity. Its initial successes in cosmology and then physics generally prompted the idea that reduction to well-behaved variables and the ensuing rigorous use of the hypothetico–deductive method were universally applicable to all fields of inquiry. An underlying assumption here, from the Pythagoreans on to Kandel's demand that psychoanalysis joins the neurosciences' search for 'the elementary mechanisms of psychic processes', is that the whole of empiry rests on a yet-to-be-found system of simple elements. Popper's core demarcational idea that only the fully deductive consequences of hypotheses allow for their verification or refutation, and therefore only such hypotheses can be deemed scientific, is a rather extreme case of rationalism.

Reduction to 'variables' holds a central place in the empirical use of the hypothetico–deductive method, given that in order to fit formal systems, the complexities of the field of study must be reduced to assumedly homogeneous, universally applicable, measurable, logically independent, context-free dimensions (so-called 'well-behaved' or 'projectible' variables). A classical example is given by Ptolemy's astronomy, which reduced the complexities of the cosmos to a highly intricate formal system of epicycles, which retains at its conceptual base the simplest movement: uniform circular movement. In classical physics so-called Humean variables were required to be independent of one another: in this conceptual context space, mass, and gravity were thought to be independent of each other.

Tautology: According to Bateson, description and explanation are connected by a tautology, ranging from the simplest 'if P is true, then P is true', through elaborate structures, to Euclidean geometry or the axioms, definitions, postulates, and theorems of von Neumann's Theory of Games. All that a tautology claims is that 'if the axioms are such and such and the postulates such and such, then the theorems be so and so'; all it affords is connections between propositions and in itself contains no information. An explanation is a mapping of the pieces of a description into a tautology.

Theory is a term caught in the never-ending strife between rationalism and empiricism. So on one side of the fence 'theory' is – as it was for the Pythagoreans – a formal edifice built deductively, on whose nets depends what is to be acknowledged as empirical in the proper scientific sense: such is the Popperian stance. On the other side of the fence, from Aristotle to Darwin, formal theory holds no primacy, and theories themselves, informal as they be, are, in Freud's famous words, 'scaffoldings ready to be discarded' as soon as new findings require it.

Variables: See **Reduction to 'variables'**.

Notes

Introduction

1 As much use is made, throughout the book, of concepts coming from logic and philosophy of science, a Sceptic Glossary on such terms has been added for the reader's convenience.

1 Logical types and ostensive insight

1 For introductory studies on Matte-Blanco's notions, see Rayner (1981) and Rayner and Tuckett (1988); for a fuller consideration, see Rayner (1995). For joint studies on Matte-Blanco and Bateson, see Arden (1984) and Etchegoyen and Ahumada (1990).
2 According to Bateson (1979, p. 50fn) any explanation involves 'mapping' the phenomena to be described onto a matrix or system of coordinates, whose formal characteristics will, to a greater or lesser degree, tend to distort the phenomena themselves. It is clear from Russell's idea of ostensive definition that he sees language as a matrix for the mapping of experiences.
3 The sentence 'Socrates is mortal' is a *proposition*; '*x* is mortal' is not a proposition, but a *propositional function*, which makes no assertion at all. It becomes a proposition when the variable *x* is given a fixed meaning, when it is settled who *x* is. The collection of all the values that satisfy a propositional function (or 'property') is a *class*. I am using the terms 'unconscious propositional forms (or 'relational unconscious propositions') instead of 'unconscious propositional functions', as Matte-Blanco does, because in strict logical terms propositional functions do not *state* anything, while unconscious pragmatic propositions are concrete enacted relational statements, which can only 'affirm'.

2 Interpretation and creationism

1 Aristotle, who was aware of this, expressed valid forms of syllogisms in letters to show that the conclusion results from their form and composition and not from the matter of the premises (Lukasiewicz, 1957, pp. 7–8).

2 In contrast to propositions ('Socrates is mortal'), it is deemed in logic that propositional functions (' '*x*' is mortal') make no assertions and therefore are neither true nor false. The collection of all values that satisfy '*x*' is a class. In the Mattian–Batesonian frame I am using here, unconscious propositional 'forms' denote pragmatic action-and-emotion messages.

3 As I have argued elsewhere (Ahumada, 1992), such a repudiation of psychic reality leads Lacanianism to an 'active technique' and to a variant of narcissistic identification as 'cure'.

3 What is a clinical fact?

1 For Money-Kyrle the unconscious operates in terms of 'class' notions, imageless preconceptions of the objects or situations of major biological import. These 'class' notions we cannot consciously imagine, although we can recognize their members: what may later become a representation of an absent or separate object is, he says (1965, p. 400), first experienced concretely as an identification, introjective or projective, with the object, in a kind of 'concrete representation by identification', to which much of Melanie's Klein's work belongs. The second stage, of 'ideographic representation', occurs mainly through 'visual metaphors'; to this level pertains Freud's dream-thinking. The third stage, of 'verbal thought', rules consciousness.

2 I often find it unavoidable in my present practice, with so many patients presenting what amount to *interpersonal claustrophobias* in which intimacy and the ensuing dependency are felt as annihilating, to start with less than the optimum frequency of sessions. In such cases a proper analytic setting must be constructed over time.

3 The capital 'O' will indicate that I am referring to a primary, psychic Object.

4 Body, meaning and language

1 I shall only mention in passing Balint's (1968) idea of three coexistent 'theories of origins' in Freud's works: primary narcissism, primary auto-erotism, and primary object linking.

2 Narcissistic identification as described by Freud in *Leonardo* (1910) at the source of a type of male homosexuality, involves concrete representation by identification (see Ahumada, 1990).

3 Though I cannot go into this, ethology of 'play' as a logical frame modulating aggression (see Bateson, 1955) coincides with Freud's (1914a) idea of transference as 'playground" where meanings unfold midway between phantasy and reality.

4 That experience is not univocal is plain to that father of empiricism, John Stuart Mill, who holds in *On Liberty* (1859) that 'there must be discussion to show how experience is to be interpreted' (see also Feyerabend, 1981, p. 67). What, in terms valid for formal logic but *not* for inductive ones, Blackburn condemns as an 'infinite regression' is exalted by other linguistic currents to the range of premise, under the label of 'infinite semiosis'.

5 Fact, context, image, narrative

1 The use of human observers in confrontational strategies is often observed in chimpanzees. When accustomed to human observers, they ignore them, but this changes when a group of males goes to patrol its territory's periphery: they wait for human observers and come back to fetch them, the more so the more anxious they are about meeting an enemy patrol. The hypothesis is that they assume that rival patrols are not used to humans and will flee as soon as they encounter them; which happens when rival groups meet (see Goodall, 1986).

2 My paper 'On the Unconscious Delusion of 'Goodness' (Ahumada, 1982) shows such an example, in a little girl's link to her turtle.

6 Toward the epistemology of clinical psychoanalysis

1 I shall not enter into the polemics on the implications of the Freudian use of the terms *Instinkt* and *Triebe*, this last to refer to unconscious drives as part of psychoanalytic findings. In any case, that for Freud the psychic apparatus' id–ego–superego structure 'may be supposed to apply as well to the higher animals that resemble man mentally' (1940, p. 147) precludes attributing to him any radical distinction between animal and human at the level of drives, as is done by Lacan, among others.

2 Evans (1978) emphasizes, however, that the Henle-Koch postulates (that the specific germ be present in every case of the disease and in no other disease, that it be isolated in pure culture and repeatedly passed, inducing the disease anew) were not regarded as rigid causal criteria by Koch. I must thank Spruiell (1987) for calling to my attention Evans' paper.

8 Counterinduction in psychoanalytic practice

1 My thanks to Professor Georg-Henryk von Wright for his reading of the manuscript and the important stimulus given by his opinion that, as far as he understands the operation of clinical psychoanalysis, counterinduction seems to him its most likely logical operation.

2 Bateson (1979, p. 50n) uses the term 'map onto' because description, explanation, or representation being a mapping of derivatives from the phenomena onto some matrix or system of coordinates, the formal characteristics of the receiving matrix, be it a language or a tautological network of propositions, will distort the phenomena mapped onto it. To me it indicates, additionally, that the formal characteristics of the tautology can themselves be modified by the phenomena it contacts, of which more later when I refer to language as a component of enactment.

3 In an important paper, Anzieu (1975) uses the term 'paradoxical transference' for those forms of transference that derive from a paradoxical injunction (*double bind*) and lead to a negative therapeutic reaction. In my rather more general use, 'paradox' is seen to emerge at the interface of consciousness and unconscious transference and often to become more noticeable as insight is approached.

10 The double work on the clinical evidences, and the nature and limits of symbolization

1 In the same way as her marriages were built as a function of her fitting in and fulfilling her husbands' needs, so these role reversals follow the line I described as 'delusional goodness' (Ahumada, 1982): centrally a splitting-off into others of unconscious needy-deprived infantile self-aspects, which allows magical relief while it lasts.

2 The term counterinduction was introduced by the Finnish logician Georg-Henryk von Wright (1957), though its roots are traceable to Aristotle. As I use it, it refers to evidences impinging *against* our previously held informal theories, be they conscious or unconscious.

11 The analytic mind at work

1 See Busch de Ahumada (2003) for a detailed clinical exposition of the process of analysis in a case of transvestism in a 5-year-old child in which projection of oral anxieties in the female genital was central to the dynamics.

Postscript

1 What follows partly draws from other contributions on media society and its psychopathologies (Ahumada, 1997c, 2001a, 2001b, 2004a, 2004b, 2006b, 2010; Ahumada & Busch de Ahumada, 2010; Ahumada & Carneiro, 2006; Busch de Ahumada & Ahumada, 2005, 2009; Etchegoyen & Ahumada, 2002).

References

Ahumada, J. L. (1982). The unconscious delusion of 'goodness'. In *The Logics of the Mind: A Clinical View* (pp. 65–82). London: Karnac, 2001.

Ahumada, J. L. (1990). On narcissistic identification and the shadow of the object. *International Journal of Psychoanalysis*, 17: 177–186. Also in *The Logics of the Mind: A Clinical View* (p. 93–113). London: Karnac, 2001.

Ahumada, J. L. (1991). Logical types and ostensive insight. *International Journal of Psychoanalysis*, 72: 683–691.

Ahumada, J. L. (1992). De l'ange déchu et du 'sujet': Une critique des bases de la pensée de Jacques Lacan et de sa technique. *Revue française de psychanalyse*, 56: 425–442.

Ahumada, J. L. (1994a). Interpretation and creationism. *International Journal of Psychoanalysis*, 75: 695–707.

Ahumada, J. L. (1994b). What is a clinical fact? Clinical psychoanalysis as inductive method. *International Journal of Psychoanalysis*, 75: 949–962. Also in *The Logics of the Mind: A Clinical View* (pp. 15–36). London: Karnac, 2001.

Ahumada, J. L. (1995). Cuerpo, significación y lenguaje. *Revista de Psicoanálisis, Número Especial Internacional*, 4: 9–30.

Ahumada, J. L. (1996). Níveis logicos e comunicacionais da transferência. *Revista de Psicanálise (Porto Alegre)*, 3: 82–91.

Ahumada, J. L. (1997a). Toward the epistemology of clinical psychoanalysis. *Journal of the American Psychoanalytic Association*, 45: 507–530.

Ahumada, J. L. (1997b). Disclosures and refutations: Clinical psychoanalysis as a logic of enquiry. *International Journal of Psychoanalysis*, 78: 115–118.

Ahumada, J .L. (1997c). Counterinduction in psychoanalytic practice: Epistemic and technical aspects. In J. L. Ahumada, J. Olagaray, A. K. Richards, & A. D. Richards (Eds.), *The Perverse Transference and Other Matters: Essays in Honor of R. Horacio Etchegoyen* (pp. 181–202). Northvale, NJ: Aronson.

Ahumada, J. L. (1997d). Introduction: The crisis of culture and the crisis of psychoanalysis. In *The Logics of the Mind: A Clinical View* (pp. 1–13). London: Karnac, 2001.

Ahumada, J. L. (1998). Fato, contexto, imagem, relato: Uma aproximaçâo bio-lógica. *Revista Brasileira de Psicanálise*, 32: 9–27.

Ahumada, J. L. (2001a). On E-growth, education and E-sanity. *Journal of the American Psychoanalytic Association*, 49: 1035–1040.

Ahumada, J. L. (2001b). *The Logics of the Mind: A Clinical View.* London: Karnac.

Ahumada, J. L. (2004a). Posfazione all' edizione italiana. In V. Bonaminio (Ed.), *Scoperte e confutazioni. La logica dell' indagine psicoanalitica* (pp. 111–120). Milan, Italy: Franco Angeli.

Ahumada, J. L. (2004b). From insight to self-begetting: On the postmodern vicissitudes of psychoanalytic ownership. In A. Casement (Ed.), *Who Owns Psychoanalysis?* (pp. 61–79). London: Karnac.

Ahumada, J. L. (2005). Il doppio lavoro sulle prove cliniche. Natura e limite della simbolizzazione. *Rivista di Psicanalisi*, 51: 1065–1086.

Ahumada, J. L. (2006a). The analytic mind at work: Counterinductive knowledge and the blunders of so-called 'theory of science'. In J. Canestri (Ed.), *From Practice to Theory: The Analyst's Mind at Work.* London: Whurr.

Ahumada, J. L. (2006b). La dynamique mimesis-autisme dans les psychopathologies d'aujourd'hui. In A. Green (Ed.), *Les voies nouvelles de la thérapeutique psychanalytique. Le dedans et le dehors* (pp. 661–694). Paris: Presses Universitaires de France.

Ahumada, J. L. (2010). La dinámica mimético-autística y la reacción terapéutica negativa en los pacientes de hoy. *Revista de Psicoanálisis*, 67: 275–287.

Ahumada, J. L., & Busch de Ahumada, L. C. (2010). Further comments on Sophia's mimetic autism, with special reference to Bion's theory of thinking. In M. Leuzinger-Bohleber, J. Canestri, & M. Target (Eds.), *Early Development and Its Disturbances: Clinical, Conceptual and Empirical Research on ADHD and Other Psychopathologies and Its Epistemological Reflections* (pp. 155–174). London: Karnac.

Ahumada, J. L., & Carneiro, M. I. (2006). Tradition and truth in psychoanalysis: Everyday life, the academy, and psychoanalysis. *American Imago*, 63: 293–314.

Álvarez de Toledo, L. G. de (1954). The analysis of 'associating', 'interpreting' and 'words'. *International Journal of Psychoanalysis*, 77 (1996): 291–317.

Anzieu, D. (1975). Le transfert paradoxal. *Nouvelle revue de psychanalyse*, 12: 49–72.

Arden, M. (1984). Infinite sets and double binds. *International Journal of Psychoanalysis*, 65: 443–452.

Aristotle (1995). *Treatise on Rhetoric.* Amherst, NY: Prometheus.

Austin, J. L. (1954). Unfair to facts. In *Philosophical Papers* (pp. 154–174). Oxford, UK: Oxford University Press, 1979.

Austin, J. L. (1956–57). A plea for excuses. In *Philosophical Papers* (3rd. edn., pp. 175–204). Oxford, UK: Oxford University Press, 1979.

Austin, J. L. (1962). *How to Do Things with Words*. Oxford, UK: Clarendon Press.

Avtonomova, N. (1991). Lacan avec Kant: L'idée du symbolisme. In Collège International de Philosophie (Ed.), *Lacan avec les philosophes* (pp. 67–86). Paris: Albin Michel.

Ayer, A. J. (1956). *The Problem of Knowledge*. London: Routledge.

Balint, M. (1968). *The Basic Fault*. London: Tavistock Publications.

Barlow, N. (1958a). Charles Darwin and his grandfather. In C. Darwin, *The Autobiography of Charles Darwin 1809–1882* (N. Barlow, Ed.) (p. 149–166). New York, NY: Norton, 1993.

Barlow, N. (1958b). The Butler controversy. In C. Darwin, *The Autobiography of Charles Darwin 1809–1882* (N. Barlow, Ed.) (pp. 167–219). New York, NY: Norton, 1993.

Bateson, G. (1955). A theory of play and phantasy. In *Steps to an Ecology of Mind* (pp. 150–166). Hertfordshire: Paladin.

Bateson, G. (1973). *Steps to an Ecology of Mind*. St Albans, UK: Paladin.

Bateson, G. (1979). *Mind and Nature: A Necessary Unity*. Toronto, Canada: Bantam, 1988.

Bion, W. R. (1959). Attacks on linking. In *Second Thoughts* (pp. 93–109). London: Heinemann, 1967.

Bion, W. R. (1962). *Learning from Experience*. New York, NY: Basic Books.

Bion, W. R. (1963). *Elements of Psycho-Analysis*. New York, NY: Basic Books.

Bion, W. R. (1965). *Transformations*. London: Heinemann.

Bion, W. R. (1970). *Attention and Interpretation*. London:. Tavistock, 1975.

Bion, W. R. (1975). *Brazilian Lectures 2: Rio/São Paulo 1974*. Rio de Janeiro, Brazil: Imago.

Bion, W. R. (1977). *Two Papers: The Grid and Caesura*. Rio de Janeiro, Brazil: Imago.

Bion, W. R. (1979). *The Dawn of Oblivion*. Strath Tay, UK: Clunie Press.

Bion, W. R. (1992). *Cogitations*. London: Karnac.

Black, M. (1961). *Models and Metaphors*. Ithaca, NY: Cornell University Press.

Blackburn, S. (1984). *Spreading the Word: Groundings in the Philosophy of Language*. Oxford, UK: Clarendon Press.

Blackburn, S. (1994). *The Oxford Dictionary of Philosophical Terms*. Oxford, UK: Oxford University Press.

Blackburn, S. (1999). *Think: A Compelling Introduction to Philosophy*. Oxford, UK: Oxford University Press.

Blight, J. G. (1981). Must psychoanalysis retreat to hermeneutics? *Psychoanalysis and Contemporary Thought*, 4: 147–205.

Boesky, D. (2008). *Psychoanalytic Disagreements in Context.* Lanham, MD: Aronson.

Bouchard, A.-M. (1995). The specificity of hermeneutics in psychoanalysis: Leaps on the path from construction to recollection. *International Journal of Psychoanalysis*, 76: 533–546.

Bouveresse, J. (1991). *Wittgenstein Reads Freud: The Myth of the Unconscious.* Princeton, NJ: Princeton University Press.

Braithwaite, R. (1953). *Scientific Explanation.* New York, NY: Random House, 1960.

Breuer, J., & Freud, S. (1895). *Studies on Hysteria. S.E.* 2.

Bricmont, J. (1996). Science of chaos or chaos in science? In P. L. Gross et al. (Eds.), *The Flight from Science and Reason* (pp. 131–175). *Annals of the New York Academy of Sciences* (Vol. 775). New York, NY: The New York Academy of Sciences.

Bruner, J. (1993). Loyal opposition and the clarity of dissent: Commentary on Donald P. Spence's 'The hermeneutic turn'. *Psychoanalytic Dialogues*, 3: 11–19.

Busch de Ahumada, L. C. (2003). Clinical notes on a case of child transvestism. *International Journal of Psychoanalysis*, 83: 293–313.

Busch de Ahumada, L. C., & Ahumada, J. L. (2005). From mimesis to agency: Clinical steps in the work of psychic two-ness. *International Journal of Psychoanalysis*, 86: 721–736.

Busch de Ahumada, L. C., & Ahumada, J. L. (2009). Autistische Mimesis im Medienzeitalter: Eine Fallgeschichte. In B. Nissen (Ed.), *Zur Entstehung des Seelischen. Psychoanalytische Perspektiven*. Gissen, Germany: Psychosozial-Verlag.

Call, J. D. (1980). Some prelinguistic aspects of language development. *Journal of the American Psychoanalytic Association*, 28: 259–289.

Caper, R. (1995).On the difficulty of making a mutative interpretation. *International Journal of Psychoanalysis*, 76: 91–101.

Carnap, R. (1932–33). Psychology in physical language. In A. J. Ayer (Ed.), *Logical Positivism* (pp. 165–198). Glencoe, IL: The Free Press; London: Allen and Unwin, 1959.

Carnap, R. (1937). *The Logical Syntax of Language.* London: Routledge.

Castoriadis, C. (1996). *La Montée de l'Insignifiance.* Paris: Seuil.

Cavell, M. (1991). The subject of mind. *International Journal of Psychoanalysis*, 72: 141–153.

Cheshire, N., & Thomä, H. (1991). Metaphor, neologism and 'open texture': Implications for translating Freud's scientific thought. *International Review of Psychoanalysis*, 18: 429–455.

Collingwood, R. G. (1937). *The Principles of Art.* London: Oxford University Press, 1958.

Collingwood, R. G. (1945). *The Idea of Nature.* London: Oxford University Press, 1960.

Collingwood, R. G. (1946). *The Idea of History*. Oxford, UK: Oxford University Press, 1994.

Cottingham, J. (1986). General introduction. The Meditations and Cartesian philosophy. In R. Descartes, *Meditations on First Philosophy* (J. Cottingham, Ed.) (pp. xviii–xlii). Cambridge, UK: Cambridge University Press, 1997.

Cottingham, J. (1992). Introduction. In J. Cottingham (Ed.), *The Cambridge Companion to Descartes* (pp. 1–20). Cambridge, UK: Cambridge University Press.

Christakis, D. A., Zimmerman, F. J., DiGuiseppe, D. L., & McCarthy, C. A. (2004). Early infantile autism and subsequent attentional defects in children. *Pediatrics*, 113: 708–713.

Croce, B. (1910). Il Vico e lo svolgimento posteriore del pensiero logico e filosofico. In *Filosofia, Poesia, Storia* (pp. 126–131). Milan, Italy: Ricciardi, 1951.

Cronk, N. (1994). Introduction. Voltaire: An Augustan author. In Voltaire, *Letters Concerning the English Nation* (pp. vii–xxvii). Oxford, UK: Oxford University Press, 1999.

Darnston, R. (1997). Free spirit. *The New York Review of Books*, 26 January, p. 9.

Darwin, C. (1859). *On the Origin of Species by Means of Natural Selection*. London: Murray.

Darwin, C. (1879). *The Descent of Man, and Selection in Relation to Sex* (2nd. ed.) London: Penguin, 2004.

Darwin, C. (1887). *The Autobiography of Charles Darwin 1802–1882* (N. Barlow, Ed.). New York, NY: Norton, 1993.

Demos, R. (1959). Psychoanalysis: Science and philosophy. In S. Hook (Ed.), *Psychoanalysis: Scientific Method and Philosophy* (pp. 329–335). New York, NY: Grove Press.

Descartes, R. (1637). *Discours de la méthode/Discourse on the Method* (G. Heffernan, Ed.). Notre Dame, IN: University of Notre Dame Press, 1994.

De Waal, F. (1983). *Chimpanzee Politics*. London: Unwin.

Dosse, F. (1992). *Histoire du structuralisme* (Vol. I): *Le champ du signe 1945–1966*. Paris: La Decouverte.

Duhem, P. (1906). *La Théorie Physique. Son Objet. Sa Structure*. Paris: Vrin, 1993.

Duncan, D. (1993). Theory in vivo. *International Journal of Psychoanalysis*, 73: 25–32.

Eckert, H. (2005). Editorial: On course for the poorhouse. *Swiss Review*, 3, July. Available at www.revue.ch

Eco, U. (1973). *Segno*. Milan, Italy: ISEDI.

Eco, U. (1990). *The Limits of Interpretation*. Bloomington, IN: Indiana University Press, 1994.

Edelson, M. (1983). Is testing psychoanalytic hypotheses really impossible? *Psychoanalytic Study of the Child*, 38: 61–79.

Edelson, M. (1984). *Hypothesis and Evidence in Psychoanalysis*. Chicago, IL: University of Chicago Press.

Edelson, M. (1988). *Psychoanalysis: A Theory in Crisis*. Chicago, IL: University of Chicago Press.

Einstein, A. (1954). *Ideas and Opinions* (C. Seelig, Ed.). New York, NY: Wings Books.

Eisenbud, J. (1978). Descartes and Shaw: Some spatial aspects of object loss. *International Review of Psychoanalysis*, 5: 285–296.

Etchegoyen, R. H. (1982). The relevance of the 'here and now' transference interpretation for the reconstruction of early psychic development. *International Journal of Psychoanalysis*, 63: 65–75.

Etchegoyen, R. H. (1983). Fifty years after the mutative interpretation. *International Journal of Psychoanalysis*, 64: 445–459.

Etchegoyen, R. H. (1986). *Fundamentals of Psychoanalytic Technique* (Rev. ed.). London: Karnac, 1999.

Etchegoyen, R. H., & Ahumada, J. L. (1990). Bateson and Matte-Blanco: Bio-logic and bi-logic. *International Review of Psychoanalysis*, 17: 493–502.

Etchegoyen, R. H., & Ahumada, J. L. (2002). Que faire? Le rôle de la psychanalyse dans la posmodernité. In C. Botella (Ed.), *Penser les limites. Essais en l'honneur d'André Green* (pp. 418–423). Paris: Delachaux et Niestlé.

Evans, A. S. (1978). Causation and disease: A chronological journey. *American Journal of Epidemiology*, 108: 249–258.

Fenichel, O. (1974). A review of Freud's 'Analysis terminable and interminable'. *International Review of Psychoanalysis*, 1: 109–116.

Ferenczi, S. (1909). Introjection and transference. In *First Contributions to Psychoanalysis* (Chapter 2). London: Hogarth Press, 1953 [reprinted London: Karnac, 1980].

Ferenczi, S. (1914). The nosology of male homosexuality (homoerotism). In *First Contributions to Psychoanalysis* (Chapter 12). London: Hogarth Press, 1952 [reprinted London: Karnac, 1980].

Ferenczi, S. (1924). *Thalassa, a Theory of Genitality*. New York, NY: Psychoanalytic Quarterly, 1938 [reprinted London: Karnac, 1980].

Ferenczi, S. (1932a). Confusion of tongues between the adult and the child. *International Journal of Psychoanalysis*, 30 (1949): 225–230.

Ferenczi, S. (1932b). Notes and fragments. In *Final Contributions to the Problems and Methods of Psychoanalysis*. London: Hogarth Press, 1955 [reprinted London: Karnac, 1980].

Ferraro, F. (2001). Vicissitudes of bisexuality: Crucial points and clinical implications. *International Journal of Psychoanalysis*, 82: 485–499.

Feyerabend, P. (1962). Explanation, reduction and empiricism. In *Realism, Rationalism and Scientific Method: Philosophical Papers* (Vol. 1, pp. 44–96). Cambridge, UK: Cambridge University Press, 1993.

Feyerabend, P. (1963). Materialism and the mind-body problem. In *Realism, Rationalism and Scientific Method: Philosophical Papers* (Vol. 1, pp. 161–175). Cambridge, UK: Cambridge University Press, 1993.

Feyerabend, P. (1969). Linguistic arguments and scientific method. In *Realism, Rationalism and Scientific Method: Philosophical Papers* (Vol. 1, pp. 146–160). Cambridge, UK: Cambridge University Press, 1993.

Feyerabend, P. (1978). Philosophy of science versus scientific practice. In *Problems of Empiricism: Philosophical Papers* (Vol. 2, pp. 80–88). Cambridge, UK: Cambridge University Press, 1994.

Feyerabend, P. (1980). Mach, Einstein and the Popperians. In *Problems of Empiricism: Philosophical Papers* (Vol. 2, pp. 89–98). Cambridge, UK: Cambridge University Press, 1994.

Feyerabend, P. (1981). Historical background. Some observations on the decay of the philosophy of science. In *Problems of Empiricism: Philosophical Papers* (Vol. 2, pp. 1–33). Cambridge, UK: Cambridge University Press, 1994.

Feyerabend, P. (1987). *Farewell to Reason*. London, Verso.

Feyerabend, P. (1988). *Against Method* (3rd rev. ed.). London: Verso.

Feyerabend, P. (1995). Science, history of the philosophy of. In T. Honderich (Ed.), *The Oxford Companion to Philosophy* (pp. 806–809). Oxford, UK: Oxford University Press.

Fonagy, P. (2006). The failure of practice to inform theory and the role of implicit theory in bridging the transmission gap. In J. Canestri (Ed.), *Psychoanalysis: From Practice to Theory* (p. 69–86). London: Wiley.

Frank, P. (1959). Psychoanalysis and logical positivism. In S. Hook (Ed.), *Psychoanalysis, Scientific Method and Philosophy* (pp. 308–313). New York, NY: Grove Press, 1960.

Freud, S. (1891). The unconscious. Editor's Appendix C. Words and things. *S.E.* 14.

Freud, S. (1895). Project for a scientific psychology. *S.E.* 1.

Freud, S. (1896). The aetiology of hysteria. *S.E.* 3.

Freud, S. (1900). *The Interpretation of Dreams. S.E.* 5.

Freud, S. (1905). Three essays on a theory of sexuality. *S.E.* 7.

Freud, S. (1910). Leonardo da Vinci and a memory of his childhood. *S.E.* 11.

Freud, S. (1912). The dynamics of transference. *S.E.* 12.

Freud, S. (1912–13). *Totem and Taboo. S.E.* 13.

Freud, S. (1913). The disposition to obsessional neurosis. *S.E.* 12.

Freud, S. (1914a). Remembering, repeating and working-through. *S.E.* 12.

Freud, S. (1914b). On narcissism: an introduction. *S.E.* 14.

Freud, S. (1915a). Instincts and their vicissitudes. *S.E.* 14.

Freud, S. (1915b). The unconscious. *S.E.* 14.

Freud, S. (1916–17). Introductory Lectures on Psycho-Analysis. *S.E.* 16.

Freud, S. (1917a). Mourning and melancholia. *S.E.* 14.

Freud, S. (1917b). A difficulty in the path of psychoanalysis. *S.E.* 17.

Freud, S. (1919). Lines of advance of psycho-analytic therapy. *S.E.* 17.

Freud, S. (1923a). The ego and the id. *S.E.* 19.

Freud, S. (1923b). Two encyclopaedia articles. (A) Psychoanalysis. *S.E.* 18.

Freud, S. (1925). An autobiographical study. *S.E.* 20.

Freud, S. (1926). The Question of Lay Analysis. *S.E.* 20.

Freud, S. (1930). *Civilization and Its Discontents. S.E.* 21.

Freud, S. (1933a). New introductory lectures on psychoanalysis. *S.E.* 22.

Freud, S. (1933b). The question of a Weltanschauung. *S.E.* 21.

Freud, S. (1937). Analysis terminable and interminable. *S.E.* 23.

Freud, S. (1940). An outline of psychoanalysis. *S.E.* 23.

Gadamer, H. G. (1960). *Truth and Method* (2nd rev. ed.). New York, NY: Continuum, 1994.

Gadamer, H. G. (1976). On the philosophic element in the sciences and the scientific character of philosophy. In *Reason in the Age of Science* (pp. 1–20). Cambridge, MA: MIT Press.

Gadamer, H. G. (1986). Supplement II: To what extent does language preform thought? In *Truth and Method* (pp. 542–549). New York, NY: Continuum, 1994.

Gadamer, H. G. (1992). El otro puede tener razón. *La Nación Cultura*, 12 July.

Gaddini, E. (1984). Changes in psychoanalytic patients up to the present day. In R. S. Wallerstein (Ed.), *Changes in Analysts and Their Training* (pp. 6–19). IPA Monograph N° 4. London: International Psychoanalytical Association.

García Márquez, G. (1996). En busca del Silva perdido. *La Nación Cultura*, Buenos Aires, 27 October.

Garma, A. (1974). Mis investigaciones psicoanalíticas originales en el curso de cuarenta y cinco años. *Revista de Psicoanálisis*, 31: 141–175.

Goodall, J. (1986). *The Chimpanzees of Gombe*. Boston, MA: Belknap/Harvard University Press.

Gooding, D. (1992). Putting agency back into experiment. In A. Pickering (Ed.), *Science as Practice and Culture* (pp. 65–112). Chicago, IL: University of Chicago Press.

Green, A. (1980). Passions and their vicissitudes. On the relation between madness and psychosis. In *On Private Madness* (p. 214–253). Madison, CT: International Universities Press, 1986.

Green, A. (1984). Le langage dans la psychanalyse. In A. Green et al. (Eds), *Langages* (pp. 19–250). Paris: Les Belles Lettres.

Green, A. (1993). *Le travail du négatif.* Paris: Éditions de Minuit.

Green, A. (2002). *Idées directrices pour une psychanalyse contemporaine*. Paris: Presses Universitaires de France.

Gribinski, M. (1994). The stranger in the house. *International Journal of Psychoanalysis*, 75: 1011–1021.

Griffin, D. R. (1992). *Animal Minds*. Chicago, IL: University of Chicago Press.

Grinberg, L. (1956). Sobre algunos problemas de la técnica psicoanalítica determinados por la identificación y la contraidentificación proyectivas. *Revista de Psicoanálisis*, 13: 507–511.

Grünbaum, A. (1984). *The Foundations of Psychoanalysis: A Philosophical Critique*. Berkeley, CA: University of California Press.

Grünbaum, A. (1993). *Validation in the Clinical Theory of Psychoanalysis*. Madison, CT: International Universities Press.

Grubrich-Simitis, I. (1985). Six letters of Sigmund Freud and Sándor Ferenczi on the interrelationship of psychoanalytic theory and technique. *International Review of Psychoanalysis*, 13: 259–277.

Habermas, J. (1959). *Knowledge and Human Interests*. Boston, MA: Beacon, 1971.

Hacking, I. (1983). *Representing and Intervening: Introductory Topics in the Philosophy of Natural Science*. Cambridge, UK: Cambridge University Press, 1999.

Hacking, I. (1992). The self-vindication of the laboratory sciences. In A. Pickering (Ed.), *Science as Practice and Culture* (pp. 29–64). Chicago, IL: University of Chicago Press.

Hamilton, V. (1993). Truth and reality in psychoanalytic discourse. *International Journal of Psychoanalysis*, 74: 63–79.

Hanly, C. (1990). The concept of truth in psychoanalysis. *International Journal of Psychoanalysis*, 71: 375–383.

Hanly, C. (1992). Inductive reasoning in clinical psychoanalysis. *International Journal of Psychoanalysis*, 73: 293–301.

Hanly, C. (1995). Facts and ideas in psychoanalysis. *International Journal of Psychoanalysis*, 76: 901–908.

Hardin, H. T., & Hardin, D. H. (2000). On the vicissitudes of early primary surrogate mothering. II: Loss of surrogate mother and arrest of mourning. *Journal of the American Psychoanalytic Association*, 48: 1227–1258.

Hersbach, D. R. (1996). Imaginary gardens with real toads. In P. L. Gross (Ed.), *The Flight from Science and Reason* (pp. 11–30). *Annals of The New York Academy of Sciences* (Vol. 775). New York, NY: The New York Academy of Sciences.

Holland, R. (1990). Scientificity and psychoanalysis: Insights from the controversial discussions. *International Review of Psychoanalysis*, 17: 133–158.

Home, H. J. (1966). The concept of mind. *International Journal of Psychoanalysis*, 47: 42–49.

Hook, S. (1959). Science and mythology in psychoanalysis. In S. Hook (Ed.), *Psychoanalysis: Scientific Method and Philosophy* (pp. 212–224). New York, NY: Grove Press.

Hume, D. (1717). *Enquiries Concerning Human Understanding* (L. A. Selby-Bigge & P. H. Nidditch, Eds.). Oxford, UK: Clarendon, 1994.

Husserl, E. (1954). *The Crisis of European Science and Trascendental Phenomenology.* Evanston, IL: Northwestern University Press, 1970.

Huxley, A. (1932). *Brave New World.* New York, NY: Harper, 1946.

Jiménez, J. P. (1990). Some technical consequences of Matte-Blanco's theory of dreaming. *International Review of Psychoanalysis*, 7: 455–469.

Jones, E. (1957). *The Life and Work of Sigmund Freud* (Vol. 3): *The Last Phase 1919–1939.* New York, NY: Basic Books.

Joseph, B. (1985). Transference: The total situation. *International Journal of Psychoanalysis*, 66: 447–454.

Joseph, H. W. B. (1916). *An Introduction to Logic* (2nd ed.). London: Oxford University Press.

Julien, P. (1985). Hainamouration et réalité psychique. *Littoral*, 15–16: 5–19.

Julien, P. (1986). *Le retour à Freud de Jacques Lacan. L' application au miroir.* Toulouse, France: Érès.

Kandel, E. R. (1998). A new intellectual framework for psychiatry. *The American Journal of Psychiatry*, 155: 457–469.

Kandel, E. R. (1999). Biology and the future of psychoanalysis: A new intellectual framework for psychiatry revisited. *The American Journal of Psychiatry*, 156: 505–524.

Kermode, F. (1985). Freud and interpretation. *International Review of Psychoanalysis*, 12: 3–12.

Kernberg, O. (1993). Convergences and divergences in contemporary psychoanalytic techniques. *International Journal of Psychoanalysis*, 74: 659–673.

Klein, M. (1952). The origins of transference. In *The Writings of Melanie Klein* (Vol. 3, pp. 48–52). London: Hogarth, 1975.

Klimovsky, G. (1984). Símbolo, lenguaje y metalenguaje. *Psicoanálisis*, 6: 45–55.

Kuhn, T. (1962). *The Structure of Scientific Revolutions.* Chicago, IL: University of Chicago Press, 1970.

Kuhn, T. (1964). A function for thought experiments. In *The Essential Tension: Selected Studies in Scientific Tradition and Change* (pp. 240–265). Chicago, IL: University of Chicago Press, 1977.

Kuhn, T. (1970a). Logic of discovery or psychology of research? In I. Lakatos & A. Musgrave (Eds.), *Criticism and the Growth of Knowledge* (pp. 1–23). Cambridge, UK: Cambridge University Press, 1994. Also in *The Essential Tension: Selected Studies in Scientific Tradition and Change* (pp. 266–292). Chicago, IL: University of Chicago Press, 1977.

Kuhn, T. (1970b). Reflections on my critics. In I. Lakatos & A. Musgrave (Eds.), *Criticism and the Growth of Knowledge* (pp. 231–278). Cambridge, UK: Cambridge University Press, 1994.

Kuhn, T. (1974). Second thoughts on paradigms. In *The Essential Tension: Selected Studies in Scientific Tradition and Change* (pp. 293–319). Chicago, IL: University of Chicago Press, 1977.

Lacan, J. (1951). Intervention sur le transfert. In *Ecrits* (pp. 215–225). Paris: Seuil, 1966.

Lacan, J. (1954–55). *Le Séminaire Livre II: Le moi dans la théorie de Freud et dans la technique de la psychanalyse.* Paris: Seuil, 1978.

Lakatos, I. (1968). Changes in the problem of inductive logic. In *Mathematics, Science and Epistemology: Philosophical Papers* (Vol. 2, pp. 128–200). Cambridge, UK: Cambridge University Press, 1993.

Lakatos, I. (1970). Falsification and the methodology of scientific research programmes. In I. Lakatos & A. Musgrave (Eds.), *Criticism and the Growth of Knowledge* (pp. 91–196). Cambridge, UK: Cambridge University Press, 1994.

Lakatos, I. (1976). *Proofs and Refutations: The Logic of Mathematical Discovery.* Cambridge, UK: Cambridge University Press.

Landsberg, P. T. (2000). An uncertainty principle for geometry. *Nature*, 404: 705–706.

Langer, S. (1953). *An Introduction to Symbolic Logic.* New York, NY: Dover.

Laor, N. (1985). Psychoanalysis as science: The inductivist's resistance revisited. *Journal of the American Psychoanalytic Association*, 32: 149–166.

Laplanche, J. (1992). Interpretation between determinism and hermeneutics: A restatement of the problem. *International Journal of Psychoanalysis*, 73: 429–445.

Laplanche, J., & Pontalis, J.-B. (1967). *The Language of Psychoanalysis.* London: Hogarth Press, 1973.

Lasch, C. (1979). *The Culture of Narcissism. American Life in an Age of Diminishing Expectations.* New York, NY: Norton, 1991.

Lasch, C. (1984). *The Minimal Self: Psychic Survival in Troubled Times.* New York, NY: Norton.

Leupold-Löwenthal, H. (1987). Analysis finite and infinite. In J. Sandler (Ed.), *A Study of Freud's 'Analysis Terminable and Interminable'* (pp. 56–75). IPA Educational Monograph No. 1.

Levin, F. M. (1991). *Mapping the Mind.* Hillsdale, NJ: Analytic Press.

Lévi-Strauss, C. (1974). *Anthropologie structurale.* Paris: Plon.

Lévy-Leblond, J.-M. (1996). *Aux contraires. L'exercise de la pensée et la pratique de la science.* Paris: Gallimard.

Lifton, R. J. (1968). *Revolutionary Immortality.* Harmondsworth, UK: Penguin.

Lindberg, D. C. (2007). *The Beginnings of Western Science* (2nd ed.). Chicago, IL: University of Chicago Press.

Lorenzer, A. (1969). *El lenguaje destruído y la reconstrucción psicoanalítica.* Buenos Aires, Argentina: Amorrortu, 1977.

Lorenzer, A. (1973). Advertencia para la reedición alemana. In *El lenguaje destruído y la reconstrucción psicoanalítica* (pp. 9–37). Buenos Aires, Argentina: Amorrortu, 1977.

Lukasiewicz, J. (1957). *Aristotle's Syllogistic from the Standpoint of Modern Formal Logic.* London: Oxford University Press.

Matte-Blanco, I. (1975). *The Unconscious as Infinite Sets*. London: Duckworth.

Matte-Blanco, I. (1978). Un contributo psicanalitico al pensiero logico e matematico. In F. Ferrari (Ed.), *Psicoanalisi e Instituzioni* (pp. 314–337). Florence, Italy: Le Monnier.

Matte-Blanco, I. (1988). *Thinking, Feeling and Being*. London: Routledge.

Meltzer, D. (1986). *Studies in Extended Metapsychology: Clinical Applications of Bion's Ideas*. Strath Tay, UK: Clunie Press.

Meltzer, D. (1993). Implicancias psicosomáticas en el pensamiento de Bion. *Psicoanálisis*, 15: 315–338.

Mill, J. S. (1852). *A System of Logic, Ratiocinative and Inductive* (4th ed.). New York, NY: Harper.

Mill, J. S. (1859). *On Liberty*. London: Penguin, 1985.

Modell, A. H. (1978). The nature of psychoanalytic knowledge. *Journal of the American Psychoanalytic Association*, 26: 641–658.

Money-Kyrle, R. (1955). An inconclusive contribution to the problem of the death instinct. In D. Meltzer (Ed.), *The Collected Papers of Roger Money-Kyrle* (pp. 285–296). Strath Tay, UK: Clunie Press, 1978.

Money-Kyrle, R. (1965). Success and failure in mental maturations. In D. Meltzer (Ed.), *The Collected Papers of Roger Money-Kyrle* (pp. 397–406). Strath Tay, UK: Clunie Press, 1978.

Money-Kyrle, R. (1968). Cognitive development. In D. Meltzer (Ed.), *The Collected Papers of Roger Money-Kyrle* (pp. 416–433). Strath Tay, UK: Clunie Press, 1978.

Money-Kyrle, R. (1978a). On being a psycho-analyst. In D. Meltzer (Ed.), *The Collected Papers of Roger Money-Kyrle* (pp. 457–465). Strath Tay, UK: Clunie Press, 1978.

Money-Kyrle, R. (1978b). *The Collected Papers of Roger Money-Kyrle* (D. Meltzer, Ed.). Strath Tay, UK: Clunie Press.

Moore, G. (1925). A defence of common sense. In *Philosophical Papers* (pp. 32–59). London: Allen and Unwin; New York, NY: Macmillan, 1959.

Moore, G. (1939). Proof of an external world. In *Philosophical Papers* (pp. 127–150). London: Allen and Unwin; New York, NY: Macmillan, 1959.

Nagel, E. (1959). Methodological issues in psychoanalytic theory. In S. Hook (Ed.), *Psychoanalysis: Scientific Method, and Philosophy* (pp. 38–57). New York, NY: Grove Press, 1960.

Nagel, E. (1961). *The Structure of Science: Problems in the Logic of Scientific Explanation*. New York, NY: Harcourt, Brace and World.

Nanda, M. (1996). The science question in postcolonial feminism. In P. L. Gross, N. Levitt, & M. W. Lewis (Eds.), *The Flight from Science and Reason* (pp. 420–436). *Annals of the New York Academy of Sciences* (Vol. 775). New York, NY: The New York Academy of Sciences.

New Shorter Oxford English Dictionary (Vol. 2). (1995). Oxford, UK: Oxford University Press.

Nichols, R.W. (1996). Kelvin's injunction. *The Sciences*, July–August, p. 4.

Nissen, B. (2008). On the determination of autistoid organizations in non-autistic adults. *International Journal of Psychoanalysis*, 89: 261–277.

Pap, A. (1958). *Semantics and Necessary Truth*. New Haven, CT: Yale University Press.

Parmat, S. (2010). El difícil camino a la universidad. *La Nación*, 12 October, p. 13.

Parsons, M. (1992). The refinding of theory in clinical practice. *International Journal of Psychoanalysis*, 73: 103–105.

Peirce, C. S. (1868). Some consequences of four incapacities. In P. Wiener (Ed.), *Charles S. Peirce: Selected Writings* (pp. 39–72). New York, NY: Dover, 1966.

Peirce, C. S. (1877). The fixation of belief. In J. Buchler (Ed.), *Philosophical Writings of Peirce* (pp. 5–22). New York, NY: Dover, 1955.

Peirce, C. S. (1883). The general theory of probable inference. In J. Buchler (Ed.), *Philosophical Writings of Peirce* (pp. 190–217). New York, NY: Dover, 1955.

Peirce, C. S. (1897). Concerning the author. In J. Buchler (Ed.), *Philosophical Writings of Peirce* (pp. 1–4). New York, NY: Dover, 1955.

Peirce, C. S. (1901). Abduction and induction. In J. Buchler (Ed.), *Philosophical Writings of Peirce* (pp. 150–156). New York, NY: Dover, 1955.

Peirce, C. S. (1905). The principles of phenomenology. In J. Buchler (Ed.), *Philosophical Writings of Peirce* (pp. 74–97). New York, NY: Dover, 1955.

Poincaré, H. (1902). *La science et l'hypothèse*. Paris: Flammarion, 1968.

Popper, K. R. (1945). *The Open Society and its Enemies. Vol. II Hegel and Marx*. London, Routledge, 1993.

Popper, K. R. (1957a). *The Poverty of Historicism*. London: Routledge, 1994.

Popper, K. R. (1957b). Science: Conjectures and refutations. In *Conjectures and Refutations: The Growth of Scientific Knowledge* (5th rev. ed., pp. 33–65). London: Routledge, 1989.

Popper, K. R. (1963). *Conjectures and Refutations*. London: Routledge, 1991.

Popper, K. R. (1979). *Objective Knowledge: An Evolutionary Approach* (Rev. ed). Cambridge, UK: Cambridge University Press.

Popper, K. R. (1982). Introduction, 1982. In *Realism and the Aim of Science* (pp. xix–xxxix). London: Routledge, 1992.

Popper, K. R. (1983). *Realism and the Aim of Science*. London: Routledge, 1992.

Popper, K. R. (1994). *The Myth of the Framework: In Defense of Science and Rationality* (M. A. Notturno, Ed.). London: Routledge.

Postman, N. (1982). *The Disappearence of Childhood*. New York, NY: Vintage, 1994.

Quine, W. O. (1957). Carnap and logical truth. In. *The Ways of Paradox and Other Essays* (Rev. ed., pp. 107–132). Cambridge, MA: Harvard University Press, 1976.

Quine, W. O. (1960). *Word and Object*. Boston, MA: MIT Press.

Quine, W. O. (1961). *From a Logical Point of View*. Cambridge, MA: Harvard University Press.

Quine, W. O. (1962). The ways of paradox. In *The Ways of Paradox and Other Essays* (pp. 1–18). Cambridge, MA: Harvard University Press, 1976.

Quine, W. O. (1964). Implicit definition sustained. In *The Ways of Paradox and Other Essays* (pp. 133–137). Cambridge, MA: Harvard University Press, 1976.

Quine, W. O. (1978). On the nature of moral values. In *Theories and Things* (pp. 55–66). Cambridge, MA: Belknap/Harvard University Press, 1981.

Quine, W. O. (1980). Foreword, 1980. In *From a Logical Point of View* (pp. vii–ix). Cambridge, MA: Harvard University Press.

Quine, W. O. (1981). Empirical content. In *Theories and Things* (pp. 24–30). Cambridge, MA: Belknap/Harvard University Press.

Quinodoz, J.-M. (1994). Clinical facts or psychoanalytical clinical facts. *International Journal of Psychoanalysis*, 75: 393–396.

Racker, H. (1952). Considerations on the theory of transference. In *Transference and Countertransference*. New York, NY: International Universities Press, 1968.

Racker, H. (1968). *Transference and Countertransference*. New York, NY: International Universities Press.

Rado, S. (1926). The psychic effects of intoxicants: An attempt to evolve a psychoanalytical theory of morbid cravings. *International Journal of Psychoanalysis*, 7: 396–413.

Rayner, E. (1981). Infinite experiences, affects and the characteristics of the unconscious. *International Journal of Psychoanalysis*, 62: 403–412.

Rayner, E. (1992). Matching, attunement and the psychoanalytic dialogue. *International Journal of Psychoanalysis*, 73: 39–54.

Rayner, E. (1995). *Unconscious Logic: An Introduction to Matte-Blanco's Bi-Logic and Its Uses*. London: Routledge.

Rayner, E., & Tuckett, D. (1988). An introduction to Matte-Blanco's reformulation of the Freudian unconscious and his conceptualization of the internal world. In I. Matte-Blanco, *Thinking, Feeling and Being* (pp. 3–42). London: Routledge.

Reichenbach, H. (1927). *The Philosophy of Space and Time*. New York, NY: Dover, 1956.

Reichenbach, H. (1947). *Elements of Symbolic Logic*. New York, NY: Macmillan.

Rescher, N. (1999). *The Limits of Science*. Pittsburgh, PA: University of Pittsburgh Press.

Rescher, N. (2009). *Aporetics: Rational Deliberation in the Face of Inconsistency*. Pittsburgh, PA: University of Pittsburgh Press.

Richards, A. D. (1995). *A. A. Brill: The politics of exclusion and the politics of pluralism*. 47th A. A. Brill Conference, New York Psychoanalytic Society, 28 November.

Richfield, J. (1954). An analysis of the concept of insight. *Psychoanalytic Quarterly*, 23: 398–408.

Ricoeur, P. (1970). *Freud and Philosophy: An Essay on Interpretation*. New Haven, CT: Yale University Press.

Ricoeur, P. (1991). *From Text to Action: Essays in Hermeneutics, II*. Evanston, IL: Northwestern University Press.

Riesman, D., with Glatzer, N., & Denney, R. (1960). *The Lonely Crowd: A Study of the Changing American Character.* New Haven, CT: Yale University Press, 1989.

Riviere, J. (1937). A contribution to the analysis of the negative therapeutic reaction. *International Journal of Psychoanalysis*, 17: 304–320.

Rorty, R. (1975). Diez años después. In *El giro lingüístico* (pp. 135–158). Barcelona, Spain: Paidós, 1990.

Rorty, R. (1990). Veinte años después. In *El giro lingüístico* (pp. 159–167). Barcelona, Spain: Paidós, 1990.

Rosenfeld, H. (1964). An investigation into the need of psychotic and neurotic patients to act out during analysis. In *Psychotic States* (pp. 202–216). London: Hogarth, 1965.

Rosenfeld, H. (1972). A critical appreciation of James Strachey's paper on the nature of the therapeutic action of psychoanalysis. *International Journal of Psychoanalysis*, 53: 455–461.

Rosser, J. B. (1953). *Logic for Mathematicians*. New York, NY: McGraw-Hill.

Roudinesco, E. (1991). Vibrant hommage de Jacques Lacan à Martin Heidegger. In Collège International de Philosophie (Ed.), *Lacan avec les philosophes* (pp. 225–236). Paris: Albin Michel.

Roudinesco, E. (1993). *Jacques Lacan*. Paris: Fayard.

Rougier, L. (1960). *La Métaphysique et le Langage*. Paris: Flammarion.

Russell, B. (1897). *An Essay on the Foundations of Geometry*. New York, NY: Dover, 1956.

Russell, B. (1903). *The Principles of Mathematics*. New York, NY: Norton, n/d.

Russell, B. (1911). Knowledge by acquaintance and knowledge by description. In *Mysticism and Logic* (pp. 200–221). London: Unwin Paperbacks, 1989.

Russell, B. (1938). Introduction to the Second Edition. In *The Principles of Mathematics* (pp. v–xiv). New York, NY: Norton, n/d.

Russell, B. (1948). *Human Knowledge: Its Scope and Limits*. London: Routledge, 1992.

Russell, B. (1950). *An Enquiry into Meaning and Truth*. London: Routledge, 1989.

Russell, B. (1959a). *Wisdom of the West*. London: Macdonald.

Russell, B. (1959b). *My Philosophical Development*. London: Unwin Hyman.

Searle, J. (1965). What is a speech act? In M. Black (Ed.), *Philosophy in America* (pp. 221–239). Ithaca, NY: Cornell Univesity Press.

Sebeok, T. A., & Umiker-Sebeok, J. (1980). *You Know My Method.* Bloomington, IN: Gaslight.

Sharpe, E. F. (1940). Psycho-physical problems revealed in language: An examination of metaphor. In *Collected Papers on Psycho-Analysis* (pp. 155–169). London: Hogarth Press, 1950.

Singh, S. (1997). *Fermat's Enigma.* New York, NY: Anchor.

Smith, H. F. (1995). Analytic listening and the experience of surprise. *International Journal of Psychoanalysis*, 76: 67–78.

Spence, D. (1991a). Teorias da mente: fato o ficçao. *Ide*, 21: 104–115.

Spence, D. (1991b). Review of S. E. Goldberg, Two Patterns of Rationality in Freud's Writings. *International Review of Psychoanalysis*, 18: 281–283.

Spence, D. (1993). The hermeneutic turn: Soft science or loyal opposition. *Psychoanalytic Dialogues*, 3: 3–12.

Spence, D. (1994). The special nature of psychoanalytic facts. *International Journal of Psychoanalysis*, 75: 915–925.

Spillius, E. (2007). *Encounters with Melanie Klein.* London: Routledge.

Spruiell, V. (1987). The foundations of psychoanalysis: An essay on a philosophical book by Adolf Grünbaum. *International Review of Psychoanalysis*, 14: 169–183.

Steele, R. (1979). Psychoanalysis and hermeneutics. *International Review of Psychoanalysis*, 6: 389–411.

Stewart, H. (1990). Interpretation and other changes for psychic change. *International Review of Psychoanalysis*, 17: 61–69.

Strachey, J. (1934). The nature of the therapeutic action of psychoanalysis. *International Journal of Psychoanalysis*, 15: 127–159 [reprinted 1969, 50: 275–292].

Strachey, J. (1937). Symposium on the theory of the therapeutic results of psychoanalysis. *International Journal of Psychoanalysis*, 18: 139–145.

Symington, N. (1991). *Narcissism: A New Theory.* London: Karnac.

Tarski, A. (1931). The concept of truth in formalized languages. In *Logic, Semantics, Metamathematics* (pp. 152–278). Oxford, UK: Clarendon, 1956.

Toulmin, S. (1990). *Cosmopolis: The Hidden Agenda of Modernity.* Chicago IL, University of Chicago Press.

Tuchman, B. (1978). *A Distant Mirror: The Calamitous 14th Century.* New York, NY: Ballantine.

Tuckett, D. (1983). Words and the psychoanalytic interaction. *International Review of Psychoanalysis*, 10: 407–413.

Tully, R. E. (1995). Logic, informal. In T. Honderich (Ed.), *The Oxford Companion to Philosophy* (p. 500). Oxford, UK: Oxford University Press.

Turkle, S. (1995). *Life on the Screens: Identity in the Age of the Internet.* New York, NY: Touchstone.

Tustin, F. (1981a). The asymbolic nature of autistic states. In *Autistic States in Children* (pp. 123–134). London: Routledge & Kegan Paul.

Tustin, F. (1981b). Transference phenomena in autistic states. In *Autistic States in Children* (pp. 163–172). London: Routledge & Kegan Paul.

Tustin, F. (1986). *Autistic Barriers in Neurotic Patients*. New Haven, CT: Yale University Press.

Tustin, F. (1991). Revised understandings of psychogenic autism. *International Journal of Psychoanalysis*, 72: 585–591.

Urtubey, L. de (1994). Le travail de contre-transfert. *Revue française de psychanalyse*, 58: 1271–1372.

Valls, J. L. (1995). *Diccionario Freudiano*. Madrid, Spain: Julián Yébenes.

Vargas Llosa, M. (1996). El canto de las sirenas. *La Nación*, Buenos Aires, 27 July.

Vattimo, G. (1985). *El Fin de la Modernidad. Nihilismo y Hermenéutica en la Cultura Posmoderna*. Barcelona, Spain: Gedisa, 1986.

Vattimo, G. (1994). *Más allá de la interpretación*. Barcelona, Spain: Paidós.

Viderman, S. (1970). *La Construction de l'Espace Analytique*. Paris: Denoël.

von Wright, G. H. (1957). *The Logical Problem of Induction*. New York, NY: Macmillan.

von Wright, G. H. (1971). *Explanation and Understanding*. Ithaca, NY: Cornell University Press.

Waelder, R. (1962). Psychoanalysis, scientific method, and philosophy. *Journal of the American Psychoanalytic Association*, 10: 617–637.

Wallace, E. R. (1989). Pitfalls of a one-sided idea of science: Adolf Grünbaum's *Foundations of Psychoanalysis*. *Journal of the American Psychoanalytic Association*, 37: 493–529.

Wallerstein, R. S. (1986). Psychoanalysis as science: A response to the new challenges. *Psychoanalytic Quarterly*, 55: 414–451.

Wallerstein, R. S. (1988). One psychoanalysis or many? *International Journal of Psychoanalysis*, 69: 5–21.

Whewell, W. (1849). Mill's logic. In R. E. Butts (Ed.), *William Whewell: Theory of Scientific Method* (pp. 265–308). Indianapolis, IN: Hackett, 1989.

Whewell, W. (1850). Criticism of Aristotle's account of induction. In R. E. Butts (Ed.), *William Whewell: Theory of Scientific Method* (pp. 311–321). Indianapolis, IN: Hackett, 1989.

Whewell, W. (1858). Novum Organum Renovatum. In R. E. Butts (Ed.), *William Whewell: Theory of Scientific Method* (pp. 103–249). Indianapolis, IN: Hackett, 1989.

Whitehead, A. N., & Russell, B. (1912). *Principia Mathematica* (Vol. 1, 2nd rev. ed.). Cambridge, UK: Cambridge University Press, 1960.

Williams, B. (2002). *Truth and Truthfulness: An Essay in Genealogy*. Princeton, NJ: Princeton University Press.

Williams, M. (2000). Epistemology and the mirror of nature. In R. B. Brandom (Ed.), *Rorty and his Critics* (pp. 191–213). London: Blackwell.

Winnicott, D. W. (1951). Transitional objects and transitional phenomena. In *Playing and Reality* (Chapter 1). London: Routledge, 1994.

Winnicott, D. W. (1967). Postscript: DWW on DWW. In C. Winnicott, R. Shepherd, & M. Davis (Eds.), *Psychoanalytic Explorations*. London: Karnac, 1989.

Winnicott, D. W. (1969). James Strachey. Obituary. In C. Winnicott, R. Shepherd, & M. Davis (Eds.), *Psychoanalytic Explorations*. London: Karnac, 1989.

Winnicott, D. W. (1971). *Playing and Reality*. London: Routledge, 1994.

Wittgenstein, L. (1938). *Lectures and Conversations on Aethetics, Psychology and Religious Belief* (C. Barrett, Ed.). Berkeley, CA: University of California Press, n/d.

Wittgenstein, L. (1980). *Culture and Value* (G. H. von Wright, Ed.). Chicago, IL: University of Chicago Press.

Wurmser, L. (1989). 'Either/or': Some comments on Professor Grünbaum's critique of psychoanalysis. *Psychoanalytic Inquiry*, 9: 220–248.

Index